East Central European C

Studies on Language and Culture in Central and Eastern Europe

Edited by
Christian Voß

Volume 41

PETER LANG

Ferdinand Kühnel / Soňa Mikulová / Snežana Stanković (eds.)

East Central European Cemeteries

Ethnic, Linguistic, and Narrative Aspects of Sepulchral Culture
and the Commemoration of the Dead in Borderlands

PETER LANG

Bibliographic Information published by the Deutsche Nationalbibliothek
The Deutsche Nationalbibliothek lists this publication in the Deutsche
Nationalbibliografie; detailed bibliographic data is available
online at http://dnb.d-nb.de.

Library of Congress Cataloging-in-Publication Data
A CIP catalog record for this book has been applied for at
the Library of Congress.

This project received generous financial support from the Central European
Network for Teaching and Research in Academic Liaison (CENTRAL), the Humboldt University of Berlin, the Faculty of Historical and Cultural Studies at the University of Vienna, and the Viennese Austrian and Central European Center at the Institute of East
European History at the University of Vienna.

ISSN 1868-2936
ISBN 978-3-631-78448-8 (Print) · E-ISBN 978-3-631-89340-1 (E-PDF)
E-ISBN 978-3-631-89341-8 (EPUB) · DOI 10.3726/b20382

© Peter Lang GmbH
Internationaler Verlag der Wissenschaften
Berlin 2023
All rights reserved.

Peter Lang – Berlin · Bruxelles · Lausanne · New York · Oxford

This publication has been peer reviewed.

www.peterlang.com

CONTENTS

Editorial

Today more than ever, with the experience of the COVID-19 pandemic, we may say that one dies alone and distant from the eyes of surrounding society. Moreover, the full-scale Russian invasion of Ukraine reminds us how cultures of commemoration and remembrance work. Although lived out differently, grief has befallen both countries, collectively and individually. Those who died in war—known and unknown—shape burial practices on battlefields. War-related deaths bring family members and various communities together. Thus, grief, memories, commemoration and remembrance work in manifold ways: privately, socially, politically and historically.

With this in mind, what can earlier, contemporary, and future cemeteries and memorials tell us in general? Their boundaries are mostly explicit, but there are cases where military dead are laid to rest amongst civilian graves. These delineations and nets refer to past events, while the inscribed names may divulge life circumstances: family relations, marital status, profession, waves of migration or (even) changing state structures. The cemetery lays open both strategies of social bordering and implicit mutual acceptance. But in a sense, it is a visible mark of a borderless world: Although the names of the deceased may refer to people with different cultural backgrounds, their memory can be kept alive within the same space and cherished by the same community. However, some persons and communities may be subjected to gradual self-evolving or forced oblivion, as was the case with some German minorities in post-war East Central Europe. Here, we encounter contradictory dimensions of memorial behavior: from commemoration or celebration to forgetting.

The material work of memory and honoring is an appropriate departure point to enquire into sepulchral culture—its forms, roles and changes over time. While some graves, memorials and whole cemeteries can become pilgrimage sites, conveying specific cultural or historical value, others simply reflect individual or communal lifeworlds.

The edited volume *East Central European Cemeteries: Ethnic, Linguistic, and Narrative Aspects of Sepulchral Culture and the Commemoration of the Dead in Borderlands* engages with various forms of cemetery landscapes. It originated from two CENTRAL-*Kollegs* projects based at the Humboldt University of Berlin in 2016 and 2017. Both *Kollegs* were organized by the editors who at that time were early career researchers based at three Central European universities: Ferdinand Kühnel, University of Vienna; Soňa Mikulová, Charles University

(Prague); and Snežana Stanković, Humboldt University of Berlin. Although the scholars were from different disciplines—social sciences, history, literary studies and anthropology—they shared research interest in the two-fold function of cemeteries as artifacts and *lieux de mémoire* [realms of memory] within individual and social mourning, often embedded respectively in the collective national past and history.

Generous financial support from the Central European Network for Teaching and Research in Academic Liaison (CENTRAL) enabled us to develop a project in collaboration with our students. Our shared learning, based on field research and theoretical discussions, has evolved into this publication. We had the good fortune to enjoy the long-term supervision of Professor Christian Voß (Humboldt University of Berlin). Christian Voß and Stefan Karsch (International Department, Humboldt University of Berlin) facilitated financial support and publishing with the Peter Lang series *Studies on Language and Culture in Central and Eastern Europe*.

All individual projects focused on cemeteries, gravestones, and other artifacts featuring remembrance of the dead, on the one hand, and conveying the dynamics of borderland multi-ethnic and multilingual areas, on the other. Studying these manifestations of past times allowed us to deconstruct how narratives and specific cultures of remembrance connected to various minority groups evolve. In this vein, we may speak of private and public realms of memory that translocally synchronize different pasts.

Therefore, *lieux de mémoire* imply two main intertwining structures: the tangible, *i. e.*, the materiality, and the intangible residing in the system of visible signs (semiotics) tied to hidden lifeworlds of memories, emotions, stories, and various interpretations of history. The book follows these entanglements in a way that each chapter attempts to reveal a particular layer within the various regional "palimpsests." Each author adopted a unique methodological and conceptual language to convey their own approach.

The regions examined in this book are southern Carinthia in Austria, Croatia, Czech Silesia, Eastern Slovakia, Upper Lusatia in Germany, and Southeastern Banat in Serbia. All these areas share similar experiences: From the second half of the nineteenth century, particularly after both world wars, they were affected by various assimilation processes, homogenization, and mass violence that would erupt into deportation, expulsion, and murder. Twentieth-century East Central Europe bears dramatic scars of forced displacement and ethnic homogenization. Our reading and telling of the past based on East Central European cemetery, therefore, involved two aspects: On one level, it considers gravestone design and language, while, on the other, it studies past events, practices and collective awareness developed around the sites.

Martina Mirković (University of Vienna) deals with the so-called *Bleiburška tragedija/Pliberška tragedija* [Bleiburg tragedy] and seeks to find indications of historical revisionism which glorifies the fascist past in today's Croatia by analyzing specific manifestations of the culture of remembrance since Yugoslavia's disintegration. The chapter focuses on symbols and inscriptions of three plaques commemorating victims of the mass killings, installed at the cemetery in Unterloibach/Spodnje Libuče, the Loibacher Feld/Libuško polje in Austrian Carinthia, and the Mirogoj cemetery in Zagreb. Furthermore, she analyzes the speeches the highest Croatian political and clerical representatives gave at the annually held commemoration in Austrian Carinthia and symbols that appeared at the event—used either by official representatives or the numerous visitors.

Anežka Brožová (Charles University) writes about World War II monuments and graves in the Hlučín Region (Hlučínsko/Hultschiner Ländchen) and their contested importance within the Czech culture of remembrance. World War II plays a significant role in the collective memory of inhabitants of the Hlučín Region who identify with former Prussian inhabitants. Due to different historical experiences, their interpretation departs from the dominant narrative constructed in the postwar period in communist Czechoslovakia and adopted by the successor state, the Czech Republic, as Hlučín soldiers, i. e., inhabitants of the Hlučín Region, fought in the German *Wehrmacht* and either survived or fell in the war. This chapter analyzes the alternative Hlučín narrative manifested on graves and monuments dedicated to the fallen World War II Hlučín soldiers.

Tereza Juhászová (Charles University) examines different manifestations of identity in cemeteries in the eastern Slovak town of Medzev, where until today, the German minority, so-called *Mantaks*, descendants of German immigrants from the thirteenth century, live and still use a specific German dialect (*Mantakisch*). Her contribution asks if and how the identity of the Germans/*Mantaks* in Medzev manifests via inscriptions on gravestones. She argues that categories based on language or nationality are not always relevant in a multilingual space and that gravestones represent only one level of the multilayered identities of the German minority members.

Michał Piasek (Humboldt University of Berlin) explores how shifting borders and religion in German Upper Lusatia are entangled with the current use of the Sorbian language on gravestones. Throughout history, the different areas of Upper Lusatia have undergone specific historical and religious changes, which the chapter aims to make visible through a cartographic approach combined with the *phantom borders* theory. The author has designed a map as a narrative tool that helps read how different states, their language policies and extensive coal mining impacted the use of Sorbian in the explored areas over time. This approach enables the author to track down continually evolving phantom borders.

Snežana Stanković (Friedrich Schiller University of Jena) explores the preserved, abandoned, vandalized, destroyed, and vanished German cemeteries as a source of memories of the absent German/Danubian Swabian minority in Southeastern Banat in Serbia. How the absence of the Germans/Danubian Swabians was both silenced and transposed onto public knowledge during the years after World War II, and today, forms the central question of this chapter.

We would especially like to thank the Humboldt University of Berlin for hosting our workshops and helping develop the project; especially Aleksandra Laski, Lucy Häntschl, Nenad Stefanov, Christian Voß, and Stefan Karsch; Konrad Petrovszky (Austrian Academy of Sciences, ÖAW), the Faculty of Historical and Cultural Studies at the University of Vienna; the Austrian and Central European Center (Wiener Österreich und Ostmitteleuropa Zentrum) at the University of Vienna and its director Marija Wakounig; Alojz Ivanišević; the Institute of East European History at the University of Vienna; Kateřina Králová, the Faculty for Social Sciences at Charles University; the CENTRAL-Network, the German Academic Exchange Service (Deutscher Akademischer Austauschdienst, DAAD); Gisela Lindeque for English proofreading; the reviewers for their thorough work. Last but not least, we are grateful to our colleagues, the then students, many of whom have become early career researchers. Thank you for your inspiring enthusiasm, hard work, patience and endurance, without which this volume would not have been possible.

This publication has undergone the process of anonymous peer review.

Ferdinand Kühnel, Soňa Mikulová, and Snežana Stanković

Vienna, Berlin, and Jena, September 2022

The (Newly) Negotiated Remembrance of the *Bleiburška Tragedija*: Parallels and Discontinuities

Martina Mirković

In recent years, a wide range of publications on the so-called *Bleiburška tragedija/ Pliberška tragedija* [Bleiburg tragedy] has been published. The authors of these books and articles mainly focused on the Croatian politics of memory as there are reasonable grounds to assume that this official policy followed and still follows the specific and highly controversial tendency of historical revisionism. According to Ivo and Slavko Goldstein, revisionism in Croatia was first voiced publicly in 1989/1990 and "[...] the post-1990 political authorities in Croatia encouraged it and to some degree incorporated it in their political program."[1]

During Yugoslavia's disintegration in the 1990s, the Croatian public perception of World War II changed abruptly. As Holm Sundhaussen states, it passed through a "Croatian filter,"[2] when historians started questioning the Yugoslav myth[3] of its foundation.[4] It was the period when around 3,000 Croatian partisan monuments that commemorated the Yugoslav foundation myth were damaged or demolished. At the same time, the socialist symbolism was rewritten into an explicit national one.[5] Moreover, the number of World War II victims was renegotiated as the original communist victim myth was divided into a plurality of national victim myths.[6] One such created myth concerned the 1945 mass killings of around 50,000 *ustaše, domobrani* (regular army members) and civilians who had left the territory of the Independent State of Croatia in order to

---

1   Ivo Goldstein and Slavko Goldstein, "Revisionism in Croatia. The Case of Franjo Tuđman," *East European Jewish Affairs* 32, no.1 (Fall 2002): 52.

2   Holm Sundhaussen, "Jugoslawien und seine Nachfolgestaaten. Konstruktion, Dekonstruktion und Neukonstruktion von 'Erinnerungen' und Mythen," in *Mythen der Nationen: 1945 Arena der Erinnerung*, ed. Monika Flacke (Berlin: Deutsches Historisches Museum, 2004), 393.

3   The Yugoslav founding myth is going to be discussed below in detail.

4   Ljiljana Radonić, *Krieg um die Erinnerung: Kroatische Vergangenheitspolitik zwischen Revisionismus und europäischen Standards* (Frankfurt am Main: Campus Verlag, 2010), 385.

5   Ibid., 393.

6   Holm Sundhaussen, *Jugoslawien und seine Nachfolgestaaten 1943–2011. Eine ungewöhnliche Geschichte des Gewöhnlichen* (Wien, Köln, Weimar: Böhlau, 2014), 60.

surrender to the Allies in British-occupied Carinthia. Arriving in the Austrian border town Bleiburg/Pliberk, their aim of surrendering was foiled: The British Allies denied their capitulation and extradited them to the Yugoslav partisans, who subsequently perpetuated mass killings. Although most of these killings were not committed in Bleiburg/Pliberk, but on the Yugoslav side of the border, the Austrian town became a significant symbol and a synonym for "the biggest tragedy in the history of the Croatian people."[7] Furthermore, "[...] the myth of Bleiburg is not only important in understanding Croatian interpretations of the Second World War II but rather symbolizes a much broader period of communist violence and repression lasting up until the Croatian War of Independence [...]."[8]

This study seeks to find indications of historical revisionism, which glorifies the fascist past in today's Croatia by analyzing specific manifestations of the culture of remembrance since Yugoslavia's disintegration. Firstly, the analysis will briefly introduce the attempted capitulation in Bleiburg/Pliberk in 1945. Secondly, it will try to outline the Yugoslav and Croatian politics of memory, focusing on the commemoration of this event and its significance for the research subject. Here, the theoretical concepts of cultures of remembrance, *e. g.*, Maurice Halbwachs' *collective memory*, Aleida Assmann's *kulturelles Gedächtnis* [cultural memory] and *Gedenkort* [place of commemoration],[9] will be applied accordingly.

In the third part, the methodological approach will be defined along with the empirical analysis of the sources. Firstly, it focuses on symbols and inscriptions of three commemorative plaques installed for the victims of the mass killings (at the cemetery in Unterloibach/Spodnje Libuče, at the Loibacher Feld/Libuško polje and the cemetery Mirogoj in Zagreb). Secondly, it analyzes the speeches—given by the highest Croatian political and clerical representatives at the annually held commemoration in Austrian Carinthia—and symbols that appeared at the event, used by either official representatives or the numerous visitors. The significance of the commemoration is considered multidimensional: The ceremony not only reflects Croatia's interpretation of history, or more precisely, the mass killings in 1945, but since the highest Croatian representatives regularly attend the ceremony, this specific reading of the past is (re-)affirmed and acknowledged every year. Thus, the innovative approach of this study is its comparison of the three commemorative plaques with an in-depth analysis of the speeches.

Other questions that are relevant in the context of the empirical analysis would be: What can be said about the Croatian government since the 1990s, considering

---

7   Speech of Željko Raguž, Bleiburg/Pliberk, Mai 13, 2017. See further this chapter's analysis of the speeches held at the annual commemoration in Bleiburg/Pliberk 2017.

8   Vjeran Pavlaković, Dario Brentin, Davor Pauković, "The Controversial Commemoration: Transnational Approaches to Remembering Bleiburg," *Croatian Political Science Review* 55, no. 2 (February 2018): 8–10.

9   Aleida Assmann, *Cultural Memory and Western Civilization. Functions, Media, Archives* (Cambridge: Cambridge University Press 2001), 292.

its wreath-laying ceremonies during the commemoration in Bleiburg/Pliberk in front of symbols, which can be clearly embedded in a fascist setting? What symbols were used on the commemorative plaques and during the commemoration? In what context do they appear, and how do they refer to Croatia's history? The final subchapter will then present the research results and show how this case study can be integrated into current controversies on Croatian politics of memory and whether it confirms the prevailing Croatian perspective on the "Bleiburg tragedy."

Historical Contextualization

From 1941 to 1945, the *Nezavisna Država Hrvatska* (Independent State of Croatia, NDH) existed as a vassal state of Nazi Germany and fascist Italy.[10] Its army took part in World War II under the command of the German *Wehrmacht*. With the last order in May 1945, it was forced to withdraw from the NDH territory to the Austrian borders. A group consisting of about 150,000 *ustaše*[11] and *domobrani* (the NDH's regular army members),[12] NDH administrative employees and civilians, Serbian četniks along with četniks, and a group of around 300,000 German *Wehrmacht* soldiers followed this command and set off to Austrian territory. They aimed to surrender to the British Allies, who were occupying Carinthia in Austria at that time. They expected the Allies to treat prisoners of war better than partisans gathered under Josip Broz Tito (1892–1980) in *Narodnooslobodilačka vojska* (People's Liberation Army) would do. Yet, as soon as the first soldiers and civilians crossed the Austrian border, the British Allies denied their capitulation, sent them back to Yugoslav territory and extradited them to the (Yugoslavian) People's Liberation Army.[13] Reasons for the denial have been widely discussed by scholars and in popular literature:[14] While the Croatian diaspora community would condemn it as

---

10 The NDH was not just a collaborator but, at the same time, a rare example of a European state that engaged in death camps on its own; in other words, the Croatian regime practiced the mass killings of Jews, Serbs, Romani people, political opponents and others sovereignly from Nazi Germany, see Radonić, *Krieg um die Erinnerung*, 15; Alexander Korb, *Im Schatten des Weltkriegs. Massengewalt der Ustaša gegen Serben, Juden und Roma in Kroatien 1941–1945* (Hamburg: Hamburger Edition, 2013).

11 The ideological movement underlying the NDH was called *Ustaša – Hrvatska revolucionarna organizacija* and its members were called *ustaše*. See: Arnold Suppan, *Hitler—Beneš—Tito. Konflikt, Krieg und Völkermord in Ostmittel- und Südosteuropa*, vol. 2 (Wien: Verlag der Österreichischen Akademie der Wissenschaften, 2014), 1064 f.

12 Korb, *Im Schatten des Weltkrieges*, 101.

13 Sundhaussen, *Jugoslawien und seine Nachfolgestaaten*, 62; Radonić, *Krieg um die Erinnerung*, 98 f.

14 In Great Britain, Nikolai Tolstoy's book *The Minister and the Massacres* led to his punishment. The court made him pay 1.5 million Pounds, as he claimed that the majority of the 200,000 Croats were murdered by Tito's partisans immediately after the British extradited them and therefore accused the British politicians and military. See Nikolai Tolstoy, *The*

a betrayal of the Croatian people,[15] some historians such as Robert Knight argued that the British Allies' decision needs to be seen in a specific context:

> Die Auslieferung der Kosaken und dissidenter Jugoslawen aus dem südlichen Österreich im Mai und Juni 1945 wurde beschlossen in einer Zeit der Krise und des Druckes. Die Verantwortung für die Bevorzugung einer "bequemen" Lösung in einer Zeit der akuten Schwierigkeiten lag in erster Linie bei den damit befaßten Militärs. Die Frage nach dem moralischen Aspekt der Auslieferung [...] muss die Frage stellen, wie viel die Entscheidungsträger über das wahrscheinliche Schicksal der Ausgelieferten wussten [...].[16]

Ljiljana Radonić, in turn, quotes the responsible British officer Thomas Patrick David Scott (1905–1976), who argued that according to the ceasefire agreement, the NDH army should have laid down its weapons earlier and surrendered in front of the moving partisan troops but instead they kept fighting them.[17] However, after the British denial, the group was kept from crossing the borders and capitulated to the (Yugoslavian) People's Liberation Army, both outside and inside the British occupation zone. What followed is known in Croatia as the *Bleiburška tragedija*: The partisans carried out mass killings on Yugoslav territory of members of the abovementioned group, who were forced to return to Yugoslavia. Later, this event was named *križni put* [Way of the Cross] or *smrtni put* [death march] in Croatia.[18]

Minister and the Massacres (London: Century Hutchinson, 1986); Sundhaussen, *Jugoslawien und seine Nachfolgestaaten*, 64.

15 Robert Knight points further that, in their view, Bleiburg/Pliberk became a symbol for "[...] a colossal national tragedy and a monstrous Allied betrayal." See Robert Knight, "Transnational Memory from Bleiburg to London (via Buenos Aires and Grozny)," *Zeitgeschichte* 38, no.1 (2010): 41. See further the empirical analysis on the speeches held at the 2017 commemoration in Bleiburg/Pliberk.

16 Robert Knight, "Kosaken und Kroaten in Kärnten. Vernachlässigte Perspektiven," in *Zweiter Weltkrieg und ethnische Homogenisierungsversuche im Alpen-Adria-Raum*, eds. Brigitte Entner and Valentin Sima (Klagenfurt/Wien: Drava Verlag, 2012), 129; [The extradition of [...] dissident Yugoslavs from southern Austria in May and June 1945 was decided in a time of crisis and pressure. The military was responsible for a "more comfortable" solution in a time of acute difficulties [...] the question about the moral aspect of the extradition [...] must be followed by another question: how much the decision makers knew about the probable fate of the extradited [...].] All translations by the author unless otherwise noted.

17 Radonić, *Krieg um die Erinnerung*, 100; Sundhaussen too argued that the capitulation was refused because of the instructions given by commander-in-chief Harold Macmillan (1894–1986, Conservative Party) and because of the "Allies' arrangement." Sundhaussen, *Jugoslawien und seine Nachfolgestaaten*, 62.

18 Sundhaussen, *Jugoslawien und seine Nachfolgestaaten*, 62–64; See also Martina Grahek Ravančić, "The Historiography of Bleiburg and the Death Marches since Croatian Independence," *Croatian Political Science Review* 55, no. 2 (March 2018): 133.

It is difficult to estimate how many Croatian *ustaše, domobrani,* Slovenian *domobranci,*[19] Serbian *četniks* and civilians were killed. While the Croatian *diaspora* community has overstated the number of victims,[20] the official Yugoslav historiography did quite the opposite, if it mentioned this at all.[21] According to Vladimir Žerjavić's calculation, 45,000–55,000 *ustaše* and *domobrani*; 8,000–10,000 Slovenes and 2,000 Serbian Montenegrin četniks were killed.[22]

Theoretical Contextualization

Before giving a brief overview of Croatia's politics of memory within a theoretical framework, it should be emphasized that cultures of remembrance consist of far more than the aspects outlined in this text.[23] Concerning the empirical analysis, just two of these aspects will be outlined specifically since they appeared as the most significant ones in the results: Symbols, which include not just signs,

---

19 During World War II Slovenia was occupied by Nazi Germany and Fascist Italy and therefore considered as collaborators by the partisans. The *Slovensko domobranstvo* was an anticommunist military organization that collaborated with the Nazis and therefore also fought the partisans. See Tamara Griesser-Pečar, *Das zerrissene Volk—Slowenien 1941–1946: Okkupation, Kollaboration, Bürgerkrieg, Revolution* (Wien, Graz: Böhlau 2003); Sabrina Petra Ramet, "Confronting the past: The Slovenes as subjects and objects of history," *Družboslovne razprave* 59, no. 24 (2008): 31. In May 1945, About 17,000 Slovene people, including members of the *Slovensko domobranstvo* and civilians, fled to Carinthia, where they wanted to surrender to the British Allies in Viktring/Vetrinj. Similarly, to the events in Bleiburg/Pliberk, that capitulation was also denied and the group was extradited to the Yugoslav partisans who then started killing the group's members in Yugoslavia. See: Griesser-Pečar, *Das zerrissene Volk,* 480–516; Arnold Suppan, "Kärnten und Slowenien. Die Geschichte einer schwierigen Nachbarschaft im 20. Jahrhundert," in: *Kärnten und Slowenien—"Dickicht und Pfade,"* eds. Stefan Karner and Janez Stergar, vol. 5 (Klagenfurt: Hermagoras, Heyn, 2005), 40.
20 According to their estimates, around 600,000 people were killed in Bleiburg/Pliberk. See Sundhaussen, *Jugoslawien und seine Nachfolgestaaten,* 64.
21 Radonić, *Krieg um die Erinnerung,* 102.
22 Vladimir Žerjavić, "Opsesije i megalomanije oko Jasenovca i Bleiburga. Gubici stanovništva Jugoslavije u drugom svjetskom ratu," *Radovi Zavoda za hrvatsku povijest Filozofskoga fakulteta Sveučilišta u Zagrebu* 25, no.1 (1992): 286–89.
23 See, *e.g.,* Katrin Hammerstein, Ulrich Mählert, Julie Trappe, and Edgar Wolfrum, eds. *Aufarbeitung der Diktatur—Diktat der Aufarbeitung. Normierungsprozesse beim Umgang mit diktatorischer Vergangenheit* (Göttingen: Wallstein Verlag, 2009); Claus Leggewie, *Der Kampf um die europäische Erinnerung. Ein Schlachtfeld wird besichtigt* (München: Beck Verlag, 2011); Ulf Brunnbaucher and Stefan Troebst, eds. *Zwischen Amnesie und Nostalgie. Die Erinnerung an den Kommunismus in Südosteuropa* (Köln, Weimar, Wien: Böhlau 2007); Harald Welzer, *Der Krieg der Erinnerung. Holocaust, Kollaboration und Widerstand im europäischen Gedächtnis* (Frankfurt am Main: Fischer Taschenbuch Verlag, 2007); Lars Alberth, *Die Fabrikation europäischer Kultur. Zur diskursiven Sichtbarkeit von Herrschaft in Europa* (Bielefeld: transcript Verlag 2013).

but also language/speeches as a symbolic and performative act,[24] and Bleiburg/ Pliberk as a *Gedenkort*.[25]

According to Maja Brkljačić and Holm Sundhaussen's definition, for most of the population, national symbols are *Identitätszeichen* [marks of identity][26] that evoke certain feelings like a sense of community and/or exclusion of foreigners. In periods of transformation, national symbols obtain an additional function of existential importance, as their meanings and significance need to be transformed. For a brief time, they can evolve into highly polarizing objects of the meta-symbolic discourse.[27]

The nation was staged symbolically as a central feature of politics, not only in Croatia. As Peter Niedermüller points out, the usage of national history to present political visions of the future happened in the post-socialist societies all over Eastern Europe:

Post- symbolisiert und repräsentiert einen grundsätzlichen Bruch, eine absolute Grenze, die den alten Zustand, den Sozialismus von dem neuen, dem Postsozialismus trennt und die historische und politische Kontinuität zwischen den beiden Perioden aufhebt [...]. Die neue Gesellschaft entsteht nämlich durch die symbolische und politische Wiederbelebung der Nation bzw. durch die Nationalisierung der Geschichte und Vergangenheit.[28]

What emerges during the transition from a socialist to a "new post socialist society" is, according to Niedermüller, an "ontological uncertainty" as the previous narratives, values, visions, security concepts and cultural codes lose their validity. To overcome this uncertainty, new narratives are created, countering the former ones by implying that socialism did not just cause this uncertainty but that it destroyed "the nation as a historic and political reality"[29] for ideological reasons, for which

---

24   Aleida Assmann, *Einführung in die Kulturwissenschaft. Grundbegriffe, Themen, Fragestellungen* (Berlin: Erich Schmidt Verlag, 2011), 45.

25   Assmann, *Cultural Memory,* 292.

26   Maja Brkljačić and Holm Sundhaussen, "Symbolwandel und symbolischer Wandel. Kroatiens 'Erinnerungskulturen'," *Osteuropa. Zeitschrift für Gegenwartsfragen des Ostens* 53, no. 7 (July 2003): 934.

27   Ibid., 934.

28   Peter Niedermüller, "Der Mythos der Gemeinschaft. Geschichte, Gedächtnis und Politik im heutigen Osteuropa," in *Umbruch im östlichen Europa. Die nationale Wende und das kollektive Gedächtnis,* eds. Andrei Corbea-Hoisie, Rudolf Jaworski, and Monika Sommer (Innsbruck: Studien Verlag, 2004), 2; [Post- symbolizes and represents a fundamental break, or absolute boundary, separating the old status, socialism, from the new one, post-socialism, and setting off the historical and political continuity between those periods [...]. The new society evolves through a symbolic and political revival of the nation or through nationalizing the history and the past]].

29   Ibid.

the authorities rewrote history and suppressed certain traditions, values, memories and narratives. Consequently, the symbolic "Wiederbelebung der Nation" [revival of the nation] in post-socialist societies is carried out by undermining the history told by the former governments and by restoring the "historische Wahrheit" [historic truth] and the "Geschichtsbewusstsein" [historical awareness].[30] Therefore, and based on these assumptions, socialism is seen as a political and historical dead end that could only be abandoned by going back to the point, "wo man in die Sackgasse geraten ist" [where we blundered into that dead end][31]—a process that Niedermüller calls *rethinking history*.[32] In the practice of official commemorations, as shown below, this often meant re-discovering the pre-socialist times, as they occurred in Croatia in the 1990s: The Yugoslav war in Croatia was constantly connected to World War II, with the NDH regime connoted symbols, persons, notions returned in the form of renamed street names or erected monuments.[33]

Within this process of *rethinking history*, Niedermüller defined three techniques: *Textualisierung* [textualiziation] and *Diskursivierung* [discoursivation] of history and the past by, *e. g.,* rewriting the history schoolbooks.[34] The second method is called *Ritualisierung* [ritualization] of history and the past, in which the cult of death, cemeteries, and reburials play a significant role. The last method of *rethinking history* is *Visualisierung* [visualization], the visual representation of the aforementioned "historic truth."[35]

Croatia's first president, Franjo Tuđman (1922–1999, *Hrvatska Demokratska Zajednica*/Croatian Democratic Union, HDZ), played an active role in the process of all three methods. As for *Diskursivierung* and *Textualisierung* of the history, Tuđman was accused of revisionism[36] mainly because of his book *Horrors of War: Historical Reality and Philosophy*.[37] Therein, he relativized the concentration camp complex Jasenovac[38] in Croatian public discourse by calling it a labor camp rather than a death camp. He even understated the number of victims killed by the NDH there.[39]

---

30 Ibid., 2.
31 Ibid., 5.
32 Ibid.
33 Niedermüller, "Der Mythos der Gemeinschaft," 28.
34 For further details see this chapter's conclusions.
35 Niedermüller, "Der Mythos der Gemeinschaft," 28.
36 Goldstein and Goldstein, "Revisionism in Croatia," 52.
37 Franjo Tuđman, *Bespuća povijesne zbiljnosti* (Zagreb: Nakladni zavod Matice hrvatske, 1989).
38 For further information about Jasenovac see Korb, *Im Schatten des Weltkrieges*, 390–428.
39 As mentioned above, the numbers of victims played a significant role during and after the disintegration of Yugoslavia. See Sundhaussen, "Jugoslawien und seine Nachfolgestaaten. Konstruktion, Dekonstruktion und Neukonstruktion von 'Erinnerungen' und Mythen," 378 f. Furthermore, Tuđman cited three survivors of the camp who allegedly claimed that the "[...] administration was run by Jews [and] they were the inner authority in the camp"; that there

The second example of Niedermüllers' *Ritualisierung* can be illustrated with Tuđman's plan of *pomirba* [reconciliation].[40] He intended to narrow the gaps among Croatians and their different interpretations of history (such as the Croatian fascist and Croatian antifascists, the victims and the perpetrators, *ustaše* and communist resistance fighters) by establishing an "all reconciliatory-nationalism."[41] This reconciliation should have been represented by redesigning the memorial in Jasenovac in the 1990s, which is in accordance with the last method of *rethinking history: visualization* of the new "historical awareness", by erecting new memorials[42] and rebuilding and/or damaging already existing ones. As mentioned above, thousands of socialist monuments have been destroyed or damaged since Croatia's independence in 1991, primarily during Tuđman's presidency.[43]

Starting this process of *rethinking history* in Croatia, therefore, did not just entail rewriting the history told before but highlighting those aspects that had not been described: With the establishment of Socialist Yugoslavia (Federal People's Republic of Yugoslavia 1945–1963; Socialist Federal Republic of Yugoslavia 1963–1992) the communist party conceived and enforced its interpretation of World War II. Divergent memories were suppressed and criminalized.[44] The mass killings in 1945 represented a memory that did not fit into the Yugoslav official narrative of the people's liberation: Added to the mass liquidations committed by Tito's partisans after the end of World War II,[45] persecutions and expropriations of alleged collaborators proceeded, carried out by the Yugoslav secret police and secret service (*Uprava državne bezbednosti, Služba državne bezbednosti*). Holm Sundhaussen concluded that "[...] there is no doubt that the Yugoslav Communist Party enforced its claim to power violently [...]."[46]

---

were "links between the camp administration and the Ustasha administration; that Jewish camp officials had 'participated in the killing' and were in large measure responsible for 'Selection' [...]." See Goldstein and Goldstein, "Revisionism in Croatia," 57.

40 He suggested bringing back the remains of Tito from Serbia to bury him in Kumrovec (Tito's birth town) in Croatia and to bring back the remains of *ustaše* killed after the attempted surrender in Bleiburg/Pliberk to bury them in Croatia. This should have represented his reconciliation plan to narrow the gaps but was never realized. Sundhaussen, "Jugoslawien und seine Nachfolgestaaten. Konstruktion, Dekonstruktion und Neukonstruktion von 'Erinnerungen' und Mythen," 402 f.

41 Brkljačić and Sundhaussen, "Symbolwandel und symbolischer Wandel," 946.

42 In Slunj, a monument for Jure Francetić, an NDH military general and first commander of the *Crna Legija*, was erected in June 2000 with the inscription "Slava, ovdje umrlomu legendarnom borcu protiv četnika" [Glory to the here perished, legendary fighter against the *četniks*]. See Sundhaussen, "Jugoslawien und seine Nachfolgestaaten. Konstruktion, Dekonstruktion und Neukonstruktion von 'Erinnerungen' und Mythen," 394.

43 Brkljačić and Sundhaussen, "Symbolwandel und symbolischer Wandel," 946.

44 Sundhaussen, "Jugoslawien und seine Nachfolgestaaten. Konstruktion, Dekonstruktion und Neukonstruktion von 'Erinnerungen' und Mythen," 377.

45 See Sundhaussen, *Jugoslawien und seine Nachfolgestaaten,* 64.

46 Ibid., 69.

However, in the sense of a culture of remembrance, this "claim to power" was also maintained and achieved through the references to World War II, the National Liberation and, in particular, the number of victims that had lost their lives for the victory.[47] Moreover, with "supranational partisans" under the slogan *bratstvo i jedinstvo* [fraternity and unity],[48] the nationalist controversies that already existed in Yugoslavia before 1945 were meant to be overcome. Public ceremonies, museums, memorials,[49] partisan movies,[50] partisan songs, history schoolbooks, and other representations, realized these aims, as previously discussed; memories that did not fit into the Yugoslav official interpretation of history were suppressed. Therefore, the mass killings in 1945 were kept quiet, only to emerge once the communist culture of remembrance had collapsed. Until then, this topic had been dominant only within the Croatian diaspora community abroad:[51] "Thus, Bleiburg and its pre-existing commemorative practices were uploaded into Croatia's repertoire of collective remembrance [...]."[52]

Ljiljana Radonić analyzed Bleiburg's/Pliberk's changing—or rather growing—significance and discourse in considerable detail by studying Croatian newspapers. She marked the break with the Yugoslav narrative in 1990 when the first report about the commemoration in Bleiburg/Pliberk was published in the Croatian newspaper *Vjesnik*. Not only did the report express a fondness for the commemoration, but it also did not conceal the victim's belonging to the NDH.[53] Articles and the public discussion published afterward were characterized by a glorification of the NDH "[...] those who fought for the NDH were not interested in fascism but rather in the Croatian state [...] the movement [*ustaša*] was established because of the great-Serbian state terrorism [...]."[54] and by a religious ductus.[55] Finally, the victims of Bleiburg/Pliberk were equated with the

---

47 The number of 1.7 million—almost eleven percent of the Yugoslav population—war victims was claimed by Tito and was not questioned (officially) in Yugoslavia whereas calculations from abroad were already challenging this claim in the 1950s; see Sundhaussen, "Jugoslawien und seine Nachfolgestaaten. Konstruktion, Dekonstruktion und Neukonstruktion von 'Erinnerungen' und Mythen," 398.

48 Radonić, *Krieg um die Erinnerung*, 384.

49 A prominent example is the Šumarice Memorial Park in Kragujevac, *i. e.,* "interrupted flight" (architect Miodrag Živković, officially unveiled in 1963); see "Kragujevac," *spomenikdatabase.org*, November 11, 2017, accessed August 31, 2022, http://www.spomenikdatabase.org/kragujevac.

50 *E. g., Bitka na Nerveti, Kozara*.

51 Sundhaussen, "Jugoslawien und seine Nachfolgestaaten. Konstruktion, Dekonstruktion und Neukonstruktion von 'Erinnerungen' und Mythen," 402.

52 Pavlaković, Brentin, Pauković, "The Controversial Commemoration," 11 f.

53 The definition of the victims varied in the 1990s. See Radonić, *Krieg um die Erinnerung*, 237 f.

54 Ibid., 234.

55 The sufferings of Jesus were compared to the history of the Croatians as a "resurrection of the Croatian state" (*Via dolorosa* of the Croatian state); Ibid., 235. The religious aspect will be discussed below.

Croatian people (the escape to Austria is mentioned among others as the "exodus of the Croatian people," "genocide of Croatians," and "severe tragedy of the Croatian people")[56] which suggests that all Croatians had supported the NDH as they were included in the public discourse in their entirety.[57] Radonić concludes: "Bleiburg was the most important national realm of memory during the Tuđman era in which—from uncontested international norms[58]—the focus of the politics of memory lay."[59]

As for the mentioned realm of memory, both Aleida Assmann and Pierre Nora stressed the importance of a specific distinction: Nora's concept of *lieux de mémoire* stems from his differentiation between *history* and *memory*, based on the assumption of a growing "distance" between *real memory* and *memory without past*. While archaic societies embodied the first one, *memory without past* "[...] eternally recycles a heritage, relegating ancestral yesterdays to the undifferentiated time of heroes, inceptions, and myth."[60] *Memory without past* is, therefore, "how modern societies organize a past they are condemned to forget." Hence, memory does not exist.[61] Consequently, the concept of *lieux de mémoire* does not examine the "historical events" and the actions that remain as memories themself but their construction and changing meaning in time.[62]

Assmann refers to Nora's approach by asking whether memory truly ceased to exist.[63] While her conclusions do not contradict the "end of memory" completely, Assmann broadened the functions and impacts of memory that she identified as *kulturelles Gedächtnis* [cultural memory]:[64] "Individuals and cultures construct their memories interactively through communication by speech, images, and rituals. Without such representations, it is impossible to build a memory that can transcend generations and historical epochs."[65] If assumed that the mentioned representa-

---

56 Ibid., 235.

57 Ibid., 238.

58 The mentioned "international norms" will be discussed below in the Conclusion.

59 Radonić, *Krieg um die Erinnerung*, 386; Josip Hrgović, "Orte der Erinnerung und das Problem der Gegenerinnerung. Der 'Platz der Opfer des Faschismus' in Zagreb," in *Die Besetzung des öffentlichen Raumes. Politische Plätze, Denkmäler und Straßennamen im europäischen Vergleich*, eds. Rudolf Jaworski and Peter Stachel (Berlin: Bohemia, 2007), 116.

60 Pierre Nora, *Realms of Memory* (New York: Columbia University Press 1992), 2.

61 "Memory is constantly on our lips because it no longer exists." Ibid., 1.

62 Pierre Nora, *Erinnerungsorte Frankreichs* (München: Beck 2005), 16. "Lieux de mémoire arise out of a sense that there is no such thing as spontaneous memory, hence that we must create archives, mark anniversaries, organize celebrations, pronounce eulogies, and authenticate documents because such things no longer happen as a matter of course." Ibid., 7.

63 Aleida Assmann, *Erinnerungsräume. Formen und Wandlungen des kulturellen Gedächtnisses* (München: C. H. Beck, 2010), 11.

64 Ibid.

65 Assmann, *Cultural Memory and Western Civilization*, 10.

tions, which Assmann calls "Medien" [media], constitute *kulturelles Gedächtnis*, then "[…] every medium opens up its own access to cultural memory."[66]

Therefore, analyzing *kulturelles Gedächtnis* means approaching *Medien* or *Gedächtnisstützen* [memory aids],[67] of which one is the *Gedenkort* [place of commemoration].[68] Such places, *Gedenkorte*, are characterized by the blatant difference between the past and the present. A place in which a specific history did not continue but instead became interrupted through violence, conquest, or loss and cannot be "[…] restored; however, in the medium of memory, we can connect with it. Places of commemoration—where something has been preserved from what has gone forever but can be reactivated through memory—are markers of discontinuity."[69]

Thus, a narrative needs to be created around it to retain and continue something that ended or got demolished.[70] As shown in the empirical analysis below, Bleiburg/Pliberk became such a narrative and *Gedenkort* that is being maintained, *inter alia*, by yet another two *Medien* (*Gedächtnisstützen*): the commemorative plaques and the annual commemoration that are both analyzed here.

Empirical Analysis

The following section analyzes symbols and inscriptions on three commemorative plaques, symbols used either by official representatives of the Croatian government or by representatives of the Croatian Catholic church and visitors during the 2017 commemoration or in the speeches given there. The aim is to identify references relating to the previously-mentioned context of historical revisionism. The commemorative plaques and inscriptions chosen for this research and their relevance as sources of empirical analysis comply with Assmann's claim: "Writing is not only a means of immortalization; it is also an aid to memory. The process of writing on something, or inscribing into something, is the oldest […] and still the most salient metaphor for memory,"[71] which is why writings/inscriptions also constitute part of the *kulturelles Gedächtnis*.[72]

---

66 Ibid., 11.
67 Ibid., 171.
68 Assmann, *Erinnerungsräume*, 309.
69 Assmann, *Cultural Memory and Western Civilization*, 292.
70 Ibid. Assmann distinguishes between different places according to their function of the respective memory—*das Gedächtnis der Orte* [the memory of places]. Beside the mentioned *Gedenkorte*, Assmann identified *Generationenorte* [generational places], *heilige Orte und mythische Landschaften* [holy places and mythical landscapes], *exemplarische Gedächtnisorte* [exemplary place of memory], *Gräber und Grabsteine* [graves and gravestones] and *traumatische Orte* [places of trauma]. Ibid., 281–324.
71 Ibid., 174. Note that according to Assmann, graves and gravestones are also *Gedächtnisorte* that "guarantee the presence of the dead" in contrast to a monument that "distracts attention from the place and onto itself as a representative symbol." Ibid., 309.
72 Ibid., 169.

The following three commemorative plaques were analyzed:

1. The commemorative plaque at the cemetery in Unterloibach/Spodnje Libuče, Carinthia, Austria (erected in 1977 by Petar Miloš, member of the *Počasni bleiburški vod*).
2. The commemorative plaque at the Loibacher Feld/Libuško polje, Carinthia, Austria (erected in 1987 by Petar Miloš, member of the *Počasni bleiburški vod*).
3. The commemorative plaque at the Mirogoj cemetery in Zagreb, Croatia (erected in 1994 by "Hrvati iz domovine i iz inozemstva").[73]

Written and symbolic elements are not the only *Medien* to constitute *kulturelles Gedächtnis;* places and rituals also complete the corpus. Furthermore, following Maurice Halbwachs' concept of *collective memory*, symbols and pictures, along with monuments, places, and rituals, have an essential impact on establishing and maintaining a community's self-perception.[74]

This chapter's aim is neither to reconstruct the events of Bleiburg/Pliberk nor to question what is remembered by individual visitors. Instead, based on the concept of *kulturelles Gedächtnis* and, more specifically, *Gedenkorte*, it seeks to reconstruct the circumstances and requirements of commemoration practices and the process and setting of how something should be remembered.

The commemoration was initially organized by representatives of the Croatian diaspora community, starting with the first ceremony in 1952.[75] The commemoration was organized by the association *Bleiburger Ehrenzug/Počasni Bleiburški vod*[76] under the patronage of the Croatian Parliament and the Parliament of the Croatian people in Bosnia and Hercegovina. It takes place at the Loibacher Feld/ Libuško polje, south of the Carinthian town Bleiburg/Pliberk, near the border with Slovenia. It is held annually on the weekend before Mother's Day as this day is considered the day closest to the actual historical event.[77] The commemoration itself consists of three parts: It begins at the cemetery in Unterloibach/Spodnje Libuče, then the "procession" moves to the Loibacher Feld/Libuško polje where the main part of the commemoration, the holy mass and the speeches, take place.

---

73 As written on the commemorative plaque: [Croats from the homeland and from abroad].
74 Aleida Assmann, *Der lange Schatten der Vergangenheit. Erinnerungskultur und Geschichtspolitik* (München: C. H. Beck, 2006), 30.
75 Kolstø, "Bleiburg," 1161.
76 The *Počasni Bleiburški vod* (PBV) was founded as an association in 1953 by Croatian emigrés Ante Mikrut, Ilija Abramović, Jakov Radoš, and Mirko Karačić, who were former *ustaše* and "who left no doubt that they [...] embellished and glorified the NDH [...]." See *Bericht der ExpertInnen "Bleiburg"* (Wien: Bundesministerium für Inneres, 2021), 30 f., accessed August 31, 2022, https://bmi.gv.at/Downloads/Expertenbericht_Bleiburg.pdf.
77 The Croatian parliament has even proclaimed May 15 an official *spomen dan* [memorial day], Kolstø, "Bleiburg," 1161 f.

Methodical Approach

To analyze the research objects systematically, the following multilayered method was applied to examine the (contemporary) hypothesis of historical revisionism in Croatia:

I. **Symbolic approach**: In the first step, the chosen symbols from the commemorative plaques were screened and put in their historical context to interpret them properly. The interpretation was accompanied by the already published literature.

II. **Semantic approach**: This methodological approach followed a process similar to the symbolic approach. Consequently, it analyzed the engraved scriptures, contextualized them, and interpreted them to decode their specific meaning and function.

III. **Performative approach**: In a third step, performative aspects were focused on, rather than the materiality, *i.e.,* the annual commemoration in Bleiburg/Pliberk. This approach is again subdivided along the three main methodical paths: symbolic, semantic, and performative.

For this purpose, the commemoration held in Bleiburg/Pliberk on May 13, 2017, was visited by the author and two additional persons, who were briefed in advance.[78] The author developed a guideline to observe the commemoration

---

78 In recent years, more critical attention to Austria's role in the commemoration has arisen. In 2018, representatives of 21 organizations (political and cultural) presented a petition in which they protested the commemoration. The *Landesamt für Verfassungsschutz und Terrorismusbekämpfung* (Carinthian Office for the Protection of the Constitution and Counterterrorism) argued, in turn, that the commemoration is a clerical event that had been taking place for 30 years. See "Protest gegen kroatische Gedenkfeier," *orf.at*, accessed November 16, 2017, http://kaernten.orf.at/news/stories/2842236/. However, the 2017 commemoration was the last one to be declared and celebrated as a bishop's mass. As such, it required the permission of the Austrian diocese Gurk-Klagenfurt/Krška škofija. However, in 2018 the diocese refused to approve the commemoration as a bishop's mass, citing the "lacking distance to fascist *Gedankengut*." In 2019 the organizers of the commemoration, the PBV, bypassed this prohibition by declaring the bishop's sermon as a speech rather than a bishop's mass. In addition to the diocese's reaction, an amendment of the federal law was passed in March 2019, banning specific symbols that are "explicitly" related to "terrorism" and "extremism." These include two *ustaše* symbols: See "Gesamte Rechtsvorschrift für Symbole-BezeichnungsV," *Rechtsinformationssystem des Bundes*, accessed April 8, 2021, https://www.ris.bka.gv.at/GeltendeFassung.wxe?Abfrage=Bundesnormen&Gesetzesnummer=20009091; "Extremismus: Welche Symbole verboten sind," *Die Presse*, February 13, 2019; "Ustascha-Gedenkfeier in Bleiburg: Weniger Besucher als erwartet," *Der Standard*, May 18, 2019. In July 2020, the Austrian parliament filed a motion for a resolution that commissioned the Austrian government to prove if the commemoration in Bleiburg could be prohibited (see "Entschließung des Nationalrates vom 9. Juli 2020 betreffend Untersagung der Feier im Gedenken an das 'Massaker von Bleiburg'," *Republik Österreich: Parlament*, accessed June 14, 2022, https://www.parlament.gv.at/

structurally.[79] The analysis results of the symbolic and semantic approach are presented in the following table:

Table 1: Results of symbolic and semantic approach. Source: Author.

Commemorative Plaque	Symbols	Semantic inscriptions
Cemetery in Unterloibach/ Spodnje Libuče	Coat of arms (white-red), crescent moon, Catholic-Christian symbols (Jesus, Mary, rosary, bible)	"U čast i slavu poginuloj i u domovinu izručenoj, te nestaloj hrvatskoj vojsci u borbi za hrvatsku domovinu svibnja 1945."[80] "Majka Hrvata tuguje i plače. I Blajburško polje ovo gorka nam je uspomena, vječnog mira Domobrana, ko i ratnog pobratima svoga."[81]
Loibacher Feld/Libuško polje	Coat of arms (white-red), crescent moon, cross	"U čast i slavu poginuloj hrvatskoj vojsci svibanj 1945."[82]
Cemetery Mirogoj, Zagreb	Picture (see interpretation below), coat of arms, cross	"Hrvatskim žrtvama u Bleiburgu i na križnim putovima 1945."[83]

PAKT/VHG/XXVII/E/E_00081/index.shtml). Based on this motion, the Austrian Federal Ministry of the Interior assigned a group of experts to prove a possible ban on the commemoration. The experts concluded the following: "In result, the group of experts came to the decision that a gathering, as it occured in 2019 and the years prior, should be banned." See *Bericht der ExpertInnen "Bleiburg,"* 102. The commemorations were canceled in 2020 and 2021 due to the covid-19-pandemic restrictions. The commemoration was held in Sarajevo in 2020 and in the Croatian Udbina, and at the Mirogoj cemetery in Zagreb in 2021. Notwithstanding, the Croatian ambassador in Austria, Daniel Glunčić laid down wreaths in Bleiburg/Pliberk; according to the press statement, the wreaths were laid down in the name of Gordan Jandroković and Andrej Plenković. See "Bleiburg 2021—kleine Feier mit Botschafter, keine Entscheidung zum Verbot," *no-ustasa.at*, accessed June 12, 2022, https://www.no-ustasa.at/allgemein/4658/nachbetrachtung-2021/. In 2022 no commemoration took place; instead, a mass was held at the church of Bleiburg/Pliberk and in Udbina and Zagreb. See "Bleiburg 2022: Alles neu? Eher nicht ...," *no-ustasa.at*, accessed June 12, 2022, https://www.no-ustasa.at/allgemein/4753/bleiburg-update-2022/.

79   The guideline is in the author's archive.
80   [In honor and glory of the Croatian army who fell in the struggle for their Croatian fatherland as they were extradited back to the fatherland and disappeared, May 1945].
81   [Mother Croatia grieves and cries. The Bleiburg Field is a bitter memory for us, everlasting peace for the homeland-defenders and for their fellow comrades].
82   [In honor and glory of the fallen Croatian army, May 1945].
83   [For the Croatian victims in Bleiburg and on the Way of the Cross 1945].

Results

Symbolic Analysis

By analyzing the commemorative plaques and their symbolic meaning, three characteristics appeared permanently: a coat of arms, a Catholic-Christian symbol, and the Muslim emblem of the crescent moon. All three will be discussed here.

In two of the three cases, the coat of arms with a white-red sequence could be found, suggesting a symbolic connection to the NDH. Although the sequence could also refer to the medieval Croatian kingdom, the semantic inscriptions confirm these suggestions. With considerable frequency, another symbol appeared, *i.e.*, the crescent moon. The Independent State of Croatia aimed to forge a homogenous state, a "greater Croatia,"[84] specifically addressed to the Serbian Orthodox population in the NDH.[85] Muslims who lived in the state did not have a specific

Figure 1: Commemorative plaque at the cemetery in Unterloibach/Spodnje Libuče, Carinthia, Austria. Source: *bleiburgcro.blogspot.com*, May 14, 2017, accessed July 29, 2022, http://bleiburgcro.blogspot.com/2017/05/spomenik-blieburg_14.html.

Figure 2: Commemorative plaque at Loibacher Feld/Libuško polje, Carinthia, Austria. Source: Author (May 2017).

Figure 3: Commemorative plaque at the cemetery Mirogoj, Zagreb, Croatia. Source: *bleiburgcro. blogspot.com*, May 14, 2017, accessed July 29, 2022, http://bleiburgcro.blogspot.com/2017/05/spomenik-blieburg_14.html.

---

84 Korb, *Im Schatten des Weltkrieges*, 129.
85 The NDH officials persecuted not just the Serbs living within the territory but also Jews, Romani people and Communists. However, the ustaše called upon a "Volkstumskampf"

position, although "some were fond of the *ustaša* government."[86] Furthermore, the government declared them Croats with a Muslim belief.[87]

Accordingly, it can be concluded that the Croatian remembrance also includes the victims of Muslim confession. Following the culture of Croatian remembrance in terms of beliefs, the third characteristic represented here is the Catholic-Christian symbolic (cross: see Figures 1, 2, and 3; Jesus, Mary, rosaries, and the bible: see Figure 10) that appeared on all three commemorative plaques. The plaque at the cemetery in Unterloibach/Spodnje Libuče stands out as it shows more than just one related reference (see Figure 1). Considering that the official culture of remembrance is narrated in a highly Catholic-Christian ductus,[88] the symbol fits into the current state of research: The Catholic Church "has left its clearly recognizable imprint on the Bleiburg myth, which today has strong religious overtones."[89]

The commemorative plaque in Mirogoj differs from the others: The visual highlight of this memorial plaque is the image that depicts a gathering of men and women. The composition includes a priest (Catholic-Christian-reference) and a man wearing the traditional Muslim headgear, the *fez* (which refers to the victims of Muslim confession). Furthermore, the image shows a woman and a child, which one could interpret as a hint that not only members of the NDH-Army and the Government but also civilians were killed. There is a significantly different emphasis on the man on his knees and the one standing behind him. Firstly, the fact that the man is kneeling and holding his right shoulder suggests that he

---

[racial war] with Serbia, mostly because of their "[...] unpleasant Yugoslav era." Ibid., 130 f. and 195–206.

86 Marie-Janine Calic, *Geschichte Jugoslawiens im 20. Jahrhundert* (München: C. H. Beck, 2010), 139.

87 Ibid. The *ustaše* argued that the Bosnian Muslims were, in fact, "ethnic Croats" whose ancestors converted to Islam in the Middle Ages. In 1943 the *Waffen-SS* started to recruit Bosnian Muslims to expand its influence in Southeastern Europe and deployed the 1. Kroatische-SS-Freiwilligen-Divison in March 1, 1943 (which was renamed to 13. *Waffen-Gebirgs-Division der SS Handschar in* June 1944); Korb, *Im Schatten des Weltkrieges*, 84 f.

88 The discourse on the Croatian catholic church's role within the NDH is predominated by the role of the Croatian archbishop Alojzije Stepinac (1898–1960), who sympathized with the NDH as it was an independent state but simultaneously condemned its persecutions. On October 11, 1946, Stepinac was arrested and sentenced to 16 years in prison and forced labor. When the Vatican announced Stepinac's nomination for becoming a cardinal on November 29, 1952, Yugoslavia interrupted its diplomatic relations with the Vatican, re-adopting them just after Stepinac's death. Stepinac, known as an anticommunist, returned to the Croatian public as a martyr in the 1990s. In general, the relationship between the Croatian catholic church and the NDH has been considered ambivalent and "[...] ranging between apotheosis and a half-hearted distance." See Sundhaussen, "Jugoslawien und seine Nachfolgestaaten. Konstruktion, Dekonstruktion und Neukonstruktion von 'Erinnerungen' und Mythen," 396; Korb, *Im Schatten des Weltkrieges*, 274, 426.

89 Kolstø, "Bleiburg," 1154.

is wounded and has therefore suffered. Secondly, a depiction of sorrow can be understood for the man behind as his bones are more clearly depicted than those of the rest, which in turn could suggest that he suffered from starvation caused by the partisans' maltreatment.

Moreover, the attached NDH coat of arms highlights a fiercely controversial aspect of Croatia's politics of memory: Although Croatia's history dates back further than 1941, the employed coat of arms overtly refers to the events of Bleiburg/Pliberk and therefore to the NDH.

Semantic Analysis

Language *per se* always represents more than just the circumstances or items it refers to. It postulates itself as a certain act and therefore needs to be considered a "performative language"[90] or "performative act."[91] If it is presumed that a "performative act" carries not merely meanings but a certain kind of power as a discursive element[92], the analysis of semantic categories then serves the purpose of this study to examine the revisionist implications of Croatia's politics of memory with regards to Bleiburg/Pliberk.

The posthumously published book *How to Do Things in Words* is a collection of John L. Austin's lectures held at Harvard and Oxford University, in which he criticized the traditional linguistic philosophy of treating language and sentences respectively as statements or as "constative utterances."[93] In contrast, he identified the "performative utterances"[94] as its enforcement and therefore determined by an act (*e. g.*, the sentence "I am eating a fish" requires an action). Based on John L. Austin, Michel Foucault,[95] Jacques Derrida,[96] and other scholarship,[97] Judith Butler has further developed the speech act theory, which seems

---

90   John L. Austin, *Zur Theorie der Sprechakte. (How to Do Things with Words)* (Stuttgart: Reclam, 2005).
91   Judith Butler, *Hass spricht. Zur Politik des Performativen* (Frankfurt am Main: Suhrkamp, 2006).
92   Ibid., 87.
93   John A. Dinneen, "What Austin Does with Words," *Philosophy and Phenomenological Research* 32, no. 4 (Summer 1972): 515.
94   Ibid.
95   Michel Foucault, "Politics and the Study of Discourse" in *The Foucault Effect: Studies in Governmentality*, eds. Graham Burchell, Colin Gordon, Peter Miller (Chicago: The University of Chicago Press, 1991).
96   Jacques Derrida, *Grammatologie* (Frankfurt am Main: Suhrkamp, 1983); Jacques Derrida, "Die Différance," in *Postmoderne und Dekonstruktion*, ed. Peter Engelmann (Stuttgart: Reclam, 2015).
97   *E. g.*, Roland Barthes, *Das Reich der Zeichen* (Frankfurt am Main: Suhrkamp, 2015); Charles Bally and Albert Sechehaye, eds. *Ferdinand De Saussure. Grundfragen der allgemeinen Sprachwissenschaft* (Berlin, New York: Walter de Gruyter, 1967).

to precisely describe the semantic aspects of Croatia's culture of remembrance: Language is (from a poststructuralist perspective) considered as an element that constitutes the social reality by structuring and carrying meanings. As a result, things gain their meanings through invocation—therefore, they can be defined as an act. The premise for this invocation is its recognition by an authority, which has not just established a particular meaning, but a specific identity—within a discourse. Hence, the invocation does not describe an existing reality but instead creates a new one, accepted and/or created by an authority/power in conventional terms. This process culminates into a universal recognition of meanings and the resulting created reality by using the established invocations. Moreover, the usage reproduces this reality and therefore reproduces its required power.[98]

Placing the Croatian case study into these theoretical concepts, the following inscriptions gain even more importance. Especially when bearing in mind the wreath-laying ceremony in front of the commemorative plaques, which affirms the inscriptions and their meanings with not just a dynamic but also a repetitive character.

The commemorative plaque at the cemetery in Unterloibach/Spodnje Libuče was built by "preživjeli suborci" [survived fellow comrades], with "in honor and glory" referring to the NDH-Army. Literally, it says (see Figure 1): "In honor and glory of the Croatian army who fell in the struggle for their Croatian fatherland as they were extradited back to the fatherland and disappeared, May 1945." This is the only inscription that refers specifically to the extradition to the Yugoslavian Liberation Army. Furthermore, the plaque's left wing says: "Mother Croatia grieves and cries. The Bleiburg Field is a bitter memory for us, everlasting peace for the homeland-defenders and for their fellow comrades." Apart from the fact that the semantics here refer to the NDH Army (and therefore to the *Waffen-SS* that fought alongside the NDH Army)[99] and that the inscriptions suggest that the "Bleiburg Field" was a site of mass killings, in this context, the commemorative plaque suggests that the "Blessed Mother Mary" simultaneously symbolizes the alleged Mother of Croatia which would again point to a Catholic-Christian relatedness. What stands out particularly is the German translation of the Croatian inscription as it does not refer to the "hrvatskoj vojsci" [Croatian army] but to the "kroatischen Soldaten" [Croatian soldiers] (see Figure 1). Furthermore, while the

---

98 Butler, *Haß spricht*, 125.
99 One of the German *Waffen SS* Mountain Divisions was deployed to Bosnia as the *Waffen SS Gebirgs-Division Handschar*. It was composed mostly out of volunteers from the NDH and *Volksdeutsche*. See Holm Sundhaussen, "Zur Geschichte der Waffen-SS in Kroatien. 1941–1945," *Südost-Forschungen* 30 (January 1971); Calic, *Geschichte Jugoslawiens im 20. Jahrhundert*, 141.

Croatian inscription contains the phrase "za hrvatsku" [for the Croatian], this is missing in the German translation.[100]

The German inscription at the second commemorative plaque at the Loibacher Feld/Libuško polje also substantially deviates from the Croatian one because it does not "honor" the NDH army specifically but "the fallen Croats May 1945" instead. Similar to the first plaque, it, therefore, insinuates that the killed individuals (or individual soldiers) are being remembered. At the same time, the Croatian version "openly reveals the honoring of the *ustaša* Army and its declaration as the 'croatian army' which in turn conceals the Croatian anti-fascist fight."[101] The inscription says: "In honor and glory of the fallen Croatian army 1945" (see Figure 2). It also remembers the *ustaša* militia and, therefore, clearly refers to the soldiers of a fascist state ("in honor and glory").

Considering that the highest political representatives of Croatia annually visit all three commemorative plaques,[102] this semantic remembrance seems to correspond perfectly with the assumed hypothesis of today's sustaining role of historical revisionism among Croatian political elites and vast parts of society.

A special and rather undefined expression is placed on the third memorial plaque at the cemetery Mirogoj in Croatia's capital Zagreb: The inscription "For the Croatian victims in Bleiburg and on the Way of the Cross 1945" (see Figure 3) clearly refers to the Croatian victims among the rather heterogeneous group of all victims. Since the NDH-government eliminated the linguistic usage of the Bosnian geographical parts, Bosna i Hercegovina, and declared its population as Croatians with a Muslim confession,[103] this inscription does not necessarily exclude the Muslim victims, at least geographically. Furthermore, the fact that the image shows a man wearing a *fez* confirms this assumption.

An even more clearer reference in terms of confessions is the expression of *križnim putovima* [Way of the Cross], which exclusively limits the memory to the Catholic victims. At the same time, it does not exclude the orthodox, therefore Serbian, ones.

To summarize and conclude the semantic approach: Two (Figures 1 and 2) out of the three commemorative plaques are connected to the remembrance of the NDH Army, with the important exception of the German inscriptions. These deviations were made deliberately and suggest that the official remembrance is

---

100 The Croatian word *domovina* can be translated as "homeland" as well as "fatherland." The latter (*Vaterland*) is used in the German inscription of the plaque. See also: *Bericht der ExpertInnengruppe "Bleiburg,"* 36, 51.

101 Ibid. The reason for these blatant deviations in the German inscription was the respective requirements of the Austrian local authorities. These entailed that the commemoration plaque could not be dedicated to the "Croatian army." See ibid., 36; "Veränderung des Gedenkorts Bleiburg/Pliberk seit 1945," *no-ustasa.at*, accessed June 14, 2022, https://www.no-ustasa.at/allgemein/577/veraenderungen-des-gedenkorts-bleiburg-pliberk-set-1945/.

102 See the next subchapter.

103 Calic, *Geschichte Jugoslawiens im 20. Jahrhundert*, 139.

solely focused on the individual "soldiers" and "Croats," whereas the Croatian part exclusively highlights the NDH Army. Considering that wreaths were annually laid down in front of all three commemorative plaques (not just by relatives of the victims but also by Croatian politicians), it must be concluded that a fascist state's armed forces are officially commemorated, and the fascist state is part of the collective memory.

Performative Analysis

This part of the research focused solely on the annual commemoration ceremony in Bleiburg/Pliberk. Three observers, including the author, attended the ceremony on May 13, 2017.[104] The scheme for monitoring the ceremony was divided into three parts—symbolic objects (*e. g.*, flags), semantic things (speeches), and performative objects (structure of the event). Each observer had to focus on one of these aspects.

Symbolic analysis: The observers were briefed to focus on symbols related to the NDH state, especially on clothes and flags.

Besides the version of the coat of arms used by the *ustaša* government, another clear reference to the NDH is the salute *Za dom spremni* [for the homeland—ready], which is the Croatian equivalent to the German *Hitlergruß*[105] and can be read on the black flag (see Figure 4). In today's Croatia, this expression is prohibited by law but only if used in the context of the NDH. Since the phrase *Za dom spremni* was also used during the Yugoslav war in the 1990s, the execution of this law is rather complicated. It cannot be applied if the slogan refers to the 1990s war. Furthermore, since the commemoration took place in Austria, its usage was not prosecuted until the 2019 amendment to the law that banned two *ustaše*-related symbols.[106]

---

104 The underlying system of the observation was ensured by a preceding briefing and guideline, which the author developed to assure that the seen and heard objects get documented properly.

105 Radonić, *Krieg um die Erinnerung*, 345.

106 The following example shows how controversial and difficult it is to execute the law: As of June 2020, the Croatian Supreme Court decided that the Croatian Singer Thompson would be allowed to use the expression *Za dom spremni* In his song *Bojna Čavoglave* [Čavoglave Battalion] legally. This decision was made after the police raised charges against him for using the expression during a concert in 2016. In its statement, the Supreme court referred to the Croatian constitution in which Croatia's sovereignty is based on a "series of historical events" that include the 1990s election as well as the NDH. Since the expression *Za dom spremni* was also used during the war in the 1990s, the court argued that the song and this expression refer to the war in the 1990s rather than its usage in the NDH. The constitutional court, in turn, contradicted: "Regarding the greeting *Za dom spremni* the constitutional court has already expressed its standpoint through decision a few times after which it is the NDH's greeting and that it is not in accordance with Croatia's constitution." See "Ustavni sud još jednom ustvrdio 'za dom spremni' je

Figure 4: *HOS, Za dom spremni I*, Loibacher Feld/ Libuško polje, Carinthia, Austria. Source: Author (May 2017).

Figure 5: *HOS, Za dom spremni II*, Loibacher Feld/Libuško polje, Carinthia, Austria. Source: Author (May 2017).

Another association with NDH can be found on the flag, which has two meanings: During the NDH period, the abbreviation HOS labeled the military force *Hrvatske oružane snage* (Croatian Armed Force). However, it also relates to the *Hrvatske obrambene snage* (Croatian Defensive Force), a Croatian paramilitary organization during the Yugoslav war of the 1990s.[107] Although the usage in this picture (see Figure 4) does not necessarily rely on the NDH-Version of the HOS, despite what the coat of arms and the phrase *Za dom spremni* suggest. Nevertheless, it does mean that a connection between the two wars was made. This linkage recurred systematically throughout all three parts of the performative analysis.

The symbols mentioned above can all be found several times in Figure 5. It is also worth noticing the prevalence of black clothing. Again, this reference has two denotations, depending on the period. An elite force of the NDH state was called *crna legija* [Black Legion] or, in short: *crnci* [the Blacks].[108] Similarly, the paramilitary force *Hrvatske obrambene snage* from the war of the 1990s was also called *crnci*,[109] which is the second direct link between World War II and the Yugoslav war.

ustaški pozdrav i nije u skladu s Ustavom," *dnevnik.hr*, June 5, 2020, accessed August 31, 2022, https://dnevnik.hr/vijesti/hrvatska/ustavni-sud-jos-jedom-ustvrdio-za-dom-spremni-je-ustaski-pozdrav-i-nije-u-skladu-s-ustavom---608157.html; Enis Zebić, "Zašto se Thomsonu dozvoljava upotreba pozdrava 'za dom spremni'?," *slobodnaevropa.org*, June 4, 2020, accessed August 31, 2022, https://www.slobodnaevropa.org/a/zašto-se-thompsonu-dozvoljava-upotreba-pozdrava-za-dom-spremni-/30652940.html. For the Croatian constitution see "Ustav Republike Hrvatske," *verfassungen.eu*, accessed April 8, 2021, http://www.verfassungen.eu/hr/verf90-i.htm.

107 For further information, see Rene Toth, *Zwischen Konflikt und Kooperation. Fünfzehn Jahre Friedenskonsolidierung in Bosnien und Herzegowina* (Wiesbaden: Springer VS, 2011).

108 See Kolstø, "Bleiburg," 1161; Suppan, *Hitler—Beneš—Tito*, 1066.

109 Toth, *Zwischen Konflikt und Kooperation*, 85.

Figure 6: *Za dom spremni III*, Loibacher Feld/Li-
buško polje, Carinthia, Austria. Source: *stopptdie-
rechten.at*, May 23, 2017, accessed July 29, 2022,
https://www.stopptdierechten.at/2017/05/23/die-
bleiburg-pilger_innen/.

Figure 7: Ante Pavelić, Loibacher Feld/Libuško
polje, Carinthia, Austria. Source: Author (May
2017).

In addition to the previously mentioned symbols, the last one captured at the commemoration was the *Reichsadler* (the "Imperial Eagle," which resembles the Emblem of the "Third Reich") that is attached to the coat of arms used by the *ustaša* and the phrase *Za dom spremni* (Figure 6).

Noticeable in this picture (Figure 7) is the imprint of the two wooden bottles with a portrait of the Croatian *poglavnik* Ante Pavelić.

Regarding the assumption of a glorification and transfiguration of the NDH regime within the remembrance of Bleiburg/Pliberk and its victims, this symbolic approach clearly shows their linkage, as connections between the two wars could be traced repeatedly.

Semantic Analysis: This part solely analyzes the speeches held at the commemoration ceremony on May 13, 2017.[110] Since the audience was mainly composed of Croats, speeches were also mostly held in the Croatian language.[111]

At noon, a catholic mass was held by the Croatian archbishop of Đakovo-Osijek, Đuro Hranić. He started the holy mass by referring to the slain "vojnici i civilisti" [soldiers and civilians][112] and their tragic fate. The victims had been condemned to be never questioned or mentioned. Currently, as the truth is coming out, "pokušava se spriječiti našu molitvu" [there is an attempt to obstruct our prayer].[113] Therefore, he asked the participants to give the opponents no reason for further criticism, be it through symbols, gestures, or words.[114]

---

110 Note the already mentioned aspects about symbolic and performative language as discussed in the subchapter "Semantic analysis."
111 All speeches held in Bleiburg/Pliberk were recorded, transcribed and translated by the author.
112 Speech of Đuro Hranić, Bleiburg/Pliberk, Mai 13, 2017.
113 Ibid.
114 Ibid.

After the catholic mass *Efendi* Idriz Bešić held a speech in the name of the Muslim community in Croatia in which he highlighted that the truth needs to be known and that no one can run away from it. The truth should be kept safe, and the victims remembered. Legitimating these events, as some tried and are still trying to do, would mean provoking misfortune. In the end, he referred to the victims of the Yugoslav war by saying that crimes similar to those committed in Bleiburg/Pliberk also happened in Vukovar and Srebrenica.[115] Before the microphone was passed to the speaker from the organizer (*Počasni bleiburški vod*), the moderator Tanja Popovec also emphasized the remembrance of the victims of the Croatian Army and civilians, which represents "najveća tragedija našeg naroda" [the greatest tragedy of our people].[116]

The PBV speaker, the priest Ante Kutleša, started off by thanking the president of the Croatian Parliament, Gordan Jandroković (HDZ) and all the other members of the Croatian Parliament and ministers, the representatives of the Croatian people in Bosnia and Hercegovina. He also expressed his gratitude to the disabled veterans of the "Domovinski rat"[117] [homeland war] and to the representatives of the Croatian diaspora community.[118] Finally, in German, he thanked the Austrian government, the Bleiburg authorities, and especially the regional administrative bodies and directorates for making the commemorative act possible. In the end, he cited the theologian Dietrich Bonhoeffer:[119] "Die Ehrfurcht vor der Vergangenheit und die Verantwortung gegenüber der Zukunft geben dem Leben die richtige Haltung."[120] In the context of Kutleša's interpretation of Bleiburg/Pliberk, the words of the prominent resistance fighter against the Nazi regime concerning the right attitude in life gained a completely different meaning from what was intended.

Afterwards, Željko Raguž, as the representative of the *Hrvatski narodni sabor Bosne i Hercegovine* (Croatian People's Parliament in Bosnia and Hercegovina), held his speech: He started by referring to the elusive injustice and to the "mračna noć povijesti" [dark night of history], which "je mijenjao lice Europe" [changed

---

115 Paraphrased from Idriz Bešić's speech. The connotation made between World War II and the Yugoslav war evidences the widely spread assumption that the partisans mainly consisted of Serbian četniks. Also, he refers to the myth of Bleiburg/Pliberk by implying that the mass killings happened in Bleiburg/Pliberk.

116 Speech of Tanja Popovec, Bleiburg/Pliberk, Mai 13, 2017.

117 *Domovinski rat* [homeland war] is the common Croatian word for Yugoslav war.

118 Speech of Ante Kutleša, Bleiburg/Pliberk, Mai 13, 2017.

119 Dietrich Bonhoeffer was not just a theologian but also participated actively in the resistance against the Nazi regime. He was sentenced to death and executed in April 1945. For further information see Eberhard Bethge, *Dietrich Bonhoeffer* (Reinbeck bei Hamburg: Rohwolt Taschenbuch Verlag, 2006).

120 [The awe of the past and the responsibility for the future provide the right attitude in life.] Speech of Ante Kutleša, Bleiburg/Pliberk, Mai 13, 2017.

Europe's face].[121] He then summarized the most important elements of his interpretation of history:

> Vrijedno je i danas prisjetiti se nekih činjenica. U drugome svjetskom ratu 1941-1943 Velika Britanija je podupirala *četničke* pokrete [...] u zimi 43. saveznici su počeli pomagati Titove partizane. Broj partizana u Srbiji 44. porastao je sa 22000, koliko je bilo 43., na 204000. Partizanski vođa Josip Broz [...] pozvao je 1944. *četnike* na suradnju. [...] te godine jugoslovenski kralj Petar iije pod Britanskim pritiskom pozvao *četnike* da se pridruže partizanima. Najveći broj *četnika* poslušao je kralja i prešao na partizansku stranu.[122]

[It is worth remembering some facts: During World War II, from 1941–1943, Great Britain encouraged the *četnik* movements [...]; in the winter of 1943, the Allies started to support Tito's partisans; the number of partisans in Serbia rose from 22,000 in 1943 to 204,000 in 1944 [...]; in 1944 the partisan's leader Josip Broz Tito [...] called the *četniks* to cooperate, the Yugoslavian king Peter also asked četniks to join the partisans under Great Britain's pressure. Most of the četniks followed the King's request and defected to the partisans.]

Željko Raguž concluded that the largest part of the četniks defected to the partisans:

> Na kraju drugog svjetskog rata veliki broj pripadnika Hrvatske Vojske i još brojni civili predali su se britanskoj vojsci u Austriji uzdajući se u njihovu zaštitu. Međutim britanski zapovjednici su ih predali na nemilost partizanima, iako su dobro znali ili su trebali znati od koga je (sic!) i kako je velikim dijelom nastala ta vojska. Uslijedila je najveća tragedija u povijesti hrvatskog naroda.[123]

[By the end of World War II, a considerable number of Croatian army members and civilians had surrendered to the British Army in Austria, believing in their protection. Meanwhile, the British commanders extradited them to the partisan's disgrace, although they certainly knew or should have known how a big part of this army had formed. The biggest tragedy in the history of the Croatian people followed.]

Raguž referred to the widespread assumption that, at that time, the partisans consisted mostly of Serbian četniks.[124] This assumption partly stems from the fact that tens of thousands of *četniks* and the Muslims formerly recruited for

---

121 Speech of Željko Raguž, Bleiburg/Pliberk, Mai 13, 2017.
122 Ibid.
123 Speech of Željko Raguž, Bleiburg/Pliberk, Mai 13, 2017.
124 *Cf.* Robert Knight's article on the extradition and the "betrayal of the Croatian people" discussed among the Croatian diaspora community, see Knight, "Kosaken und Kroaten in Kärnten."

the *Waffen-SS* in Bosnia had deserted during the war against the partisans.[125] In addition, by claiming that the "Bleiburg tragedy" was the "biggest tragedy in the history of Croatian people," he made no distinction between the members of NDH and the rest of the Croatian population during World War II and today, which suggests that all of them supported and still support the NDH.[126]

At the end of his speech, he referred to the victims of Bleiburg/Pliberk and the "Way of the Cross" again:

> Žrtve Bleiburga i križnog puta nisu bile uzalud. One su bile nadahnuće za sva hrvatska nastojanja da se dođe do slobode i hrvatske države.[127]

> [They did not die in vain as they were important for all Croatian efforts for freedom and a Croatian state.]

Besides the fact that his speech endorsed the Bleiburg myth, insinuating that the Austrian town was a site of the 1945 mass killings, when in fact it was not, he also declared the victims' death "an effort" for the "Croatian State" which, in a certain way legitimizes or neglects the NDH and the crimes it committed.

Finally, the last speaker, president of the Croatian Parliament Gordan Jandroković, greeted the participants personally as well as in the name of the Croatian Parliament, which, together with the Croatians people's Parliament in Bosnia and Hercegovina,[128] formed the patronage of the commemoration for the victims of the "Bleiburg tragedy" and the victims of all post-war communist regimes. As the president of the Parliament, he promised that the patronage would be kept in the future:[129]

---

125 See Korb, *Im Schatten des Weltkrieges*, 435.
126 *Nota bene*: No difference was made between the members of NDH and the rest of the Croatian population during World War II and today, which suggests that all of them supported and still support the NDH. *Cf.* Radonić, *Krieg um die Erinnerung*, 238.
127 Ibid. Note the emphasis on the victims of World War II and the Yugoslav war.
128 The head organization of all Croatian political parties in Bosnia and Herzegovina.
129 Between 2012 and 2016 the Croatian parliament terminated its patronage for the commemoration as the 2012 government considered it as a place where "not the victims are remembered but the end of NDH is mourned." (This statement originated from Zoran Milanović, Croatia's prime minister from 2011–2016, chair of the *Socijaldemokratska partija Hrvatske*/Socialdemocratic Party Croatia). See "Sabor vratio pokroviteljstvo nad Bleiburgom, Milanović: Tamo idu oni koji žale za NDH," *IndexHR*, February 2, 2016, accessed August 31, 2022, https://www.index.hr/vijesti/clanak/cetiri-glasa-za-i-dva-protiv-sabor-ce-opet-biti-pokrovitelj-bleiburga/872849.aspx. Up to that point Croatian authorities played an important role in the commemoration considering that their donations in 2004 and 2007 enabled the *Počasni bleiburški vod* to purchase an additional piece of land at the Bleiburg fields. Kolstø, "Bleiburg," 1162.

Okupili smo se ovdje da se podsjetimo, ali i da još jednom potvrdimo našu obavezu i odgovornost čuvanja istine i aktivnog suprotstavljanja svim oblicima totalitarne vladavine.[130]

[We came here together to remember and confirm once again our responsibility to keep the truth alive and to actively oppose every form of totalitarian government.]

Furthermore, he referred to hundreds of thousands of victims consisting of disarmed soldiers and unarmed people who crossed the entire former country on foot until death overtook them: "I svakako su jedan od najtežih događaja (sic!) u našoj povijesti" [These sorrows are absolutely among the most fatal in our history]."[131] He also emphasized a connection between World War II and the Yugoslav war pointing out the sacrifice for an independent Croatian state:

Na ovom mjestu hodamo u počasti i svim naraštajima Hrvata koji su daleko od Domovine čekali dan kada će Hrvatska postati suverena nacija, usidrena u europski prostor mira i demokracije. Danas, kada imamo svoju državu, obaveza je svih nas stalno se podsjećati na sve žrtve koje su pali za nju. Obaveza je svih učiniti da se više nikada ne ponove strašne zločini, učinjeni iz zbog bilo kojeg razloga, zbog bilo koje ideologije.[132]

[In this place, we are walking in honor of every Croat who waited far away from their home until Croatia became a sovereign nation, anchored in the European area of peace and democracy. Today, as we have our country, our duty is to remember all those victims who fell for their homeland. Our duty is to do everything to avoid atrocities, induced for any reason, by any ideology.]

Before Jandroković ended his speech, he referred to those who had committed the crimes by saying that they had liquidated those people without any fair trial and that this fact had been one of the best-hidden secrets during communism. If there is a will to sincerely deal with the past, there is a need for acknowledgment and remembrance of the victims. Croatia, as a sovereign and democratic country, has the responsibility to expedite and preserve freedom and democracy and to respect human rights.[133]

Jandroković finished his speech by again amalgamating the Yugoslav war and World War II, using the victims of both as a common denominator:

---

130 Speech of Gordan Jandroković, Bleiburg/Pliberk, Mai 13, 2017.
131 Ibid.
132 Ibid.
133 Paraphrased from Gordan Jandroković' speech.

Žrtve tragedije na Bleiburgu i svim križnim putovima, žrtve Domovinskog rata, u kojem je izborena naša sloboda i neovisnost, kao i sve žrtve totalitarnih vladavina moraju se uvijek spominjati da se njihova priča i tragedija više nikada ne ponove, ali i ne zaborave. Jer kao što je poznato, narodi koji zakopavaju istinu (sic!), koje zaboravljaju svoju povijest, osuđeni su na svoje ponovne tragedije.[134]

[The victims of Bleiburg, the victims of the Way of the Cross, the victims of the Homeland War, in which people fought for our freedom and independence, as well as all victims of totalitarian governments need to be mentioned for not having repeated their tragedy again and for never having forgotten their story. People who bury the truth, who forget their past, are repeatedly condemned to their tragedies.]

Similar to Raguž, Jandroković directly implied the Bleiburg myth by saying that "hundreds of thousands of victims" were killed in Bleiburg/Pliberk after they had crossed the border. Furthermore, he indicated that the reason for their escape was the "fight for freedom and independence," therefore as honorable as the "fight for freedom and independence" in the 1990s. Ironically, while Jandroković condemned the repression of "the truth" during the "communist regime," no remarks were made about the atrocities the *ustaše* had committed prior to 1945.

Performative analysis: The performative analysis focused on the commemoration and its organization and structure. The day of the commemoration started in the morning at the cemetery in Unterloibach/Spodnje Libuče where the participants gathered (see Figure 9). From there, the "procession" moved southwards to the Loibacher Feld/Libuško polje where the main part of the commemoration, the holy mass and the speeches, took place (see Figures 8 and 9).

The participants arrived privately in cars or in buses hired by the organizers. According to the media portal *tportal.hr*, 100 buses arrived at the venue from Croatia and another 50 from other European countries.[135] Besides the Austrian police, at least two different security agencies oversaw the safety at this event.

Noteworthy was the large number of market stands spread all over the area. Apart from Catholic-Christian memorabilia and information material, various other devotional objects that could only be illegally worn and sold in Croatia were on offer.[136]

Finally, charges were raised by the Austrian police against three participants, accusing them of re-engagement in National socialist activity (*Wiederbetätigung*)

---

134 Speech of Gordan Jandroković, Bleiburg/Pliberk, Mai 13, 2017.
135 Z. K., "Na kommemoraciji se okupilo 15.000 ljudi," *tportal.hr*, May 13, 2017, accessed August 31, 2022, https://www.tportal.hr/vijesti/clanak/na-komemoraciji-u-bleiburgu-okupilo-se-15-000-ljudi-20170513.
136 Kolstø, "Bleiburg," 1161f.

Figure 8: At the cemetery in Unterloibach/Spodnje Libuče Carinthia, Austria. Source: Author (May 2017).
Figure 9: "Bleiburg križni put" [Bleiburg Way of the Cross], Blaženi Alojzije Stepinac" [Blessed Aloijzije Stepinac], "Bog i Hrvati" [God and the Croatians], "Sveti Ante sačuvaj Hrvate" [Holy Ante take care of the Croats], Loibacher Feld/Libuško polje, Carinthia, Austria. Source: Author (May 2017). "God and the Croatians" refers to the election slogan that goes back to Ante Starčević (1823–1896, politician and co-founder of the *Hrvatska Stranka Prava*/Croatian Party of Rights). See Sundhaussen, "Jugoslawien und seine Nachfolgestaaten. Konstruktion, Dekonstruktion und Neukonstruktion von 'Erinnerungen' und Mythen," 396.

Figure 10: Bleiburg magnets and rosaries, Loibacher Feld/Libuško polje, Carinthia, Austria. Source: Author (May 2017).

Figure 11: "Bleiburg—Ostali smo Hrvati domovini vjerni 1945 2017" [Bleiburg—We remained Croats faithful to our homeland 1945 2017], Loibacher Feld/Libuško polje, Carinthia, Austria. Source: Author (May 2017).

as defined by Austrian criminal legislation.[137] Two of them got arrested when they raised their hands in the *Hitlergruß*. The third came into conflict with the Austrian criminal law because of a *Hakenkreuz* tattoo.[138]

---

137 "Gesamte Rechtsvorschrift für Verbotsgesetz 1947," *Rechtsinformationssystem des Bundes*, accessed April 7, 2021, https://www.ris.bka.gv.at/GeltendeFassung.wxe?Abfrage=Bundesnormen&Gesetzesnummer=10000207.

138 "Drei Anzeigen wegen Wiederbetätigung bei Gedenkfeier in Bleiburg," *derStandard*, May 15, 2017, accessed August 31, 2022, http://derstandard.at/2000057579296/Drei-Anzeigen-wegen-Wiederbetaetigung-bei-Gedenkfeier-in-Bleiburg.

Figure 12: *"HOS, Za dom spremni,"* Loibacher Feld/Libuško polje, Carinthia, Austria. Source: Author (May 2017).

Figure 13: *Hitlergruß*, Loibacher Feld/Libuško polje, Carinthia, Austria. Source: *stopptdierechten.at*, May 23, 2017, accessed July 29, 2022, https://www.stopptdierechten.at/2017/05/23/die-bleiburg-pilger_innen/.

Conclusion

Since the results of the empirical analysis have already been presented and concluded separately in each section, the conclusion attempts to place these results in a broader theoretical and practical framework by comparing the results of the Croatian politics of memory with the current (theoretical) state of research. Therefore, it is necessary to open a broader picture by considering Croatia's politics of memory, where revisionist tendencies are widely discussed. For this purpose, the following concepts of *negatives Gedächtnis*,[139] *memories of the 1990s war*[140] and *myths*[141] will be outlined briefly and put into the context of this study's empirical results.

Negatives Gedächtnis [negative memory]: According to Ljiljana Radonić and Heidemarie Uhl, a new trend of cultures of remembrance has developed in western Europe over the past decades. It addresses the *dark points* of one country's own history and its involvement in "crimes against humanity." It implies a critical confrontation with its "own guiltiness" instead of seeing its own society as a victim.[142] One of these *dark points* is undoubtedly the Holocaust. Still, it is not the key element of commemorations everywhere: Although this new trend has led to

---

139 Ljiljana Radonić and Heidemarie Uhl, "Zwischen Pathosformel und neuen Erinnerungskonkurrenzen. Das Gedächtnis-Paradigma zu Beginn des 21. Jahrhunderts. Zur Einleitung," in *Gedächtnis im 21. Jahrhundert. Zur Neuverhandlung eines kulturwissenschaftlichen Leitbegriffs,* eds. Ljiljana Radonić and Heidemarie Uhl (Bielefeld: transcript Verlag, 2016), 7–28.

140 Jelena Subotić, "Stories States Tell. Identity, Narrative, and Human Rights in the Balkans," *Slavic Review* 72, no. 2 (Spring 2013): 318.

141 Assmann, *Der lange Schatten der Vergangenheit*, 40.

142 Radonić, Uhl, "Zwischen Pathosformel und neuen Erinnerungskonkurrenzen," 8.

a "universalization and Europeanization of memory,"[143] especially in some East European countries, the victims of communist governments are granted more attention, which leads to the assumption among historians, that a common event, e. g., World War II, is remembered differently in various parts of Europe. Furthermore, the adoption of the Western-European focus on the Nazi and Holocaust reappraisal conceals the Eastern-European view on their own specific dictatorial history of communism and their victims.[144]

This side effect of a *negative memory* was also indicated by Aleida Assmann. She defined it as a *Viktimisierung* [victimization]:[145] "The one-sided concentration on negative references in the past often leads to a privileged status of the victim experience which defends sorrow as a precious possession and an important symbolic capital."[146] She further states that this emphasis then leads to ethnicization of sorrow and therefore "to a dangerous resistance of pluralistic tendencies in societies."[147] The case of the Bleiburg myth, along with the Croatian politics of memory show how Assmann's assessments correspond with the Croatian politics of memory, not just during Franjo Tuđman's presidency but ever since then. Regarding the research results, the "victimization" and "ethnicization of sorrow"

---

143 Ibid., 10.

144 Ibid., 16; Katrin Hammerstein and Julie Trappe, "Einleitung," in *Aufarbeitung der Diktatur—Diktat der Aufarbeitung. Normierungsprozesse beim Umgang mit diktatorischer Vergangenheit,* eds. Katrin Hammerstein, Ulrich Mählert, Julie Trappe, and Edgar Wolfrum, eds. (Göttingen: Wallstein Verlag, 2009), 12. This development of "divided memories in east and west" has been discussed widely in literature: Stefan Troebst, identified four east/west categories instead of two and concluded that by closer examination, the "east-west-gap" appears to be inadequate as, in reality, a "European patchwork respectively a center-periphery-structure" has been observed. Stefan Troebst, "Jalta versus Stalingrad, GULag versus Holocaust. Konfligierende Erinnerungskulturen im größeren Europa," in *"Transformation" der Erinnerungskulturen in Europa nach 1989,* eds. Bernd Faulenbach and Franz-Josef Jelich (Essen: Klartext-Verlag, 2006), 30. Besides the *Terror Háza* (House of Terror*)* in Budapest, another prominent example can be found in the city: At the Szabadság tér, the monument for the "Victims of the German Occupation" during World War II can be visited (This was and still is discussed as another example of historical revisionism). In 2006, the monument for the victims of the Hungarian rebellion in 1956 was built at the Ötvenhatosok tér in Budapest. These two monuments could be understood precisely in this context. Timothy Garton Ash considers Germany to be an exemption to the rule as it successfully *past-beated* not just the Nazi-regime but also the communist regime: a strategy that Garton Ash defined as *Deutsche Industrie Normen* (DIN-Standard). See Timothy Garton Ash, "Mesomnesie. Plädoyer für ein mittleres Erinnern," *Transit,* no. 22 (2002): 32 f.; Christoph Cornelißen, "'Vergangenheitsbewältigung'—ein deutscher Sonderweg?," in *Aufarbeitung der Diktatur—Diktat der Aufarbeitung. Normierungsprozesse beim Umgang mit diktatorischer Vergangenheit,* eds. Katrin Hammerstein, Ulrich Mählert, Julie Trappe, and Edgar Wolfrum (Göttingen: Wallstein Verlag, 2009).

145 Aleida Assmann, *Das neue Unbehagen an der Erinnerungskultur* (München: C. H. Beck, 2013), 144.

146 Ibid., 143.

147 Ibid., 147.

clearly come out as a vital component of collective memory, namely through the ceremonial speeches.

Especially the speeches of Gordan Jandroković and Željko Raguž highlight this by referring constantly and sympathetically to the Bleiburg/Pliberk victims, calling them "disarmed soldiers and unarmed civilians." Jelena Subotić also emphasized the Croatian trend of "victimization"—in the sense of defeating pluralistic tendencies—in Croatia. In the history schoolbooks of the 1990s and early 2000s, this narrative of victimization is consequently repeated and describes the NDH "as an internationally recognized country with a relatively developed industry, economy and especially science and culture." Furthermore, "Croats never fought aggressive but only defensive wars."[148]

Not only do the analysis results correspond with the current state of research, but the concentration on a victim's narrative also eased the way for the ongoing glorification of the NDH. This was confirmed several times: firstly, by the symbolic analysis (*e. g.,* coat of arms), secondly, by the semantic analysis, *e. g.,* "U čast i slavu poginuloj hrvatskoj vojsci svibanj 1945" [In honor and glory of the fallen Croatian soldiers May 1945], and finally through the speeches, in which, for example, the victims (soldiers and civilians) were glorified as they fought for their homeland.

"Memory of the 1990s war": Another aspect stresses the connection between World War II and the Yugoslav war in the 1990s: Croatia's commemorations of World War II are often used to promote contemporary interpretations of Croatia's 1990s war—its "Homeland War." Like in the case of Serbia, Jelena Subotić observed that "[...], Croatia built a seamless narrative connecting the events of World War II and making the recent war seem historically predetermined and inevitable."[149]

Similarly, Pål Kolstø outlines a connection as the crimes committed by the *ustaša* were emphasized by some Serbian publicists in the 1980s as the "genocidal character of the Croatian people [...]. These outrageous allegations gained strength during the Wars of Yugoslav succession in 1990–1995 which was precisely the time when the Bleiburg/Pliberk myth was imported into Croatia."[150]

---

148 Subotić, "Stories States Tell," 321. When in 2005, Croatian academics rewrote a more critical version of the history schoolbooks, their attempt got rejected by the Croatian Education Ministry with the following explanation: "History textbooks must take into consideration not only scientific and pedagogic standards but also national and state criteria." Ibid.

149 Ibid., 320.

150 Kolstø, "Bleiburg,"1154. This genocidal character of the Croatian people was postulated in the famous memorandum of the Serbian Academy of Sciences in 1986. For this purpose (to define an enemy) the authors "[...] (re)activated old enemy images, stereotypes and prejudices. They did not create new enemy images but tied up to everything which was already known somehow." See Sundhaussen, *Jugoslawien und seine Nachfolgestaaten,* 254.

The results prove this connection convincingly. Not only were names from the NDH (*e. g.,* HOS) adopted in the 1990s war and overtly shown at the commemoration, but rhetorical connotations were also employed in the speeches. As shown, the victims of the mass killings in 1945 were repetitively mentioned together with the victims of the 1990s, as both fought for an independent Croatia, so both were glorified. Alternatively, the connotation was mentioned otherwise, *e. g., Efendi* Idriz Bešić said that the crimes committed in Bleiburg/Pliberk were similar to the mass murders in Vukovar and Srebrenica. Various symbols and memorabilia sold at the commemoration should also be considered in this context (see Figures 4, 5, 11, 12 and 13).

Finally, Gordan Jandroković's last sentence in his speech seems to approve Subotić's assumption of a "historically predetermined and inevitable" recent war. As he said that "the victims of Bleiburg/Pliberk, the victims of the Way of the Cross, the victims of the Homeland War, in which people fought for our freedom and independence, as well as all victims of totalitarian governments, need to be mentioned for not having repeated their tragedy again and for never having forgotten their story. People who bury the truth, who forget their past are repeatedly condemned to their tragedies."

If it is suggested that he referred to the fact that the victims of Bleiburg/Pliberk were not allowed to be openly commemorated during Socialistic Yugoslavia,[151] then, according to Jandroković's logic, the war of the 1990s seems to be "historically predetermined" by suppressing the memories of Bleiburg/Pliberk.

Myth: Following the *Gedächtnisstützen* of the cultural memory, or, more precisely, the national or political memory,[152] the contents of these *Gedächtnisstützen* can become myths: "Within the collective memory mental images become icons, narratives and myths, of which the most important feature is their persuasive power and affective impact."[153]

Assmann refers to myths not as a "falsification of historical facts"[154] but rather as the myths' potential to function as a collective self-image, respectively, within the nation-building process.[155] Or, to express it in Ernest Renan's words, "A nation is therefore a cast solidarity, constituted by the sentiment of the sacrifices one has made and of those one is yet prepared to make."[156] Pål Kolstø points out:

---

151 Kolstø, "Bleiburg," 1158.
152 Assmann, *Der lange Schatten der Vergangenheit,* 40.
153 Ibid.
154 Ibid.
155 Ibid., cf. Benedict Anderson, *Imagined Communities. Idem, Imagined Communities. Reflections on the Origin and Spread of Nationalism* (London: Verso, 1991).
156 Ernest Renan, *What is a Nation? And other Political Writings,* ed. M. F. N. Giglioli (New York: Columbia University Press, 2018), 261.

Bleiburg is where tens of thousands of Croatian fascists—the Ustaša—and other soldiers of the collaborationist Croatian regime met their fate. To gain acceptance for a historical version that portrays people who fought on the side of Nazi Germany during World War II as innocent victims, indeed as martyrs, would presumably be an uphill battle, but that is precisely what the contemporary Croatian nationalist mythmaking is about.[157]

Considering the results of the performative analysis and especially the analyzed speeches held at the commemoration, Croatia's politics of memories seem to precisely confirm Assmann and Kolstø's assumptions in which the remembrance of the "Bleiburg Tragedy" appears as an element of Croatia's nation-building-process by (partly) relying on "nationalist mythmaking." As Željko Raguž mentioned, "[...] they [the Bleiburg victims] died not in vain as they were important for all Croatian efforts to freedom and a Croatian state."

Returning to the initial question of contemporary revisionism in Croatia, the following can be concluded: The analysis' results do not necessarily indicate that Croatia's officials glorify a fascist ideology. But they do indicate that their history with this ideology is used for specific (political) purposes, especially when bearing in mind the ambivalences and disputes frequently found in the former territory of Yugoslavia. Based on this chapter's results, the conclusion is substantiated in two ways, presuming that language is a performative act and as such an element of discursive power: Not only do the symbolic and semantic inscriptions refer plainly and "in honor and glory" to the NDH's army but those inscriptions are being affirmed by the mere attendance of Croatia's politicians, by their wreath-laying ceremonies in front of the respective plaques and their speeches held at the commemoration. When applied to the concepts of *kulturelles Gedächtnis* and *rethinking history*, it has become apparent that these specific acts are embedded in the greater context of Croatia's politics of memory in which national symbols (like the coat of arms) and semantic references ("they died for Croatia's independence") are used for particular reasons, *e. g.*, to evoke a sense of community (*Identitätszeichen*), to "revive a nation symbolically" or to establish a different interpretation of history (*neues Geschichtsbewusstsein*). Therefore, the study has shown that Bleiburg/Pliberk has not only become a *Gedenkort*, a medium of memory that conveys a specific narrative, partly through the techniques described by Niedermüller but that, as a *Gedenkort,* it also represents Croatia's *kulturelles Gedächtnis*. In this regard, it must be said that an official glorification and a transfiguration of narratives from the NDH regime to the culture of remembrance in today's Croatia has been accomplished.

---

157 Kolstø, "Bleiburg," 1153.

Selected Bibliography

Assmann, Aleida. *Erinnerungsräume. Formen und Wandlungen des kulturellen Gedächtnisses.* München: C. H. Beck, 2010.

Assmann, Aleida. *Der lange Schatten der Vergangenheit. Erinnerungskultur und Geschichtspolitik.* München: C. H. Beck, 2006.

Austin, John. *Zur Theorie der Sprechakte.* Stuttgart: Reclam, 1972.

Brkljačić, Maja and Sundhaussen, Holm. "Symbolwandel und symbolischer Wandel Kroatiens 'Erinnerungskulturen'." *Osteuropa. Zeitschrift für Gegenwartsfragen des Ostens* 53, no. 7 (February/March 2003): 933–48.

Goldstein, Ivo and Goldstein, Slavko. "Revisionism in Croatia: The case of Franjo Tuđman." *East European Jewish Affairs 32*, no. 1 (Fall 2002): 52–64.

Halbwachs, Maurice. *Das Gedächtnis und seine sozialen Bedingungen.* Berlin: Suhrkamp, 1966.

Knight, Robert. "Transnational memory from Bleiburg to London (via Buenos Aires and Grozny)." *Zeitgeschichte,* no. 38 (2010): 39–53.

Knight, Robert. "Kosaken und Kroaten in Kärnten: vernachlässigte Perspektiven." In *Zweiter Weltkrieg und ethnische Homogenisierungsversuche im Alpen-Adria-Raum,* edited by Brigitte, Entner and Valentin, Sima, 127–46, Klagenfurt/ Wien: Drava-Verlag, 2012.

Kolstø, Pål. "Bleiburg: The Creation of a National Martyrology." *Europe-Asia Studies* 60, no. 7 (2010): 1153–74.

Korb, Alexander. *Im Schatten des Weltkriegs. Massengewalt der Ustaša gegen Serben, Juden und Roma in Kroatien 1941–1945.* Hamburg: Hamburger Edition, 2013.

Niedermüller, Peter. "Der Mythos der Gemeinschaft. Geschichte, Gedächtnis und Politik im heutigen Osteuropa." In *Umbruch im östlichen Europa. Die nationale Wende und das kollektive Gedächtnis,* edited by Corbei-Hoisie, Andrei, Jaworski, Rudolf, and Sommer Monika, 1–26. Innsbruck: Studienverlag, 2004.

Nora, Pierre. *Erinnerungsorte Frankreichs.* München: C. H. Beck, 2005.

Pavlaković, Vjeran, Brentin, Dario and Pauković, Davor. "The Controversial Commemoration: Transnational Approaches to Remembering Bleiburg." *Croatian Political Science Review* 55, no. 2 (February 2018): 7–32.

Radonić, Ljiljana. *Krieg um die Erinnerung. Kroatische Vergangenheitspolitik zwischen Revisionismus und europäischen Standards.* Frankfurt am Main: Campus-Verlag, 2010.

Subotić, Jelena. "Stories States Tell. Identity, Narrative, and Human Rights in the Balkans." *Slavic Review* 72, no. 2 (Summer 2013): 306–26.

Sundhaussen, Holm. *Jugoslawien und seine Nachfolgestaaten 1943–2011. Eine ungewöhnliche Geschichte des Gewöhnlichen.* Wien, Köln, Weimar: Böhlau, 2014.

Sundhaussen, Holm. "Jugoslawien und seine Nachfolgestaaten. Konstruktion, Dekonstruktion und Neukonstruktion von 'Erinnerungen' und Mythen." In *Mythen der Nationen. 1945 Arena der Erinnerung,* edited by Flacke, Monika, 373–426. Berlin: Deutsches Historisches Museum, 2004.

Internet sources

"Entschließung des Nationalrates vom 9. Juli 2020 betreffend Untersagung der Feier im Gedenken an das 'Massaker von Bleiburg'."*Republik Österreich: Parlament*, Accessed June 14, 2022, https://www.parlament.gv.at/PAKT/VHG/XXVII/E/E_00081/index.shtml.

"Bleiburg 2021—kleine Feier mit Botschafter, keine Entscheidung zum Verbot." *no-ustasa.at.* Accessed June 12, 2022, https://www.no-ustasa.at/allgemein/4658/nachbetrachtung-2021/.

"Bleiburg 2022: Alles neu? Eher nicht ..." *no-ustasa.at.* Accessed June 12, 2022, https://www.no-ustasa.at/allgemein/4753/bleiburg-update-2022/.

"Die Bleiburg Pilger*innen." *stopptdierechten.at,* May 23, 2017. Accessed July 29, 2022, https://www.stopptdierechten.at/2017/05/23/die-bleiburg-pilger_innen/.

"Gesamte Rechtsvorschrift für Symbole-BezeichnungsV." *Rechtsinformationssystem des Bundes.* Accessed April 8, 2021, https://www.ris.bka.gv.at/GeltendeFassung.wxe?Abfrage=Bundesnormen&Gesetzesnummer=20009091.

bleiburgcro.blogspot.com, May 15, 2017. Accessed July 29, 2022, http://bleiburgcro.blogspot.com/2017/05/spomenik-blieburg_14.html.

World War II Monuments and Graves in the Hlučín Region: Fallen Hlučín Soldiers as a Contested Realm of Memory in the Czech Culture of Remembrance

Anežka Brožová

Introduction

The Hlučín Region[1] is a small area in the Czech Silesia, in the northeastern part of the Czech Republic on the border with Poland.[2] Its inhabitants are bound together by a specific regional identity.[3] This is based especially on their shared norms, values and collective memory[4] created by the oral tradition. World War II plays a significant role in the collective memory of inhabitants of the Hlučín Region. Their interpretation differs from the dominant narrative[5] constructed in the post-

---

1 In Czech called Hlučínsko, in German Hultschiner Ländchen. The Hlučín Region's administrative center is also called Hlučín in Czech or Hultschin in German. In this chapter, the term "the Hlučín Region" and other Czech toponyms relating to towns and villages in this region will be used, because nowadays the official Czech version of these names is being predominantly used by local population and visitors, too. German toponyms, historically used in the region, are attached in the Appendix to this text.

2 Speaking about Hlučín inhabitants or Hlučín soldiers refers in the following text to residents or men of the whole region, not only of the town Hlučín.

3 I comprehend and use the term "identity" as a consciousness of affiliations to a group, as an aggregate of convictions, attitudes and values common to members of a social group, in this case members of autochthonous residents of the Hlučín Region. According to Lucie Storchová, *Koncepty a dějiny: proměny pojmů v současné historické vědě* (Praha: Scriptorium, 2014), 234.

4 The term "collective memory" used here draws on the theory developed by Jan and Aleida Assmann, who elaborated the concept of *collective memory* as a social phenomenon introduced by Maurice Halbwachs. Aleida Assmann, *Der lange Schatten der Vergangenheit: Erinnerungskultur und Geschichtspolitik* (Bonn: Bundeszentrale für politische Bildung, 2007), 29. More in the following part of this chapter.

5 Dominant narrative or discourse is a narrative of the major culture which is usually challenged by counter-narratives. Gerd Baumann, *Contesting Culture: Discourses of Identity in Multi-ethnic London* (New York and Cambridge, United Kingdom: Cambridge Univer-

war period in then communist Czechoslovakia[6] and adopted by the successor state, the Czech Republic. During the time of the communist regime—from 1948 to 1989—only one narrative of World War II was acceptable in political and public discourse, while all areas of culture were united and supervised by political authorities.[7] This dominant narrative was institutionalized in the form of public holidays, museum exhibitions, political statements, schoolbooks, fiction among others. However, the margins of Czechoslovak society also contained alternative narratives of specific historical events told by political opposition groups both within the country (dissent) and abroad (exile). Since the 1960s, even more perspectives, topics and interpretations of World War II history have emerged in specific milieus of the society.

One of these alternative war narratives was that of the Hlučín Region. It was kept private until the "Velvet Revolution" in 1989 and the establishment of the democratic Czechoslovak (and later Czech) Republic. Since then, the multi-vocal character of the collective memory, typical for pluralist democracies, has enabled minor memory groups to share their specific interpretations publicly. Consequently, the communicative memory initiated by almost exclusively male World War II witnesses from the Hlučín Region has become more visible. In an attempt to challenge the institutionalized Czech cultural memory, inhabitants of the Hlučín Region have been trying ever since to extend the whole-nation discourse about the war by the motive of Hlučín soldiers, *i. e.*, inhabitants of the Hlučín Region, who fought in the German *Wehrmacht* and either survived or fell in the war.[8] Both individuals and communities started no longer merely commemorating their fallen relatives in private. Their commemoration has been presented to the public by various media, but above all via public monuments.

This chapter analyzes the alternative Hlučín narrative manifested on graves and monuments dedicated to the fallen World War II Hlučín soldiers. I collected data during three field trips in the Hlučín Region (three days in fall 2016, three days at spring 2018 and three days in summer 2018). During my fieldwork, I used participant observation methods and visited monuments, cemeteries and

sity Press, 1996). For dominant and counter-narratives in Silesia see Johana Musálková, "Silesian Identity. The Interplay of Memory, History, and Borders," (PhD diss., University of Oxford, 2018), 144–169.

6   I relate to Czechoslovakia in the period from 1945 to 1990, during which the official name of the country changed: Československá republika/ČSR between 1945 and 1960 and Československá socialistická republika/ČSSR between 1960 and 1990.

7   Ondřej Táborský, "Dějiny podle plánu. Politika dějin a paměti v normalizačním muzejnictví," in *Česká paměť: národ, dějiny a místa paměti*, ed. Radka Šustrová and Luba Hédlová (Praha: Lidice: Academia; Památník Lidice, 2014), 279–328, here 286.

8   Recent anthropological research on the memory of the Hlučín Region by Johana Wyss shows public activities in the region aiming to inform the regional and country-wide public about the Hlučín history and narrative. See Johana Musálková, "Silesian Identity," 136–209.

war graves in the region. I also conducted interviews with locals, either during the fieldwork or subsequently on the telephone. These local residents could be regarded as memory actors or persons with a living memory: two local parish priests, an employee of the Museum of the Hlučín Region and several contemporary witnesses. A part of my family comes from the region, which made some of the locals consider me a trustworthy conversation partner, enabling them to speak in the regional dialect. I also benefited from some family contacts. However, the main source of information concerning memorials of fallen Hlučín soldiers was books about particular villages by historians, most of them by Vilém Plaček[9] and Václav Štěpán.[10] As complementary data, local newspapers were analyzed.

The aim of my field research was to find out who the actors in the collective memory of the Hlučín Region have been since 1945, how its World War II narrative has been rhetorically constructed, and how it has developed over time. Furthermore, I also explored how the alternative narrative relates to the Czech dominant narrative regarding World War II and thus, what role it plays within the Czech collective memory.

Besides doing field work, I leaned on various secondary literature sources to understand the specific historical and social context of the Hlučín Region, especially the sociological study by Helena Kubátová that analyzes intergenerational changes in the way of life in the Hlučín Region.[11] In her research on the way of life in the Hlučín Region, she found out that the shared knowledge of the specific history of the region plays a major role in the construction of the specific Hlučín

9   Vilém Plaček and Pavel Kotlář, *Přehled dějin obce Hať 1250–2000* (Hať: Obecní úřad Hať, 2001); Vilém Plaček and Magda Plačková, *Dolní Benešov a Zábřeh v proměnách času* (Háj ve Slezsku, Obec Dolní Benešov, 2002); Vilém Plaček and Magda Plačková, *Ludgeřovice v sedmi staletích* (Háj ve Slezsku: Obec Ludgeřovice, František Maj, 2003); Vilém Plaček and Magda Plačková, *Oldřišov: 1234–2004* (Háj ve Slezsku: Obec Oldřišov, František Maj, 2006); Vilém Plaček and Magda Plačková, *Šilheřovice v historii a současnosti* (Háj ve Slezsku: Obec Šilheřovice, František Maj, 2006); Vilém Plaček and Magda Plačková, *Darkovice: 1250–2010* (Darkovice: Obec Darkovice, 2010); Vilém Plaček and Magda Plačková, *Vřesina: 1270–2010* (Háj ve Slezsku: Obec Vřesina, František Maj, 2010); Vilém Plaček and Magda Plačková, *Vřesina: 1270–2010, Kobeřice: 1236–2014* (Kobeřice: Obec Kobeřice, 2014); Vilém Plaček and Magda Plačková, *Vřesina: 1270–2010, Hněvošice* (Hněvošice: Obec Hněvošice, 2017); Vilém Plaček and Magda Plačková, *Vřesina: 1270–2010, Markvartovice: 1377–2007* (Háj ve Slezsku: Maj-Tiskárna, 2007); Vilém Plaček and Magda Plačková, *Vřesina: 1270–2010, Velké Hoštice 1222–2012* (Háj ve Slezsku: Maj-Tiskárna, 2012).

10   Václav Štěpán, *Dějiny obce Závada: historie hlučínské obce a jejího okolí* (Opava: Obec Závada u Hlučína, 2007); Václav Štěpán, *Dějiny obce Chuchelné: 1349–2009* (Opava: Obec Chuchelná, 2009); Václav Štěpán, *Bolatice od pravěku k současnosti* (Opava: Obec Bolatice, 2010); Václav Štěpán, *Bělá očima staletí: dějiny hlučínské obce* (Belá: Obec Bělá, AVE Centrum, 2005); Václav Štěpán, *Dějiny obce Bohuslavice* (Opava: Obec Bohuslavice 2013).

11   Helena Kubátová, *Mezigenerační proměny způsobu života na Hlučínsku* (Praha: Sociologické nakladatelství SLON, 2015).

regional identity. While conducting interviews with Hlučín residents, she noticed
that they spontaneously started talking about the history of the region in order to
express the uniqueness of the region.[12] For the historical context, works by Vilém
Plaček[13] and Jiří Neminář,[14] particularly, were considered. Additional information was provided by Dan Gawrecki in his history book about Czech Silesia.[15]

However rich the scholarship on the interpretation of Czechoslovak contemporary history and the Czech master narrative is, it deals mostly with specific
historical figures, groups and events of both world wars and with the communist
regime.[16] The Czech/Czechoslovak culture of remembrance regarding World War
II specifically, in other words the dominant narrative about World War II, has been
only partially elaborated by scholars. The most complex overview of the crucial
points of this dominant narrative—up to 1989—was presented in the exhibition
Mythen der Nationen in the German History Museum curated by Monika Flacke.[17]
The article by Barbora Spalová on *Remembering the German Past in the Czech
Lands*[18] is an inspirational work as it examines the Czech and *Sudeten*-German
narratives regarding World War II on a case study of the north Bohemian town
Nový Bor. Additional source of information concerning Czech-German realms
of memory are monographs by Tomáš Sniegoň, Pavel Mücke, Jiří Padevět and

12 Helena Kubátová, "Collective Memory and Collective Identity of Hlučín Region Inhabi-
    tants in the 20th Century," *Historická sociologie*, no. 1 (January 2016): 11–32, 11–12.
13 Vilém Plaček, *Prajzáci, aneb k osudům Hlučínska 1742–1960* (Háj ve Slezsku: František
    Maj, 2007).
14 Jiří Neminář, ed., *Hlučínsko 1920–2020* (Hlučín: Muzeum Hlučínska, 2020); Jiří Jung and
    Jiří Neminář, *Kdo jsou lidé na Hlučínsku* (Hlučín: Muzeum Hlučínska, 2016).
15 Dan Gawrecki, *Dějiny Českého Slezska 1740–2000* (Opava: Slezská univerzita v Opavě,
    2003).
16 Michal Kopeček, ed., *Past in the Making: Historical Revisionism in Central Europe after
    1989* (Budapest: Central European University Press, 2008). Several books focus also on
    features of European narratives, e. g., Arnd Bauerkämper, *Das umstrittene Gedächtnis. Die
    Erinnerung an Nationalsozialismus, Faschismus und Krieg in Europa seit 1945* (Paderborn,
    München: Schöningh, 2012); Harald Welzer, *Der Krieg der Erinnerung. Holocaust, Kolla-
    boration und Widerstand im europäischen Gedächtnis* (Frankfurt am Main: Fischer, 2007);
    Norman M. Naimark, "Die Killing Fields des Ostens und Europas geteilte Erinnerung,"
    Transit. Europäische Revue 30 (2005/2006): 57–69; Stefan Troebst, "Jalta versus Stalin-
    grad, GULag versus Holocaust. Konfligierende Erinnerungskulturen im größeren Europa,"
    in *"Transformation" der Erinnerungskulturen in Europa nach 1989*, ed. Bernd Faulenbach
    and Franz-Josef Jelich (Essen: Klartext, 2006), 23–50; Tony Judt, *Geschichte Europas von
    1945 bis zur Gegenwart* (Frankfurt am Main: Fischer, 2011), 933–66.
17 Monika Flacke, ed., *Mythen der Nationen: 1945—Arena der Erinnerungen: eine Aus-
    stellung des Deutschen Historischen Museums: Begleitbände zur Ausstellung 2. Oktober
    2004 bis 27. Februar 2005* (Berlin: DHM, 2004).
18 Barbora Spalová, "Remembering the German Past in the Czech Lands: A Key Moment
    Between Communicative and Cultural Memory," *History and Anthropology* 28, no. 1
    (2017): 84–109.

Tomáš Staněk.[19] The analysis draws on the theoretical framework of cultures of remembrance according to Jan and Aleida Assmann, whose concepts will be discussed in the following section.

Memory Studies and Realms of Memory

The field of memory studies has been drawn on ideas of Maurice Halbwachs, who first addressed the concept and came up with the term, "collective memory," in his works.[20] He claimed that individual memory is shaped by socialization and communication within the society. German scholars Aleida and Jan Assmann further elaborated this concept by including the cultural sphere. They distinguished between "communicative memory" and "cultural memory."[21]

Communicative memory contains memories of the very recent past and takes the form of autobiographical memory in a frame of history; it is based on informal traditions and storytelling. Cultural memory, on the other hand, contains representations of older, concluded history. It has highly institutionalized form and is mediated in texts, icons, and ritualized performances. The communicative memory lasts just about from eighty to hundred years until it vanishes or supplements the cultural memory.[22]

Another useful theoretical concept regarding collective memory has been defined by French historian Pierre Nora.[23] He described *lieux de mémoire* [realms of memory] as physical places (localities and locations, material objects) or metaphorical places (nonmaterial objects, human beings, historical dates, and periods), on which a particular shared vision of the past is expressed and commemorated by a group with a sense of unity. In their sum and variety, they present and symbolize the collective memory of a society. Nora's concept, originally referring to the French

---

19 Pavel Mücke, *Místa paměti druhé světové války. Svět vojáků československého zah-raničního odboje* (Praha: Univerzita Karlova, Karolinum, 2015); Jiří Padevět, *Krvavé léto 1945: poválečné násilí v českých zemích* (Praha: Academia, 2016); Tomáš Staněk, Otfrid Pustejovsky, and Walter Reichel, *Verfolgung 1945. Die Stellung der Deutschen in Böhmen, Mähren und Schlesien (außerhalb der Lager und Gefängnisse)* (Wien: Böhlau, 2002); Tomaš Sniegoň, *Vanished History: The Holocaust in Czech and Slovak Historical Culture* (New York: Berghahn Books, 2017).

20 E.g., Maurice Halbwachs, *Das Gedächtnis und seine sozialen Bedingungen* (Berlin, Neu-wied: Suhrkamp, 1966).

21 Jan Assmann, "Communicative and Cultural Memory," in *Cultural Memory Studies. An International and Interdisciplinary Handbook*, ed. Astrid Erll and Ansgar Nünning (Berlin, New York: De Gruyter, 2008), 109–119, here 109.

22 Ibid., 117.

23 Pierre Nora, *Erinnerungsorte Frankreichs* (München: C. H. Beck, 2005).

national history, inspired other historians who applied it for many local, national or even supranational realms of memory.[24]

For the purpose of further analysis, World War II is considered to be such a realm of memory in the Czech and the Hlučín collective memory as well. Today, it can be observed how collective memory is being transformed from the communicative to the cultural form, both on a nation-wide scale and locally, be it Nový Bor or the Hlučín Region. Witnesses of World War II and its immediate aftermath are dying out and can no longer report on their historical experience. Therefore, their life stories have recently been captured in books or as recordings. Many documentaries have also been produced. Also, new museums dedicated to the history before or immediately after World War II have recently been created.[25]

Other generally less considered illustrative examples of a memory transforming itself from communicative to cultural, are memorials and monuments to fallen soldiers. These are usually built to institutionalize the commemoration of fallen soldiers in the aftermath of a war, although the development of the Hlučín Region offers a specific case. As a matter of fact, some of these monuments were built after 2010, i. e., more than 65 years after the end of World War II.

Top-down constructed realms of memory define the supposed identity of a collective referring to its cultural memory. They may be used as a legitimization of the political rule of a specific political or ethnic group. On the other hand, memorialization has a multi-vocal character in democratic decentralized regimes. As a consequence, also minor groups, acting bottom-up, may succeed in creating an alternative and even contradictory narrative in order to broaden, to revise or even to challenge the dominant narrative. Following this aim, these actors may act on local, national, as well as supranational level.[26]

The Hlučín Region and its Specificities

Nowadays, the Hlučín Region comprises 27 municipalities on an area of about 316 square kilometers.[27] The administration center of the region is the town of Hlučín, however, Kravaře has traditionally had a greater importance for shaping the region's identity.[28]

---

24 Jay Winter, "Sites of Memory and the Shadow of War," in *Cultural Memory Studies*, ed. Astrid Erll, Ansgar Nünning, 61–77, here 61.

25 Spalová mentions the museum of *Sudeten*-German history in Munich and the museum dedicated to the cultural heritage of German-speaking inhabitants of Czechoslovakia in Ústí and Labem. Spalová, "Remembering the German Past in the Czech Lands," 85.

26 Winter, "Sites of Memory and the Shadow of War," 63 f.

27 There is a list of municipalities with their German toponyms in the Appendix at the end of this chapter.

28 Kubátová, *Mezigenerační proměny způsobu života na Hlučínsku*, 12–15.

Since the medieval age the Hlučín Region has been inhabited by a Slavic population, who spoke the "Moravian" dialect and referred to themselves as *Moravci* [Moravians], living in the area of the Moravian margraviate.[29] The region was part of the Lands of the Bohemian Crown (established by King Charles IV in the fourteenth century) and later of the Habsburg monarchy until the Silesian Wars (1740–1742, 1744–1745), which questioned the succession of Maria Theresa on the Austrian throne. The region was consequently acquired by the Prussian Kingdom in 1742. Because of that, people from neighboring regions referred to the Hlučín Region as *Prajzká* [Prussia]. Accordingly, the inhabitants of the region were called *Prajzáci* [Prussians]. Although some people from outside consider this marking as offensive, most of the Hlučín Region inhabitants proudly call themselves *Prajzáci* until today.[30]

The region formed an integrated part of Prussia for almost two centuries, which impacted on the use of language. The inhabitants continued to speak *po našemu* [in our way], the Moravian dialect, in their private spaces. However, German has become indispensable for them not only because of the official communication (it was the language of education and administration), but also because of work for German employers. The residents of the Hlučín Region migrated to Prussia and later to the German Empire for long-term or seasonal work.[31]

After the constitution of the German Empire, chancellor Bismarck's policy to restrict the power of the Roman-Catholic Church (the so-called *Kulturkampf*) also affected the Hlučín Region, which was mostly Catholic. In the long-term perspective, however, secularization and ongoing weakening of the Catholic Church's position in this region failed. The *Kulturkampf* also tried to annihilate Slavic languages on German territory. This endeavor failed as well, and the Moravian dialect remained the mother tongue of the people in the Hlučín Region.[32] Nevertheless, the dialect has been fading in favor of common Czech.[33]

Most of the residents of the Hlučín Region earned their living as farmers working on their own soil.[34] Seasonal agricultural work in Germany was also frequent. For industrial work, Hlučín inhabitants migrated to Prussian Silesia or even further, for example, to the Rhineland. Nonetheless, contacts with other parts of Germany as well as Austrian Silesia and Moravia were scarce, due to insufficient infrastructure. These circumstances even strengthened the compactness of the Region and the sense of community of its inhabitants.[35]

---

29 Herbert Stoklasa, *Kravařští ve víru staletí I* (Kravaře: Město Kravaře, 2009), 14.
30 Kubátová, "Collective Memory and Collective Identity of Hlučín Region Inhabitants," 13.
31 Ibid., 22–25.
32 Ibid., 24.
33 Kubátová, *Mezigenerační proměny způsobu života na Hlučínsku*, 40.
34 The Hlučín Region inhabitants call the land in their property (gardens and fields) *grunt*, coming from the German term for land *Grund*.
35 Ibid., 24.

After World War I, the newly established state of Czechoslovakia claimed the Hlučín Region, pointing at the Slavic origin of its autochthonous population. According to the Versailles Treaty, the region was annexed to Czechoslovakia in February 1920 with no plebiscite. People protested against this decision in the region as well as throughout its administrative district, Ratibor. Besides fears of local Catholic priests who warned of an anti-Catholic spirit in the newly established state, Hlučín inhabitants also complained about a supposed lack of order in Czechoslovakia, in comparison to Germany. The most important reason for their disagreement was probably the perspective of losing their access to the German labor market and its social security system.[36]

In the 1920 census, 83 percent of the region's population declared Czech or Moravian mother tongue. In the Hlučín Region, the census was carried out by census commissioners who did the questioning, which probably had an impact on the results in favor of Czech as mother tongue (mother tongue was considered as the key factor determining nationality in this census).[37] The commissioners probably recorded Czech as the mother tongue of those respondents who were able to speak Czech or a Czech dialect, even if the respondents themselves wished to state German as their mother tongue. It can be assumed that this proportion of the population had by that time mastered the Czech language or its dialect, at least on a basic level.[38] As already mentioned, the plebiscite regarding the annexation of the region to Germany or Czechoslovakia was not pursued, however, by 1922, the state let individuals opt for German citizenship and leave for Germany within twelve months. Only 13 percent opted to go to Germany while most of the Hlučín residents decided to stay and accept being a part of the Czechoslovak state.[39]

The language policy of the new state enabled the use of other languages when at least 20 percent of the minority lived in a juridical district.[40] In the Hlučín Region, the German language was excluded from official, school and religious communication as the residents were considered to be Czechs according to the census commissioners. Therefore, the language policy of the Czechoslovak state

---

36 Plaček, *Prajzáci*, 35–39.
37 "Historie sčítání lidu na území České republiky I," Český statistický úřad, accessed February 1, 2021, https://www.czso.cz/csu/czso/historie_scitani_lidu_na_uzemi_ceske_republiky_i_. See more about census in the Habsburg monarchy and inter-war Czechoslovakia in Tara Zahra, *Kidnapped Souls. National Indifference and the Battle for Children in the Bohemian Lands 1900–1948* (Ithaca, London: Cornell University Press, 2008).
38 Plaček, *Prajzáci*, 40.
39 Ibid., 26. More Pavel Kladiwa, "Odvolané opce. Snahy optantů z Hlučínska o (znovu)nabytí čs. Státního občanství," in *Hlučínsko 1920–2020. Sborník příspěvků z konference ke stému výročí vzniku Hlučínska*, ed. Jiří Neminář (Hlučín: Muzeum Hlučínska, 2020), 48–57.
40 Jaroslav Kučera, "Demokratie auf Bewährungsprobe," in *Deutsche und Tschechen. Landsleute und Nachbarn in Europa*, ed. Matthias Stickler, Jaroslav Kučera and Raimund Paleczek (München: Bayerische Landeszentrale für politische Bildungsarbeit, 2017), 187.

was perceived to be cruel and unfair to them.[41] The outcome of the land reform between 1924 and 1929, which the Hlučín Region inhabitants also experienced as unsatisfactory, interrupted economic ties to Germany and thus contributed to the growing dissatisfaction with the new state. Despite that, in the elections in the Hlučín Region, most of the votes profited German activist parties which were loyal to the Czechoslovak republic. Only from the mid-1930s, did the *Sudetendeutsche Partei* (Sudeten German Party, SdP), which supported the politics of Hitler's *Nationalsozialistische Deutsche Arbeiterpartei* (NSDAP), become the strongest party in the region, thus mirroring the development in other border regions predominantly inhabited by a German speaking population.[42]

The Munich Agreement of October 1938 between Germany, Italy, France, and Great Britain enabled Hitler's Germany to occupy Czechoslovak border regions predominantly inhabited by German speaking population, the so-called *Sudetenland*, without armed resistance of the Czechoslovak army or any reaction by its allies. Similarly, as the *Sudetenland*, the Hlučín Region was annexed to the German Empire and Hlučín inhabitants welcomed the arrival of German troops as liberators. Inhabitants born there before 1910, as well as their families and descendants, automatically acquired German citizenship with all the corresponding rights and duties, including mandatory military service in the *Wehrmacht* or other military combat units.[43]

The military service involved about 13,100 men from the Hlučín Region. During World War II, about 3,300 of these soldiers were killed and roughly 2,000 were wounded or became invalid. Many soldiers went into war captivity and returned home only after a few years.[44] The service in the *Wehrmacht* has been forming a significant part of the regional collective memory because its consequences have been continuously reflected in the postwar decades.

In the aftermath of World War II and after the re-establishment of the Czechoslovak republic, a very negative attitude of the Czech majority towards all Germans, including members of the German speaking minority, unchained and reached its peak. Such an atmosphere, nurtured by major political parties and politicians, including the President Edvard Beneš (1884–1948), simplified the implementation of his political decision on the forced transfer[45] of the German speaking

---

41 Plaček, *Prajzáci*, 42–43.

42 Gawrecki, *Dějiny Českého Slezska*, 343–44.

43 Kubátová, *Mezigenerační proměny způsobu života na Hlučínsku*, 27.

44 Aleš Binar, "Příslušníci ozbrojených sil z Hlučínska v letech 1939 až 1956," in *Mezigenerační proměny způsobu života na Hlučínsku*, ed. Helena Kubátová (Praha: Sociologické nakladatelství SLON, 2015), 292–93.

45 The process of resettlement of German-speaking population from the Czech lands in the postwar discourse has been called *odsun* [transfer]. In the German and Anglo-American scholarship, the term "expulsion"—analogous to the German expression *Vertreibung*—has been employed. However, this term in Czech (*vyhnání*) evokes the violent, non-organized part of the process which preceded the Potsdam Agreement. In this chapter, the

population from Czechoslovakia based on the principle of collective guilt.[46] His decision presented as a long-lasting solution to national disputes in Czechoslovakia was legitimized by the three Allied powers at the Potsdam Conference in August 1945. The Agreement spoke of the necessity of "the transfer of German populations" to Germany from Poland, Czechoslovakia and Hungary in "orderly and humane manner."[47] Although the practice of the "transfer" often did not fulfill these criteria, the most violent actions against Germans had already occurred in the first months after the end of the war, when several thousand alleged Germans were killed by mobs of Czech and Russian soldiers and civilians.[48]

The mass expulsions of Germans from Czechoslovakia was a part of a large-scale forced migration of Germans that affected more than twelve million people around Europe in the last stage of World War II and its aftermath.[49] The legal frame of the forced transfer from Czechoslovakia was based on the Decrees of the President of the Republic (known as the "Beneš decrees"), which substituted laws during and immediately after the war. Decree No. 5, issued by President Beneš on May 19, created the category of "unreliable population" that included people of German or Hungarian "nationality" (*i. e.*, who claimed such nationality in the previous census or were members of German or Hungarian parties or associations), and put their property under national administration. It also made property treaties concluded at a time of "non-freedom" invalid.[50] This way, the

---

process of organized resettlement of the German-speaking population from the Czech lands will be called forced transfer. For more on the forced transfer/expulsion of Germans from Czechoslovakia see Jaroslav Kučera, *Odsun nebo vyhnání? sudetští Němci v Československu v letech 1945–1946* (Praha: H & H, 1992). Tomáš Staněk, *Odsun Němců z Československa 1945–1947* (Praha: Academia, 1991).

46 Chad Bryant, *Prague in Black: Nazi Rule and Czech Nationalism* (Harvard University Press, 2007), 208–52.

47 "Potsdam Agreement," *North Atlantic Treaty Organization* Official website, accessed December 23, 2019, https://www.nato.int/ebookshop/video/declassified/doc_files/Potsdam%20Agreement.pdf, 12.

48 For more recent scholarly literature on the transfers/expulsions and repressive politics against Germans in Czechoslovakia and other countries see also: Jiří Padevět, *Blutiger Sommer 1945. Nachkriegsgewalt in den böhmischen Ländern* (Leipzig, Verlag Tschirner et Kosova 2020); Tomáš Staněk, Otfrid Pustejovsky, and Walter Reichel, *Verfolgung 1945. Die Stellung der Deutschen in Böhmen, Mähren und Schlesien (außerhalb der Lager und Gefängnisse)* (Wien: Böhlau, 2002); Adrian von Arburg *et al.*, *Německy mluvící obyvatelstvo v Československu po roce 1945* (Brno: Matice moravská); Douglas, R. M., *Orderly and Humane: The Expulsion of the Germans after the Second World War* (New Haven: Yale University Press, 2012).

49 Philipp Ther, *The Dark Side of Nation-States. Ethnic Cleansing in Modern Europe* (New York, Oxford: Berghahn, 2014), 197–98.

50 "Ústavní dekret presidenta republiky ze dne 19. května 1945 o neplatnosti některých majetkově-právních jednání z doby nesvobody a o národní správě majetkových hodnot Němců, Maďarů, zrádců a kolaborantů a některých organisací a ústavů," § 1–4. *Sbírka nařízení a zákonů republiky Československé*, § 1.

German speaking inhabitants of Czechoslovakia were deprived of their property. On August 2, Decree No. 33 followed with the loss of Czechoslovak citizenship for persons, who had gained German citizenship during Nazi occupation or claimed German nationality in previous census.[51]

Most pre-war Czechoslovaks of German nationality or people who acquired German citizenship after October 1938 were expelled, however, the Hlučín Region residents were not affected by the Beneš decrees. In their case, the interpretation of the decrees prevailed according to which the German citizenship of the Hlučín inhabitants was regarded as forced citizenship. As such they had an exception.[52] Nevertheless, some of the inhabitants of the region left or were deported and many others experienced uncertainty about whether they would be forced to leave their homes or not.[53]

The postwar history of everyday life in the Hlučín Region remains an insufficiently researched topic and findings about this period are based mostly on interviews with contemporary witnesses. According to the narrative produced by these interviews, Hlučín inhabitants remained a "mistrusted" population group. State authorities and other inhabitants of Czechoslovakia were looking at them suspiciously because of their cultural proximity to Germany and contacts to relatives living in the Federal Republic of Germany. Since the 1960s, World War II survivors and injured veterans have begun to receive pensions from the Federal Republic of Germany. As a consequence, the inhabitants of the Hlučín Region became rich compared to the neighboring Opava and Ostrava regions on the one hand, but were therefore stigmatized and discriminated against in terms of education and working places on the other hand.[54]

In the 1990s, people from the Hlučín Region gained not only the possibility to declare their German nationality in the census within Czechoslovakia (later the Czech Republic) but also to apply for German citizenship. If the application was granted, people could obtain a German passport and leave for Germany. Thus, the social and economic contacts of the Hlučín Region to Germany were restored, even before the German labor market was liberated for the rest of the Czech population due to the enlargement of the European Union. Silesian or German societies were also founded in Hlučín and Kravaře, thereby claiming a relation to German or Silesian (not Czech) identity.[55] The common historical experience described above

---

51 "Ústavní dekret presidenta republiky ze dne 2. srpna 1945 o úpravě československého státního občanství osob národnosti německé a maďarské," § 1. *Sbírka nařízení a zákonů republiky Československé*, 57.

52 František Emmert, *Češi ve wehrmachtu: zamlčované osudy* (Praha: Vyšehrad, 2005), 184 f. Aleš Binar, "Hlučínsko 1920–2020. Bilance," in *Hlučínsko 1920–2020*, ed. Jiří Neminář (Hlučín: Muzeum Hlučínska 2020), 116–39, here 129–31.

53 Kubátová, *Mezigenerační proměny způsobu života na Hlučínsku*, 28–29.

54 Kubátová, "Collective Memory and Collective Identity of Hlučín Region Inhabitants," 23.

55 Kubátová, *Mezigenerační proměny způsobu života na Hlučínsku*, 30–33.

produces mutual solidarity and a sense of cohesion within the Hlučín Region. The regional identity of Hlučíns is strengthened by other aspects, too: the long-term geographical compactness of the region, common specific vernacular language and the way of life of Hlučín residents. The latter accounts for a tight relation to the home soil/land, strong Catholicism (in comparison to other parts of the Czech Republic), firm family bonds and dense social networks within the region.[56]

Czechoslovak Dominant Narrative Regarding World War II

As already mentioned, the residents of the Hlučín Region were seen by people from outside the region as an unreliable or suspect population group because of their affiliation to Germany, their participation in World War II on the German side and links to relatives in the Federal Republic of Germany.[57] In other words, their experience of history differed heavily from the dominant Czechoslovak narrative and that made them an untrusted population group.

The dominant World War II narrative includes several significant events that were particularly remembered in Czechoslovakia and the later Czech Republic: the Munich Agreement (in the Czech culture of remembrance also referred to as the "Munich dictate" or "Munich betrayal") and the German annexation of the *Sudetenland*, the German occupation and "Protectorate of Bohemia and Moravia" civilian victims of World War II (among them political prisoners, Jews, victims of reprisal actions of German military forces and other civilians), resistance fighters supported from the Soviet Union and soldiers fighting with the Red Army, the liberation of Czechoslovakia by the Red Army and the "transfer" of the German speaking population.

During the communist regime, there was a dominant official interpretation of the most recent history, which was strictly separated from any other (political dissident or private) interpretations. However, following Nora's concept, the realms of memory have been changing slightly over time. In the following, I depict them in their strongest and more prevalent features.[58]

The Munich Agreement was interpreted as a deeply traumatizing experience, which was employed politically immediately after the end of war in order to

---

56 For more about the Hlučín regional identity, see Kubátová, *Mezigenerační proměny způsobu života na Hlučínsku*; Kubátová, "Collective Memory and Collective Identity of Hlučín Region Inhabitants in the 20th Century," 11; Jiří Neminář (ed.), *Hlučínsko 1920–2020. Sborník příspěvků z konference ke stému výročí vzniku Hlučínska* (Hlučín: Muzeum Hlučínska, 2020); Jung and Neminář, *Kdo jsou lidé na Hlučínsku*; Marcel Mečiar, *Hlučínsko: sociální identity a generace* (Ostrava: Ostravská univerzita v Ostravě, Pedagogická fakulta, 2008); Marcel Mečiar, "Mezigenerační proměny sociálních identit obyvatel Hlučínska," *Sociální studia/Social Studies*, no. 1–2 (January 2007): 97–114.

57 Kubátová, *Mezigenerační proměny způsobu života na Hlučínsku*, 31.

58 Iggers, *Tschechoslowakei/Tschechien*, 790.

legitimize the deflection from Western Europe and the shift towards the Soviet Union. According to the postwar narrative in the communist Czechoslovakia, the country was betrayed by unreliable allies of France and Great Britain. It was also associated with the traumatic abandonment of the border without resistance against the German *Wehrmacht*. The postwar alliance with the USSR and trust in the Soviet Union thus seemed to be a logical consequence of the Munich Agreement.[59] Although the remembrance of the Munich Agreement has become more complicated and differentiated in the post-communist memory, it remains a traumatic and controversial part of the Czech history.[60]

As recent academic literature shows, daily life in the "Protectorate of Bohemia and Moravia" was dominated by a fear from repression of all sorts. Therefore, Czechs were mostly passive, drew back to privacy and tried to make the least possible conflict with the Nazi power.[61] In the communist-dominant narrative, an interpretation circulated stating effective opposition to occupiers was nearly impossible because the Czech collaborating politicians did not allow the population to defend themselves against the occupiers. Only the role of the domestic communist resistance was highlighted, while noncommunist opponents and resistance against Nazism were rather neglected as could be observed in the case of Lidice.[62]

Lidice became one of the most important realms of memory to highlight the suffering of Czech civilian victims of Nazi brutality. The resistance fighters, who assassinated the *Reichsprotektor* deputy, Reinhard Heydrich (1904–1942), ordered by the Beneš exile government, became widely known as heroes only after 1989. The village of Lidice was burned down by the Nazis in 1942 as a reprisal for the alleged contact to the perpetrators of the assassination, who were connected to Edvard Beneš and the Czechoslovak exile army. The male inhabitants of Lidice were killed, women and children dragged away and deported to concentration camps.[63]

However, not all Czech civilian victims had received the same publicity in the commemorative celebrations. The Terezín ghetto and concentration camp became a memorial, however little attention was paid to the memorial or to the Holocaust as such in historiography or public discourse. The Pinkas Synagogue in Prague, the official memorial of the murdered Czechoslovak Jews, had a similar fate. This changed after 1989, when Terezín became a more popular and even-

---

59 Ibid., 774.
60 See more Hildegard Schmoller, "Der Gedächtnisort „Münchner Abkommen" als Manifestation tschechischer Selbstbildnisse," in *Nationen und ihre Selbstbilder. Post-diktatorische Gesellschaften in Europa*, ed. Regina Fritz, Carola Sachse and Edgar Wolfrum (Göttingen: Wallenstein Verlag, 2008), 90–107.
61 Bryant, *Prague in Black*, 179–207.
62 Iggers, *Tschechoslowakei/Tschechien*, 778.
63 Ibid., 780.

tually more significant realm of memory than Lidice. There were many books published about Terezín. The former concentration camp has also been renovated, and scientific activities have been supported.[64] The genocide of the Roma was ignored, if not negated, during the communist regime; the situation has improved only in recent years.[65]

After 1945, casualties among soldiers and resistance fighters were linked to the context of the liberation of Czechoslovakia and their remembrance was influenced by the Cold War perspective. Czech members of Allied armies were celebrated only when fighting on the side of the Red Army, while those fighting together with West allies were criminalized and persecuted shortly after the war, while being marginalized in the dominant narrative until the 1990s.[66] The liberation of Czechoslovakia from Nazism was mostly ascribed to the Red Army. There was no mention about Czechoslovakia being partially freed by the American army. "The Day of Liberation of Czechoslovakia by the Soviet Army" on May 9 was a national holiday celebrating the friendship of the Soviet Union, the liberation from "fascism," and expressing thanks to the Soviet Union.[67] After the "Velvet Revolution," the national symbolism changed radically. In 1990, the day was renamed "The Day of Liberation from Fascism" and one year later the holiday was moved to May 8, the usual celebration day in West European countries. The meaning of the holiday was adapted to the West as well since the holiday was renamed "Victory Day" in 2004.[68]

The expulsion of Germans from Czechoslovakia was a taboo topic in public debates for a long time. During state socialism, if it was officially mentioned at all then as "transfer of Germans." This empathy lacking, "technical" term is insufficient, since it completely conceals the dimension of suffering of Germans

---

64 E. g., Hans Günther Adler, *Terezín 1941–1945: tvář* nuceného společenství. Část 1–3 (Praha: Barrister a Principal, 2006–2007); Miroslav Kárný, *Konečné řešení. Genocida českých židů v německé protektorátní politice* (Praha: Academia, 1991); Helena Krejčová, Jana Svobodová, and Anna Hyndráková, *Židé v protektorátu: Die Juden im Protektorat Böhmen und Mähren—Hlášení Židovské náboženské obce v roce 1942* (Praha: Maxdorf a ÚSD AVČR, 1997); Livie Rothkirchenová, Eva Schmidt-Hartmannová, and Avigdor Dagan, *Osud Židů v protektorátu 1939–1945* (Praha: Ústav pro soudobé dějiny, 1991); Miroslav Kárný and Vojtěch Blodig, eds., *Terezín v konečném řešení židovské otázky. Mezinárodní konference historiků k 50. výročí vzniku terezínského ghetta 1941–1945* (Praha: LOGOS, 1992).

65 Ibid., 780–85, 791. For more see Sniegoň, *Vanished History*.

66 For more on their collective memory see Pavel Mücke, *Místa paměti druhé světové války. Svět vojáků československého zahraničního odboje* (Praha: Univerzita Karlova, Karolinum, 2015).

67 Iggers, *Tschechoslowakei/Tschechien*, 786–87.

68 "Proč slavíme 8. květen jako Den vítězství," *Aktuálně.cz*, May 2, 2011, accessed January 3, 2020, https://zpravy.aktualne.cz/domaci/proc-slavime-8-kveten-jako-den-vitezstvi/r~i:article:698911/.

and the violent role of Czechs.[69] The right to deprive a group of people of citizenship and property and to expel most of them from the state territory previously long inhabited by them, was not questioned at all. The violence and crimes of Czechs against their fellow citizens were neither discussed or punished. Instead, the "transfer" was legitimated by the consent of the Allied powers in the summer of 1945 and excused by the general violence and chaos immediately after the war. In textbooks, the expulsion was only marginally mentioned, and the topic was downplayed in the press.

Along with the expulsion, the resettlement of the border regions, known as *Sudetenland,* started. The newcomers consisted of Czech nationals loyal to the communist regime, who were praised for their work by the state propaganda and awarded with material goods, or resistant citizens who were punished by their forced relocation.[70] Thus, in the 1960s, at the time of political liberalization, the "transfer" became a public topic for a while. Following the August 1968 suppression of the reform efforts in Czechoslovakia by Soviets aided by the Warsaw Pact armies, a scientific discussion on the expulsion continued in exile and *samizdat* publications. In the 1960s, references to the expulsion occurred in fiction books and films, too.[71]

After the "Velvet Revolution," there was no political demand for a single view of history as was the case until 1989. But the long-standing unified interpretation remained deeply ingrained in the memory of Czechs. For example, the Munich Agreement and its consequences or Lidice remain living realms of memory in the Czech collective memory. Controversy still dominates the debates about the "Beneš decrees" and the expulsion of the Germans. Yet, most Czech citizens approve of the "transfer," nevertheless the majority of Czechs also condemn violent excesses that happened to Germans after the war and express their willingness to reconcile with the Germans in the future.[72] According to Spalová, Czech

---

69 As mentioned earlier, in the German and Anglo-American discourse, the term "expulsion" has been used. The different terminology describing the same process ("transfer" on the Czech side and "expulsion" on the German one) was influenced by the perceived role of particular nations. Czech perceived themselves as victors of the conflict, Germans as its victims. These views were reflected in the Czech and German cultures of remembrance, which have not been reconciled until today. Jaroslav Izavčuk, "Sémanticko-pragmatické aspekty politické korektnosti v interkulturním diskursu," in *Interculturality in Language, Literature and Education,* ed. Pavel Knápek and Bianca Beníšková (Pardubice: Univerzita Pardubice, 2014), 313–21.

70 Andreas Wiedemann, *"Komm mit uns das Grenzland aufbauen!": Ansiedlung und neue Strukturen in den ehemaligen Sudetengebieten 1945–1952* (Essen: Klartext, 2007), 235–88. Matěj Spurný, *Der lange Schatten der Vertreibung. Ethnizität und Aufbau des Sozialismus in tschechischen Grenzgebieten (1945–1960)* (Wiesbaden: Harrasowitz, 2019).

71 Iggers, *Tschechoslowakei/Tschechien,* 788.

72 ČTK, "Nevyhnutelný a spravedlivý. Násilí u odsunu Němců ale Čechům vadí," *Týden,* May 20, 2015, accessed July 5, 2018, https://www.tyden.cz/rubriky/domaci/nevyhnutelny-a-spravedlivy-nasili-u-odsunu-nemcu-ale-cechum-vadi_343464.html.

historians are divided into two groups on this issue. The major group of "apologists" agrees with most Czechs and criticizes violence during the expulsion but does not contradict the German collective guilt. "Critics of the Beneš decrees," on the other hand, condemn the expulsion as a whole.[73] Their narrative, based on moral principles, was formulated by Czechoslovak dissenters and post-revolution political leaders, such as Jiří Dienstbier and Václav Havel.[74]

The de-monopolized Czech narrative broadened out and enabled many competitive narratives to be brought to the public discourse, which is no more determined just by the state politics of memory. Various actors of civic society have contributed to the polyphonic character of the Czech culture of remembrance from the bottom up by presenting memories and stories that have been unknown to most citizens so far. Such narratives are being presented in the multimedia project *Paměť národa* [*Memory of the Nation*][75] and may become a constitutive element of the Czech cultural memory one day. The project has been collecting interviews with contemporary witnesses of significant events from Czech history and publishes it on the internet or broadcasts on Czech radio. The project focuses specifically on World War II and distributes its results via a web application and a book presenting "national realms of memory," published in 2015.[76] An interactive map and book reveal personal stories of people from different places in the whole Czech Republic related to World War II. Also, marginal or contrasting narratives are shown in this book, *i. e.,* Holocaust, bombing of Czech cities at the end of the war by American and British warplanes, resistance against the German occupation, torturing of Czech Germans immediately after the war or atrocities carried out by the Red Army. Apart from this, there have been other bottom-up activities, such as theater performances and films addressing the German past in the Czech Lands and the expulsion.[77]

Nevertheless, a Czech official governmental narrative regarding World War II has also been developed. It is reflected in the program of the Czech Ministry of Culture on the rehabilitation of memorials of the fight for freedom and democracy which was imposed in 1998 and lasted until 2009. It concentrated on the restoration of monuments commemorating the legionaries of the Czechoslovak state (World War I memory), the victims of Nazi despotism in Terezín and Lidice, allied soldiers fighting on the battlefields of the World War II (former memorial

---

73 Spalová, "Remembering the German Past in the Czech Lands," 89. Quotation marks by Spalová.

74 Ibid., 93.

75 "Slezsko: Paměť multietnického regionu," *Paměť národa*, accessed February 1, 2021, https://www.pametnaroda.cz/cs/slezsko-pamet-multietnickeho-regionu.

76 Petr Nosálek, *Místa paměti národa* (Brno: Jota, 2015). See also http://www.mistapametinaroda.cz/?lc=en, accessed July 5, 2018.

77 *E. g., Dechovka* by the Vosto5 theater company, film *Habermannův mlýn* by Juraj Herz (2010).

to the Red Army in Hrabyně), as well as memorials to commemorate the second Czechoslovak President Beneš and a memorial to the victims of communist persecution.[78] This nationalistic narrative places Czechs into the role of victims of Germans and partially of other nations.[79]

Commemoration of the *Wehrmacht* Soldiers in the Hlučín Region

The commemoration of fallen *Wehrmacht* soldiers from the Hlučín Region is unique in the Czech and Czechoslovak narrative regarding World War II. The Czech dominant narrative has never dealt with today's Czech citizens fighting in the *Wehrmacht*—among the enemy army. Until 1989, Czechoslovakian narrative underlined its role as an "antifascist state," so that the story about "Czechs" fighting in the *Wehrmacht* did not match the dominant narrative of Czechs as victims of Nazism.

It is only since 1989, that *Wehrmacht* soldiers of Czech origin have been commemorated by many different means. They are remembered on family or individual graves and collective memorials and commemorative plaques, to which commemorative events are bound. Wreaths are laid to the memorials on "Veterans Day" on November 11 and on anniversaries marking the end of World War II. The commemoration of fallen soldiers is also ensured by the Church celebrating memorial services. Other means of commemoration are based on personal memories of surviving soldiers and soldiers' family members. These include fictional and nonfictional literature and folklore,[80] web pages,[81] documentaries and TV programs,[82] and recorded memories of contemporary witnesses in the public database of *Paměť národa*.[83] The fate of *Wehrmacht* soldiers from the Hlučín

---

78 Milena Bartlová, "Národ, stát a oficiální místo paměti. Národní památník na Vítkově," in *Místa paměti česko-německého soužití. Sborník příspěvků z konference pracovní skupiny Česko-německého diskusního fóra Místa paměti v Chebu 5. 6. 2010* (Praha: Antikomplex pro Collegium Bohemicum, 2011), 91–100, here 92.

79 Spalová, "Remembering the German Past in the Czech Lands," 94.

80 Emmert, Češi ve wehrmachtu. For folklore by Jana Schlossarková see for example: Jana Schlossarková, *Co se stalo, u peřa povědalo* (Opava: Márfy Slezsko, 1999). Fictions: Eva Tvrdá, *Dědictví* (Ostrava: Littera Silesia, 2010); Anna Malchárková, *Grunt* (Ostrava: Repronis, 2011); Ludmila Hořká, *Národopisné paběrky z Hlučínska* (Kravaře: Kulturní středisko zámek Kravaře, 2002); Ludmila Hořká, *Doma* (Praha: Vyšehrad, 1947).

81 "Database of fallen soldiers from the Hlučín Region Hultschiner Soldaten," accessed January 15, 2018, http://hultschiner-soldaten.de/__de/beweggruende.php. *Memoires blog Kouty mýma očima*, accessed July 10, 2018, http://www.kuty.wbs.cz/.

82 Aleš Koudela, *Sloužil jsem ve wehrmachtu*, CZ, 2008; Daniel Krzywoň, *Prajzáci... aneb tam, kde kule letaju*, CZ, 2000; "Češi ve wehrmachtu," *Historie CS*, Czech Television, November 2, 2013, accessed July 10, 2018, http://www.ceskatelevize.cz/ivysilani/10150778447-historie-cs/213452801400032.

83 *Paměť národa*, accessed July 21, 2018, https://www.pametnaroda.cz/cs/archive.

Region is also noted in local chronicles and it is one of the main topics in the permanent exposition of the Museum of the Hlučín Region.[84]

Memorials to the *Wehrmacht* Soldiers in the Hlučín Region

Almost every city and village in the Hlučín Region has a memorial, or a commemorative plaque dedicated to the fallen World War II *Wehrmacht* soldiers from that municipality. In the Hlučín Region there are 27 municipalities. Some of them consist of more historical villages. Moreover, five villages are a part of the city of Ostrava today (Hošťálkovice, Petřkovice, Lhotka, Koblov, Antošovice), one forms part of the city of Opava (Malé Hoštice and its affiliated part Pusté Jakartice). Overall, I focused on 39 historical municipalities that belong to the region today.

Figure 1: Monument in Darkovice. Source: Author (May 2018).

Only four villages that have formed part of the city of Ostrava since 1976 have no memorial for *Wehrmacht* soldiers: Petřkovice, Lhotka, Koblov and Antošovice. Probably, due to the more significant urban district they belong to and migration to Ostrava, the original residents (*Prajzáci*) of these villages no longer have the main decision-making voice in their municipality. A memorial is also absent in Služovice, which has an affiliated village Vrbka. Apparently, Služovice and Vrbka are the only exceptions in the Hlučín Region as they do not commemorate their fallen World War II soldiers. They are affiliated to the parish in Oldřišov, but there is no sign that the fallen parishioners are commemorated there either.

However, up to 39 memorials or commemoration plaques to local fallen World War II *Wehrmacht* soldiers have been installed in the Hlučín Region. Some villages have more memorials or plaques. Most are located near the local church or in the cemetery. The following paragraphs will present and shortly characterize several typical examples of these memorials:

The most common type of memorial is a plate or a memorial with the names of the fallen soldiers from the particular village or town. These are located in twenty-one towns, villages and parts of villages: Bohuslavice, Bolatice, Darkovice, Darkovičky, Dolní Benešov, Hať, Hlučín, Hněvošice, Kobeřice, Kozmice, Ludgeřovice, Markvartovice, Píšť, Strahovice, Sudice, Svoboda, Štěpánkovice, Velké Hoštice, Vřesina, Zábřeh and Závada.

---

84 "Permanent exhibition 2014," *Muzeum Hlučínska*, accessed July 10, 2018, https://www.muzeum-hlucinska.cz/informace/stala-expozice/10.

Figure 2: Monument in Bolatice. Source: Author (May 2018).

The memorial in Darkovice stands in the middle of the village (see Figure 1). It takes the form of a wall containing plaques with a space in front of it. An information board in the village states that the memorial was built in the 1970s on the site of a demolished house. It was revealed on April 26, 1975, the 30th anniversary of the end of World War II. Originally, however, it was dedicated to fallen soldiers of the Red Army as liberators.[85] It was only in 1995 that the original memorial was replaced by memorial plaques with names of fallen soldiers and civil casualties from Darkovice. This was initiated by two locals, who compiled the names and raised the necessary funds from their families. The memorial was consecrated in the summer of 1995 during a local parish fair.[86]

In Bolatice, there is a big memorial consisting of seven memorial plaques with names of fallen soldiers (see Figure 2) entitled "Kriegsopfer. 1939–1945. Oběti války" [Victims of war 1939–1945][87] (both in German and Czech languages). *Slezsko-německý svaz* (The Silesian-German Union), an association based in the village and founded after the "Velvet Revolution," asked for permission to build a memorial as early as 1993. In 1994, it was decided that the memorial would be placed near the local cemetery. A plaque on the memorial informs that the memorial was co-financed by locals and the AGMO—an association supporting Germans and the preservation of German culture in former German areas in Poland, Russia, and Czechia.[88] The local council did not like the German title, so the title plate was turned around. Today, it has been turned back as intended.

---

85 Plaček and Plačková, *Darkovice: 1250–2010*, 326.

86 Ibid., 425.

87 All translations by the author unless otherwise noted.

88 "Die Errichtung des Ehrenmals wurde gefördert durch die AGMO – Ostdeutsche Menschenrechtsgesellschaft e. V. Bonn und ansässigen Bürgern. Na stavbu památníku přispěla AGMO – Východoněmecká společnost pro lidská práva z. s. Bonn a místní občané," [The erection of the memorial was supported by the AGMO – East German society for human rights, incorporated society, Bonn]. The AGMO was active from 1980 and dissolved in July 2017. http://www.agmo.de/, accessed July 10, 2018.

This memorial has provoked criticism from *Klub českého pohraničí* (Czech Borderlands Club, association of former guards of boards of Czechoslovakia from the Cold War times) and Československá obec legionářská (Czech Legionaries Community, association uniting Czechoslovak resistance legionaries fighting alongside the Allies or in the home resistance in World War II).[89]

There is a commemorative plaque in the new cemetery in the town district of Hlučín-Březiny, which was inaugurated at the beginning of the millennium. The plaque was placed on the side of the funeral hall and is dedicated to citizens of the town of Hlučín fallen in both world wars. Every year on "Veterans Day" wreath laying takes place there. The plate is entitled:

Figure 3: Chapel and memorial in Kobeřice. Source: Author (May 2018).

Seznam obětí I. a II. světové války
Na památku hlučínským a bobrovnickým občanům, kteří nalezli nedobrovolnou smrt v plamenech I. a II. světové války na bojištích Evropy, Asie a Afriky
Ať tam v dalekých zemích odpočívají v pokoji
V upomínku věnovalo město Hlučín L. P. 2001

[List of victims of World War I and II
In memory of the citizens of Hlučín and Bobrovníky who found involuntary death in the flames of World War I and II on the battlefields of Europe, Asia, and Africa
May they rest in peace in those distant lands
Dedicated in memoriam by the city of Hlučín in 2001]

At the end of the list of soldiers there are names of civil casualties in the town of Hlučín and two victims who died in a concentration camp. This example shows that the *Wehrmacht* soldiers are presented as victims of the war like any other war casualties—even the citizens who were murdered in Nazi concentration camps. The war as such is presented as vicious and everybody who lost their life in times of war is consequently a victim of war.

---

89 Štěpán, *Bolatice od pravěku k současnosti*, 553. The two criticizing associations represent very different groups of veterans. The Czech Borderlands Club stands for former loyal communist soldiers. The Czech Legionaries Community is based on the legionaries' tradition of the First Czechoslovak Republic (1918–1938). Czechoslovak legionaries against the Red Army at the end of World War I. However, former *Wehrmacht* soldiers represented a common opponent for both these associations.

In Kobeřice, the memorial is found in a chapel in front of the local church (see Figure 3). In its entrance there are plaques with names of soldiers from Kobeřice, who fell in World War I and II. There is no text added, just two reliefs showing an angel bending above a fallen soldier and Jesus Christ with the crown of thorns (symbol of suffering). The chapel with the memorial was built in 1933. In 1967, the plaques with names of *Wehrmacht* soldiers were added. It was financed by their families. The chapel was restored at the end of the 1980s.

The following eight villages have memorials without a list of fallen soldiers: Bělá, Chlebičov, Hošťálkovice, Malé Hoštice, Píšť, Šilheřovice, Rohov and Třebom. In Hošťálkovice the memorial is behind the church (see Figure 4). It was apparently built after World War I and dedicated to "Místním padlým 1914–1918" [[In memory of] fallen locals 1914–1918]. After World War II, the commemoration of "Padlým za osvobození naší obce I. V. 1945" [[In memory of] fallen [citizens who died] in the liberation of our village May 1, 1945] was added. The latter dedication was added even later, probably only after 1989: "Památka všem padlým z Hošťálkovic v II. světové válce" [In memory of all fallen of Hošťálkovice in World War II].

Figure 4: Monument in Hošťálkovice. Source: Author (February 2021).

Figure 5: Commemorative plaque in church in Kravaře. Source: Author (July 2018).

Five churches in the municipalities of the Hlučín Region contain plaques with a list of fallen soldiers from a particular village or town. Most of these plaques were made before the "Velvet Revolution," most probably in the late 1940s or early 1950s (the only exception is Chuchelná, where the church was built in 1997). One of the oldest plaques is located in the entrance hall of the church in Kravaře (see Figure 5).

Apart from the presented memory of fallen *Wehrmacht* soldiers from the Hlučín Region on memorials and monuments, there are also graves of individual soldiers in the local cemeteries. Some families added the name of a fallen soldier on their gravestone or even erected a gravestone, or a commemorative plaque, for him alone. Sometimes it is made clear that the soldier is not buried in his native soil.

The grave of the Otipka and Sukač family also commemorates Jan Mosler, the husband of Cecílie Moslerová, who died in 1995 (see Figure 6). There is a picture showing a grave located somewhere in a forest. It depicts the supposed grave of Jan Mosler in a foreign country. It is quite common for the widow of a soldier to live about 50 more years and never remarry.

In some cases, it is not obvious if the soldiers are buried in the grave or not. In the Hlučín Region, most churches are Roman-catholic. Only Sudice and Hlučín have protestant churches. The grave of the Proske family is located in the protestant cemetery in Sudice and has a plaque which commemorates their fallen son Martin Proske (see Figure 7). The plaque shows an angel holding a dying or a dead soldier. This scene is similar to the relief depicted on the memorial chapel in Kobeřice (see Figure 3).

Josef and Johann Koczy have their own grave in the cemetery in Píšť (see Figure 8). It is inscribed completely in German and well-kept. It is unusual for a grave-inscription to be in German, regardless of whether installed before or after 1989.

Similarly, Karl and Hubert Fischer are noted on a German grave in the cemetery in Ludgeřovice (see Figure 9). Contrastingly, this grave is not well preserved, and the gravestone contains a small, obviously ground-off square, where an iron cross or swastika might had been depicted.

Figure 6: Grave of Otipka and Sukač Family in the cemetery in Kozmice. Commemoration of Jan Mosler. Source: Author (November 2016).

Figure 7: Grave of Mosler and Proske family in the Protestant cemetery in Sudice. Source: Author (May 2018).

These examples show that the memory of fallen Hlučín soldiers is nearly omnipresent in the Hlučín Region. However, Soviet and German soldiers who were not born in the region but fell at the end of the war there are being remembered, too. From the end of March to the beginning of May 1945 the so-called Ostrava Operation took place in the region. This battle was the bloodiest one in modern history that took place in today's Czech Republic. Therefore, many bodies of Soviet and German soldiers were strewn on the fields, in forests and in the villages in the Hlučín Region. After the end of the war, the inhabitants of villages and cities buried them in local cemeteries or in separate scattered graves in the landscape throughout the whole region. Remains of Soviet soldiers were later exhumed and taken to the cemetery of the Red Army in the city of Hlučín or to the cemetery in Opava.[90] There was another approach towards the remains of German soldiers. Locals either took care of the graves, or their location has been gradually forgotten. In some villages the local communist municipal representation understood the care of German graves as veneration to Nazism, so it was prohibited. In Hlučín, for example, their graves in the local cemetery were destroyed on command of the communist mayor of the city. Yet in 1989, the city decided to restore the place.[91] Today there are plates with the soldiers' names on the ground and a memorial plaque saying:

Figure 8: Grave of Josef and Johann Koczy in the cemetery in Píšť. Source: Author (May 2018).

Na bojištích Evropy, Asie a Afriky nalezlo v plamenech II. světové války nedobrovolnou smrt 372 hlučínských občanů. Aťtam v dalekých zemích odpočívají v pokoji.

Zde ve slezské zemi na sklonku II. světové války nalezlo místo posledního odpočinku 120 německých vojáků. Jejich pozůstatky z 20 hrobů byly uloženy zde na místě, které bylo pietně obnoveno z podnětu občanů města na znamení dobré vůle a usmíření v roce 1990.

Im Zweiten Weltkrieg haben 120 deutsche Soldaten hier in Schlesien den Tod gefunden. Ihnen haben die Bürger der Stadt Hultschin im Jahre 1990 diese Gedenkstätte errichtet als Zeichen des guten Willens und zur Versöhnung der Völker.

Figure 9: Grave of Fischer Family in the cemetery in Ludgeřovice. Source: Author (May 2018).

---

90 Plaček, *Prajzáci*, 104–5.

91 Phone call with Josef Barták on July 4, 2018, who, according to his own words, suggested the restoration of the place in 1989.

Figure 10: Mass grave and memorial of German soldiers in Oldřišov. Source: Author (May 2018).

[On the battlefields of Europe, Asia and Africa 372 citizens of Hlučín found involuntary death in the flames of World War II. May they rest in peace in those distant lands.

Here in Silesia, 120 German soldiers died at the end of World War II. Their remains were collected from 20 graves and laid in this place that was transformed into a memorial site in 1990 at the initiative of the citizens of Hlučín as a sign of good will and reconciliation among peoples.]

Altogether, there are nine identifiable graves or memorials of fallen German soldiers in the villages and cities in the Hlučín Region. One of them is in Oldřišov in the local cemetery, where a mass grave with crosses and a memorial are located (see Figure 10). The memorial is inscribed with the names of the buried soldiers. The grave was built by the citizens of Oldřišov, who carefully noted all the names of the buried soldiers and placed a plate and a wooden cross on each grave. It could have served as a kind of substitute for the graves of their own relatives, who had fallen on the front. During the 1990s, the *Volksbund deutsche Kriegsgräberfürsorge* (German War Graves Commission) responsible for the maintenance and upkeep of German war graves added the current plate and iron cross. The inscription on the plaque says, "1945. Památka padlým ve 2. světové válce" [1945. Memory to the fallen in World War II]. The Commission also asked for the bodies to be exhumed, but the municipality rejected this request by stating that peace should be given to the soldiers.[92]

---

92   Plaček and Plačková, *Oldřišov: 1234–2004*, 463.

Conclusion

This chapter has offered an overview of memorials and graves of (local) soldiers fallen during World War II in the Hlučín Region and explored the regional narrative of the war. The history of the memorials' development demonstrated the dynamics of the Hlučín narrative since 1945. After World War II, newly created war memorials were mostly dedicated to the officially celebrated liberator—the Red Army—and graves of Red Army soldiers were taken care of. However, six memorials dedicated to fallen *Wehrmacht* soldiers from the Hlučín Region were also erected during the period of state socialism. Most of the Hlučín soldiers' memorials situated in the region today were built only after the "Velvet Revolution." After 1989, some earlier Red Army memorials were completed by adding new text, so that they subsequently also commemorated the fallen *Wehrmacht* soldiers. Others were completely rebuilt. This tendency corresponds with the concurrent erosion of the Czech dominant narrative which has become possible because of democratic development after 1989. The hard line of the official narrative regarding the war was called into question and public discourse regarding this topic gained new elements and narratives.

Commemoration of the fallen World War II soldiers was held mostly in families until 1989 and after the "Velvet Revolution" the need for public commemoration came into the light. Such commemoration helps locals come to terms with their loss and difficult past. This is demonstrated by the fact that besides notions on individual graves there is such a large number of memorials. They have been built on the demand of locals and mostly financed by locals, especially soldiers' family members. Additionally, locals have taken good care of graves of fallen German soldiers.

The memorials to fallen local *Wehrmacht* soldiers are mostly dedicated to "victims of war." They do not praise heroes and do not mention that soldiers fell for any country or state. Soldiers are commemorated together with civilian casualties and people killed in Nazi concentration camps. *SS* members are not mentioned on the memorials or plates if their affiliation to *SS* was known. (Similarly, German *SS* members fallen in the Hlučín Region were not buried in the cemeteries). Eventual war crimes of the soldiers are not considered. In fact, the question of responsibility for starting the war or for war crimes committed by the *Wehrmacht* is a taboo topic in the Hlučín Region. The Hlučíns commemorate lost sons, husbands, and fathers and according to the motto *De mortuis nihil nisi bene* [Of the dead, (say) nothing but good] they do not deal with possible shadows of their engagement in the war. The most important day to commemorate fallen soldiers is definitely All Souls' Day on November 2 when cemeteries and memorials in the Hlučín Region are decorated with burning candles, wreaths and flowers.

The innocence of the fallen soldiers is underlined on memorial plaques in the cemeteries in Hlučín. It is explicitly mentioned that fallen soldiers died "involuntarily," so that their position as victims of history, their innocence and suffering are stressed. The memorials and commemorative plaques do not mention the development before or after the war and the fact that inhabitants of the Hlučín Region greeted German troops coming to Hlučín after the Munich Agreement and by this supported the expansionary politics of the "Third Reich." In this regard the Hlučín narrative corresponds with the Austrian war narrative demonstrated on graves and memorials to fallen soldiers that also speak about victims of war.[93] However, a complex comparison of the culture of remembrance in the Hlučín Region and Germany or Austria is beyond the scope of this chapter.

During wreath-laying ceremonies in the cemeteries of the Hlučín Region, graves and memorials of all fallen are decorated, even graves of German and Soviet soldiers who died in the region. The memory initiators and municipal deputies try not to differentiate between the people fallen in war according to the motto *Omnia mors aequat* [Death equals all]. However, it is obvious that people from the Hlučín Region have a tight bond to German soldiers, whose graves have in a way substituted for the graves of their relatives. In comparison to other parts of the Czech Republic, people in the Hlučín Region are very religious, which leads to a strong commemoration of the fallen soldiers. Furthermore, these activities put together local people and underline their shared fate and strengthen their collective identity. Johana Wyss showed in her dissertation that "Prajzáks" (*Prajzáci*) are defined by the engagement of their ancestors in the *Wehrmacht*.[94] That makes the regional Hlučín community very exclusive.

Today, the regional Hlučín narrative stands in opposition to the Czech dominant narrative about World War II (no matter how it tries to be included) and thus creates a counter-narrative. Efforts to add the *Wehrmacht* soldiers to the national narrative have not significantly changed the Czech public discourse (the national culture of remembrance). Commemoration of fallen *Wehrmacht* soldiers and other public activities of the Hlučín Region institutions (*e. g.*, exhibitions and lectures organized by the Hlučín Museum, documentary films about the region's history or fiction and non-fiction books) familiarize Czechs with the Hlučín narrative. However, the non-Hlučín population cannot become a part of the community. There is an unresolvable dichotomy between the will to be accepted by the

---

93 For more see Reinold Gärtner, "Opfer oder Helden? Kriegerdenkmäler aus dem Zweiten Weltkrieg in Österreich," in *Die Wehrmacht im Rassenkrieg. Der Vernichtungskrieg hinter der Front*, ed. Walter Manoschek (Wien: Picus,1996), 206–20; Reinold Gärtner and Sieglinde Rosenberger, *Kriegerdenkmäler. Vergangenheit in der Gegenwart* (Innsbruck: Österreichischer Studienverlag, 1991); Heidemarie Uhl, "Vom Opfermythos zur Mitverantwortungsthese. NS-Herrschaft, Krieg und Holocaust im 'österreichischen Gedächtnis'," in *Transformationen gesellschaftlicher Erinnerungen. Studien zur „Gedächtnisgeschichte" der Zweiten Republik*, ed. Christian Gerbel *et al.* (Wien: Turia + Kant, 2005), 50–85.

94 Musálková, "Silesian Identity," 176–209.

Czech majority and the sense of uniqueness that excludes anyone who doesn't hail from the Hlučín Region. Members of the Czech majority may feel sympathy for the Hlučín soldiers and residents in general, but they do not adopt the narrative. The historical experience of Czechs with (and the Czech collective memory of) the German occupation and World War II is different from the experience of Hlučíns. Moreover, the Hlučín narrative reminds the Czech society of German heritage in the Czech Lands and expulsion controversies. The Czech majority has obviously not yet come to terms with its past and chooses to identify with victors and heroes of World War II rather than its losers and (proclaimed) victims. I agree with Barbora Spalová who showed, with the example of Nový Bor, that the German history of Czech Lands has not found a place within the Czech memory, not even on a local level. According to her, the Czech cultural memory remains nationalistic and unable to absorb transnational stories.[95]

However, it is important to perceive the Hlučín narrative in the context of the dominant Czech narrative and mention some adopted elements. Hlučíns commemorate Red Army soldiers and Nazi concentration camp prisoners along with *Wehrmacht* soldiers. They also celebrate Victory Day on May 8 and Veterans Day on November 11 and commemorate all the fallen of wars. Celebrating liberation/ victory in the war has been a tradition during the whole postwar period, whereas the latter feast of November 11 is a newly found tradition commemorating (fallen) Czech and Czechoslovak soldiers. Thus, representatives of the Czech army unit stationed in Hlučín take part in these commemorations. Moreover, Johana Wyss examined how the rhetorical strategy of Hlučín soldiers tries to reconcile Hlučín history with the Czech dominant narrative. Hlučín war stories reminded her of "Schweikism" (named after the literary character Josef Švejk by Jaroslav Hašek, meaning to avoid or sabotage fights) showing the innocence of soldiers and their reluctance to fight for the German Reich or Austria(-Hungary).[96] Despite these attempts to come closer, the Hlučín narrative remains a counter narrative in relation to the dominant Czech discourse regarding World War II.

Selected Bibliography

Assmann, Aleida. *Der lange Schatten der Vergangenheit: Erinnerungskultur und Geschichtspolitik*. Bonn: Bundeszentrale für politische Bildung, 2007.

Bryant, Chad. *Prague in Black: Nazi rule and Czech Nationalism*. Harvard University Press, 2007.

Emmert, František. *Češi ve wehrmachtu: zamlčované osudy*. Praha: Vyšehrad, 2005.

Erll, Astrid, and Ansgar Nünning, eds. *Cultural Memory Studies. An International and Interdisciplinary Handbook*. Berlin, New York: De Gruyter, 2008.

---

95 Spalová, "Remembering the German Past in the Czech Lands," 103.
96 Musálková, "Silesian Identity," 183.

Flacke, Monika, ed. *Mythen der Nationen: 1945—Arena der Erinnerungen: eine Ausstellung des Deutschen Historischen Museums: Begleitbände zur Ausstellung 2. Oktober 2004 bis 27. Februar 2005.* Berlin: DHM, 2004.

Gawrecki, Dan. *Dějiny Českého Slezska 1740–2000.* Opava: Slezská univerzita, 2003.

Kubátová, Helena. *Mezigenerační proměny způsobu života na Hlučínsku.* Praha: Sociologické nakladatelství (SLON), 2015.

Kubátová, Helena. "Collective Memory and Collective Identity of Hlučín Region Inhabitants in the 20th Century." *Historická sociologie,* no. 1 (January 2016): 11–32.

Neminář, Jiří, ed. *Hlučínsko 1920–2020. Sborník příspěvků z konference ke stému výročí vzniku Hlučínska.* Hlučín: Muzeum Hlučínska, 2020.

Nora, Pierre. *Erinnerungsorte Frankreichs.* München: C. H. Beck, 2005.

Musálková, Johana. "Silesian Identity. The Interplay of Memory, History, and Borders." PhD diss., University of Oxford, 2018.

Plaček, Vilém. *Prajzáci, aneb k osudům Hlučínska 1742–1960.* Háj ve Slezsku: František Maj, 2007.

Spalová, Barbora. "Remembering the German Past in the Czech Lands: A Key Moment Between Communicative and Cultural Memory." *History and Anthropology* 28, no. 1 (2017): 84–109.

Šustrová, Radka, and Luba Hédlová, eds. *Česká paměť: národ, dějiny a místa paměti.* Praha. Lidice: Academia, Památník Lidice, 2014.

Wiedemann, Andreas. *"Pojď s námi budovat pohraničí." Osídlování a proměna obyvatelstva bývalých Sudet 1945–1952.* Praha: Prostor, 2016.

Appendix to the Chapter: German toponyms of the Hlučín Region municipalities (in alphabetical order)

Antošovice	Antoschowitz
Bělá	Bielau
Benešov	Beneschau
Bohuslavice	Buslawitz
Bolatice	Bolatitz
Chlebičov	Klebesch/Klebsch/Klepsch
Chuchelná	Kuchelna
Darkovice	Groß Darkowitz
Darkovičky	Klein Darkowitz
Hať	Haatsch
Hněvošice	Schreibersdorf
Hošťálkovice	Hoschialkowitz
Hlučín	Hultschin
Kravaře	Deutsch Krawarn

Kobeřice	Köberwitz
Koblov	Koblau
Kozmice	Kosmütz
Lhotka	Ellguth
Ludgeřovice	Ludgierzowitz or Ludgerstal (1938–1945)
Malé Hoštice	Klein Hoschütz
Markvartovice	Marquartowitz or Markersdorf (1938–1945)
Oldřišov	Odersch
Petřkovice	Petrzkowitz/Petershofen
Píšť	Pyschcz/Pischtsch or Sandau (1938–1945)
Pusté Jakartice	Klingenbeutel/Wüst Jakartitz und Klingebeutel
Rohov	Rohow
Šilheřovice	Schillersdorf
Služovice	Schlausewitz
Štěpánkovice	Schepankowitz/Sczepankowitz
Strahovice	Strandorf
Sudice	Zauditz
Svoboda	Swoboda
Třebom	Thröm
Velké Hoštice	Groß Hoschütz
Vrbka	Wrbkau or Weidenthal/Weidental
Vřesina	Wrzessin/Wrzeschin
Zábřeh	Zabrzeg/Zabrzeh or Oppau (1938–1945)
Závada	Zawada bei Beneschau

"Bien Mantaakn":[1] The Manifestation of Identity in Cemeteries in the Eastern Slovak Town of Medzev

TEREZA JUHÁSZOVÁ

Introduction

Cemeteries are often regarded as silent and motionless witnesses of the history of particular places. People turn to the quietness of cemeteries not only to mourn and remember their loved ones and relatives but also to explore the past times or culture of contemporary society. Cemeteries and gravestones are perceived as witnesses of people's lives, beliefs, attitudes, practices, and, generally, the past. As Eva Reimers stated in her research on funerals and graves, the gravestone can feature as a "tool for presentation of self and identity" or a "device for construction of [...] identity."[2] However, other questions remain untouched: What and whose identity do gravestones represent? Do gravestones manifest the identity of deceased persons or, instead, a decision of their bereaved relatives? To what extent is the decision about the design of a gravestone intentional?

This chapter aims to flesh out and explore these questions while focusing on cemeteries in a linguistically diverse area with a range of identities—the Eastern Slovak town of Medzev.[3] This town has a significant symbolic value for the German minority in Slovakia, primarily because local inhabitants still use a specific German dialect (known as *Mantakisch*) in everyday communication. A substantial part of the Medzev population considers themselves members of the German minority, or so-called *Mantaks*, descendants of German immigrants from

---

1   "Bien Mantaakn/Wir Mantaken" [We, Mantaks] is a poem written in a German dialect *(Mantakisch)* by Peter Gallus (1868–1927), priest and poet originally from Medzev. The poem was published in Josef Roob, *Slowakei—Deutsche Anthologie der Hammerschmiede* (Košice: Vydavateľstvo Dolinár, 1994), 47.

2   Eva Reimers, "Death and Identity: Graves and Funerals as Cultural Communication," *Mortality* 4, no. 2 (1999): 164, https://doi.org/10.1080/713685976.

3   Medzev is the current name of the town. Historical toponyms are Metzenseifen (in German) or Mecenzéf (in Hungarian).

the thirteenth century. Considering the local multilinguistic context[4] of Medzev and Vyšný Medzev,[5] I already posed the questions above: Is the identity of the Germans/*Mantaks* in Medzev manifested in inscriptions on gravestones, and if yes, how? To what extent was the identity manifestation on a grave an intentional decision of the deceasedor his relatives?

During 2016 and 2017, I carried out field research in the cemeteries of Medzev and conducted interviews with members of the German/*Mantak* minority in order to explore the identification of local *Mantaks* through cemeteries and gravestones. This study of gravestones and the process of their arrangement has shown for whom and in which circumstances a specific identity is (in)significant. Considering the ambiguity between what gravestones manifest on the surface and what is symbolically expressed through the forms or words carved in granite, I argue that categories based on language or nationality are not always relevant in the context of a multilingual space. My thesis is based on the assumption that gravestones represent only one level of the identities of the German minority members. In reality, the identity of each person is multilayered and has a distinct value for each member.

This text is divided into three subchapters. The first introduces theoretical literature based on social constructivism, a theory coined by Peter L. Berger and Thomas Luckmann,[6] and focuses on the polemic between Rogers Brubaker and Richard Jenkins about relations between individuals and groups in an ethnically mixed environment. The aim is to find out how terms such as "group," "minority" and "identity" can help define the German minority in Medzev as a category of analysis. The second subchapter deals with methodological aspects of the field-

---

4   The last census in 2011 enumerated 4,261 inhabitants living in Medzev, of which 354/419 were Germans by nationality and mother tongue. The biggest group was constituted by Slovaks (2,975/2,585), followed by Roma (77/303) and Hungarians (54/100). (See website with the 2011 census results in Medzev: "Medzev," *The 2011 Population and Housing Census Slovakia*, accessed January 9, 2021, https://census2011.statistics.sk/SR/V%FD-chodn%E9%20Slovensko/Ko%9Aick%FD%20kraj/Okres%20Ko%9Aice%20-%20oko-lie/Medzev/.) However, these numbers might not correspond with the actual situation, since some of the members of German language group do not fill German nationality/ mother tongue in censuses due to persecution during the communist period (1948–1989) and persistent fear or simply because of their indifference toward the given categories. In this research, I used the numbers from the censuses only for basic orientation since I do not consider these data relevant for examining the identities of local people.

5   In the 1960s, the municipalities of Nižný and Vyšný Medzev were united into one town named Medzev. In 2000, both municipalities became separate again as Medzev and Vyšný Medzev. The research took place in both municipalities and local cemeteries—two in Medzev and one cemetery in Vyšný Medzev. See Viliam Gedeon and Valter Bistika, *Medzev: Changes of the Town from Its Origin until the Present Day* (Medzev: Tlačiareň Svidnícka, 2013), 92.

6   See Peter L. Berger and Thomas Luckmann, *The Social Construction of Reality: A Treatise in The Sociology Of Knowledge* (New York: Anchor Books, 1967).

work in Medzev. It describes the study of gravestones as well as the conduct of biographical and semi-structured interviews with the members of the *Mantak* language group. The third subchapter concentrates on the central questions and analyzes inscriptions on gravestones by comparing them with the conducted interviews. The conclusion evaluates the results of the analytical part and offers answers to the research questions.

The study of identity in cemeteries or through funeral rites is not rare in the social sciences; however, researchers usually take different approaches to the topics based on their disciplines. Eva Reimers showed which role funeral rituals play in constructing identity by examining Chilean, Pole, and Mormon funerals in a Swedish cemetery. She also noted that language and symbols written on gravestones signify ethnic or cultural membership of the deceased.[7] Ferdinand Kühnel made a similar argument while focusing on identity change through Germanization of personal names in bilingual German-Slovene areas of Carinthia (Austria). He claimed that the change of language on a gravestone means the change of ethnic identity.[8] In his next article about gravestones in the same region, Kühnel showed the reasons for the disappearance of the Slovene language—as an ethnic attribute—from the gravestones. He stated that the reason is not just an effect of enforced assimilation but also a result of a personal decision not to be identified as "Slovene" as a category presumably connected with disadvantageous positions.[9]

The way language or inscriptions are used on gravestones is examined by Snežana Stanković in her paper about the identity awareness of the German minority in Vojvodina (Serbia).[10] She dealt with the regained possibility to publicly show the German identity in Serbia after 2000 and its consequences for the people who live in the multilingual area. In conclusion, she asked what the future of German identity awareness in Serbia would be and if it would survive in the next generations. This is, in fact, a frequent question regarding all German minorities in Central, Southeastern, and Eastern Europe.[11]

---

7   Reimers, "Death and Identity," 164.

8   Ferdinand Kühnel, "The Silent Disappearance of Ethnic Minorities from Gravestones: Ethnic Homogenization in Carinthia's Bilingual Areas since 1918," in *Central Europe (Re-)Visited a Multi-Perspective Approach to a Region*, eds. Marija Wakounig and Ferdinand Kühnel (Wien, Berlin: LIT Verlag, 2016), 204.

9   Ferdinand Kühnel, "Der Friedhof als Gradmesser einer Beziehung über den Verlust der Zweisprachigkeit in Kärnten seit 1918," in *East Central Europe at a Glance. People—Cultures—Developments Europa Orientalis 18*, eds. Marija Wakounig and Ferdinand Kühnel (Wien, Berlin: LIT Verlag, 2018), 152. Kühnel elaborated recently on this topic in *Ruhe in Frieden? Počivaj v miru? Vom Verschwinden des Slowenischen auf den Friedhöfen Kärntens/Koroška* (Klagenfurt am Wörthersee: Hermagoras, 2021). See also: Theodor Veiter, *Die Identität Vorarlbergs und der Vorarlberger* (Wien: Braumüller, 1984).

10 Snežana Stanković, "Friedhöfe als Wallfahrtsstätte. Orte kollektiver Nostalgie," *Zeitschrift für Balkanologie* 51, no. 1 (2015): 103–10.

11 Stanković, 108.

As for academic research, the German minority in Slovakia and particularly its fate during the first half of the twentieth century, has been thoroughly researched, at least in the Slovak context.[12] Especially valuable are the works of Soňa Gabzdilová-Olejníková and Milan Olejník, who focused on the period of World War II and the post-war period.[13] The history of Medzev, specifically, has not yet been elaborated by historians in its complexity;[14] however, several books were published by amateur historians, those still living in Medzev or Slovakia,[15] and those who were expelled to Germany after World War II.[16] Even though these authors, to some extent, relied on archival sources besides personal testimonies, the publications often lack any references to their sources. Nevertheless, these publications show how local inhabitants reflect on historical events.

---

12   See Martin Zückert, Michal Schvarc, and Jörg Meier, eds., *Migration—Zentrum und Peripherie—Kulturelle Vielfalt: neue Zugänge zur Geschichte der Deutschen in der Slowakei* (Leipzig: Peter Lang, 2016); Jan Pešek, ed., *V tieni totality: Politické perzekúcie na Slovensku v rokoch 1948–1953* (Bratislava: Historický ústav SAV, 1996); Ján Botík, *Etnická história Slovenska: K problematice etnicity, etnickej identity, multietnického Slovenska a zahraničných Slovákov* (Nitra: Lúč, 2007); Jörg K. Hoensch and Hans Lemberg, *Begegnung und Konflikt* (Essen: Klartext, 2001); Jozef Tancer, "'Po nemecky už neviem a po slovensky ešte nie.' Strata jazyka v Bratislave po roku 1945" ["Deutsch kann ich nicht mehr und Slowakisch noch nicht." Sprachverlust in Bratislava nach 1945], in *Jazyky a jazykové ideológie v kontexte viacjazyčnosti na Slovensku.*, eds. I. Lanstyák, G. Múcsková, J. Tancer (Bratislava: Univerzita Komenského, 2018): 81–102; Ján Kokorák, *Die deutsche Minderheit in der Slowakei 1918–1945* (Hamburg: Verlag Dr. Kovač, 2013); Paul Brosz, *Die Karpaten-Deutschen in der Slowakei: 1918–1945* (Stuttgart: Arbeitsgemeinschaft der Karpatendeutschen aus der Slowakei, 1972); Adam Hudek a Peter Šoltés, *Elity a kontraelity na Slovensku v 19. a 20. storočí: Kontinuity a diskontinuity* (Bratislava: Veda, 2019).

13   Soňa Gabzdilová-Olejníková and Milan Olejník, *Karpatskí Nemci na Slovensku od druhej svetovej vojny do roku 1953, Acta Carpatho-Germanica 12* (Bratislava: Spoločenskovedný ústav SAV, Múzeum kultúry karpatských Nemcov, 2004); Soňa Gabzdilová, "Evacuation of the German Population out of Slovakia at the End of the World War II," *Človek a spoločnosť* 4, no. 4 (2001): 8–14; Soňa Gabzdilová, "Sústreďovacie tábory na Slovensku v roku 1945," *Človek a spoločnosť* 15, no. 3 (2012): 12–23; Soňa Gabzdilová, "Nemecká komunita v živote slovenskej spoločnosti 1938–1945," *Človek a spoločnosť* 7, no. 3 (2004): 139–51; Milan Olejník, "Úloha Karpatskonemeckého spolku pri výstavbe menšinového školstva a rozvoji kultúrnych tradícií nemeckého obyvateľstva na Slovensku," *Človek a spoločnosť* 3, no. 1 (2000): 74–79.

14   Here, it is also essential to mention some important scholarly works dealing with specific periods of Medzev history such as Michal Schvarc, "Guľka pre štátneho tajomníka," *Pamäť Národa* 3, no. 4 (2007): 42–50.

15   Viliam Gedeon and Valter Bistika, *Medzev: Changes of the Town from Its Origin until the Present Day* (Medzev: Tlačiareň Svidnícka, 2013), Siegfried Gašpar et al., *Vyšný Medzev: História a prítomnosť* (Košice: TypoPress, 2007).

16   Ladislaus Guzsak, *Bergstädte der Unterzips* (Stuttgart: Arbeitskreis Unterzips, 1983); Josef Kauer, Johannes Schürger, and Klement Wagner, *Metzenseifen—Stoß: Deutsche Orte im Bodwatal (Unterzips)* (Stuttgart: Hilfsbund Karpathendeutscher Katholiken e. V., 1986).

Medzev and its multilingual character also attracted the attention of a significant number of ethnologists and sociologists. Gabriela Kiliánová gained a significant place because her many articles deal with the German minority in Medzev, its cohabitation with the Slovak majority and representation of the personified figure of death in both language contexts.[17] The German identity in Medzev was also researched by Zoltán Ilyés, Máté Dávid Tamáska and Monika Bodnár.[18]

My research aims to contribute to the studies on the identification of minorities in Central Europe. This chapter focuses on the representation of identity on gravestones as a source worth examining and interpreting. Although Medzev and the local German language group have been slightly researched, the purpose of this paper is to approach this minority in a way, other than through its "ethnic identity." It attempts to emphasize the situational character of identities in arguing that coexistence within a linguistically diverse area is often based not on the affiliation of the inhabitants to a particular language group or "ethnicity," which was examined in Medzev by the authors mentioned above. On the contrary, categories other than those defined by language are relevant in the daily life of local people.

Terms and Concepts

The German minority in Slovakia has the status of a "national minority" whose rights are protected by the Constitution of the Slovak Republic. Article 34 of the Constitution guarantees rights to the "citizens belonging to national minorities or ethnic groups."[19] However, the terms "national minority" and "ethnic group" are

---

17 Gabriela Kiliánová, "Perception of Differences? One Cultural Phenomenon in Two Language Groups—Contribution to the Research of Symbolic Group Boundaries," in *Cultural Permeations: Anthropological Perspectives, Collections of Papers*, ed. Srđan Radović (Belgrade: Institute of Ethnography SAS, 2013), 137–144; Gabriela Kiliánová, "Tod und Tödin in Medzev. Interferenzen der kulturellen Repräsentation in einem mehrsprachigen Kommunikationsraum," in *Wellenschläge. kulturelle Interferenzen im östlichen Mitteleuropa des langen 20. Jahrhunderts*, ed. Ute Raßloff (Stuttgart: Franz Steiner Verlag, 2013), 183–222.

18 Zoltán Ilyés, "'Magyar lett most a mántából.' Háttérrajz a felső-Bódva-völgyi németek hungarus tudatához," *Fórum társadalomtudományi szemle* 7, no. 3 (2005): 141–50; Zoltán Ilyés, "A nemzeti identitás és az etnikus tradíció változásai és szimbolikus megjelenítésük szintjei egy szlovákiai német közösségben," in *Tér és terep: Tanulmányok az etnicitás és az identitás kérdésköréből II.*, ed. Nóra Kovács and László Szarka (Budapest: Akadémiai Kiadó, 2003), 61–75. Máté Dávid Tamáska, "Stadtbild und ethnische Identität in Untermetzenseifen (Unterzips)," in *Berichte und Forschungen. Jahrbuch des Bundesinstituts für Kultur und Geschichte der Deutschen im östlichen Europa, 18* (München: Oldenbourg Verlag, 2010), 85–101. Monika Bodnár, *Etnikai és felekezeti viszonyok a felső-Bódva völgyében a 20. században* (Dunajská Streda: Lilium Aurum, 2002).

19 *Constitution of the Slovak Republic*, accessed January 13, 2021, https://www.prezident.sk/upload-files/46422.pdf.

used more or less interchangeably in the Slovak legal context without any definition of those terms. For instance, Sergiu Constantin explained the ambiguous use of these terms in his article about the legal framework for national minorities in Slovakia. Constantin stated that the term "ethnic group" should have been initially used for the Roma minority in the Constitution, whereas other minorities in Slovakia were considered "national minorities."[20]

Since the discussed German community in Slovakia is regarded as a "national minority," without any legal definition of the term, it is useful to look into possible interpretations of this concept. The generally accepted definition of a minority was coined by Francesco Capotorti, the Special Rapporteur of the United Nations Sub-Commission on Prevention of Discrimination and Protection of Minorities, in 1977. According to Capotorti, the minority is "a group numerically inferior to the rest of the population of a State, in a non-dominant position, whose members—being nationals of the State—possess ethnic, religious or linguistic characteristics differing from those of the rest of the population and show, if only implicitly, a sense of solidarity, directed towards preserving their culture, traditions, religion or language."[21]

This broad definition may well serve official institutions, which often cannot reflect constantly changing social phenomena and the need for "hard data" collected mainly through censuses. The data gained by censuses only rarely reflect the complicated reality of national minorities, as explored in this chapter through the example of the German minority in Medzev. Instead, this study perceives national minorities through their inner dynamics, as was theorized by the sociologist Rogers Brubaker. Brubaker defined national minority as a "dynamic political stance" characterized by "(1) the public claim to membership of an ethnocultural nation different from the numerically and/or politically dominant ethnocultural nation; (2) the demand for state recognition of this distinct ethnocultural nationality; and (3) the assertion, based on this ethnocultural nationality, certain collective cultural and/or political rights."[22]

The idea of national minority as a developing political attitude may better capture the reality of minorities—not homogenous groups with a single goal, but instead internally differentiated communities, whose members may change

---

20 Sergiu Constantin, "The Legal and Institutional Framework for National Minorities in Slovakia," *Treatises and Documents: Journal of Ethnic Studies*, no. 63 (December 2010): 10, accessed January 13, 2021, https://rig-td.si/wp-content/uploads/2018/11/63_-6.pdf.

21 United Nations Human Rights Office of High Commissioner, *Minority Rights: International Standards and Guidance for Implementation* (New York, Geneva: 2010), 2, accessed January 14, 2021, http://www.ohchr.org/Documents/Publications/MinorityRights_ en.pdf.

22 Rogers Brubaker, "National Minorities, Nationalizing States, and External National Homelands in the New Europe.- Notes toward a Relational Analysis," *Institut für höhere Studien: Reihe Politikwissenschaft* 11 (1993): 11, accessed January 13, 2021, http://aei. pitt.edu/44482/1/1264675711_pw_11.pdf.

their postures according to their experiences. In order to examine this fluidity of stances in one community, I decided to abandon the top-down categorization of the local inhabitants according to their "nationality," as they would indicate on a census form. Instead, I applied a bottom-up approach and followed the reality of the German minority in a particular town from the position of the group members.[23]

This approach helped trace nuances and contexts of personal experiences and individual identities of the members of the German minority. Employing the view of the members, I looked at how they refer to the categories such as "German," "Slovak," or "*Mantak.*" *Mantak* is an expression by which the inhabitants of Medzev and its surroundings, who speak a specific German dialect (*Mantakisch*), describe themselves (and are categorized from outside). *Mantaks* are regarded as members or a subgroup of the German minority, although they often perceive themselves as autonomous. This richness of local sociolinguistic categorization brings up the following questions: Whom do these categories describe? What are the limits of these categories? For the context of this research, it is also important to ask how the categorization process works.

Social anthropologist Fredrik Barth focused mainly on categorizing people according to their "ethnicity" or "ethnic origin." According to Barth, the construction of groups relies mainly on the image of its boundaries, not on its expected inner difference. Therefore, a group cannot exist without a vision of another group, and the interaction between "us" and "them" is vital for the group's continuity.[24]

The concept of *groups* as an analytical category was provocatively challenged by Rogers Brubaker in his book *Ethnicity without groups*. He criticized *groupism*— the tendency to analyze reality only in terms of bounded groups without considering the possible irrelevance of groups in the examined reality.[25] Similar to the constructivist understanding of identity as a process, Brubaker proposed the idea of *groupness*, focusing on the situational establishment, development of groups and various degrees of adherence to particular groups.[26]

Taking the German/*Mantak* minority in Medzev as an example, this group is constantly developing and does not have fixed boundaries, yet its existence cannot be contested. Brubaker's notion of groups as imagined was criticized by Richard Jenkins, who tried to compromise between Brubaker's appeal to omit

23   See James Nazroo and Saffron Karlsen, "Patterns of Identity among Ethnic Minority People: Diversity and Commonality," *Ethnic and Racial Studies* 26, no. 5 (2003): 902–30, https://doi.org/10.1080/0141987032000109087.

24   Fredrik Barth, "Introduction," in *Ethnic Groups and Boundaries: The Social Organization of Culture Difference*, ed. Fredrik Barth (Long Grove: Waveland Press, 1998), 15f.

25   Rogers Brubaker, *Ethnicity without Groups* (Cambridge, Mass: Harvard University Press, 2006), 2.

26   Ibid., 12.

the concept of groups and the uncritical usage of the term.[27] He stressed the importance of groups in everyday life and stated that "groups are real if people think they are,"[28] and so the *Mantak* group is recognized not just by its members but also by "outsiders." As Jenkins stated, "a group does not just happen [...], it has to be continuously made and remade."[29]

The polemic between Brubaker and Jenkins also includes discussions about categorization, the process of identification or relations between individuals and groups in a linguistically or ethnically mixed environment. One of the crucial terms for this research, widely discussed in social sciences, is "identity". Rogers Brubaker and Frederick Cooper have criticized the overuse of this term, arguing that it even "loses its analytical purchase"[30] and proposing instead to use the term "identification" as a process.[31] On the other hand, Richard Jenkins tried to balance the uncritical usage of the concept of identity with its denial. He defined identity as "the human capacity [...] to know who is who."[32] After this elementary statement, Jenkins elaborated on the term and stressed that identity has a twofold meaning as a capacity by which individuals are distinguished and a process—identification—during which an individual searches and establishes their position among other individuals or collectivities.[33] However, according to Jenkins, replacing the term "identity" with "identification" is "cumbersome."[34] In his book *Social Identity,* he decided to use both terms and stressed that it is necessary to remember the limits of both terms and focus on their dynamics.[35] This chapter uses the concept of identity similarly to Jenkins. The aim is to show how the process of identification among members of the *Mantak* community occurs. How do *Mantaks* identify themselves, and how do they manifest their identity in public?

In this chapter, I highlight the main constitutive element of the *Mantak* identity—the dialect of German, *Mantakisch*. As conceptualized by Gabriela Kiliánová in her paper about "language groups" in Medzev, local groups and the identification of their members are primarily based on the knowledge of the respective language.[36] This methodological approach is the most appropriate when dealing with the specific German/*Mantak* community in the examined town of Medzev.

---

27 Richard Jenkins, *Social Identity* (New York: Routledge, 2008), 14.
28 Ibid., 12.
29 Richard Jenkins, *Being Danish: Paradoxes of Identity in Everyday Life* (Copenhagen: Museum Tusculanum Press, 2016), 13.
30 Rogers Brubaker and Frederick Cooper, "Beyond 'Identity'," *Theory and Society* 29, no. 1 (2000), 1.
31 Ibid., 14.
32 Richard Jenkins, *Social Identity* (New York: Routledge, 2008), 5.
33 Ibid., 18.
34 Ibid., 15.
35 Ibid.
36 Gabriela Kiliánová, "Perception of Differences? One Cultural Phenomenon in Two Language Groups," 140.

Therefore, the key term for this chapter is "*Mantak* language group," understood in the social constructivist view borrowed from Richard Jenkins. The *Mantak* language group is considered real because its members realize its existence. Nevertheless, my analysis is based on the assumption that the group is not homogenous, and its members can identify themselves differently. For each *Mantak*, the membership in the *Mantak* language group can mean something different, and their level of identification with the group can also vary. Precisely those various forms and layers of *Mantak* identification and the possibility of its manifestation in public are the main topic of this chapter.

Fieldwork in Medzev and Methodology

During the fieldwork in Medzev, I concentrated on the public manifestation of identity of its inhabitants, in particular members of the *Mantak* language group. I decided to study specific layers of the *Mantak* identity through local cemeteries. The cemeteries in Medzev represent the complicated history of the town and the mixture of the spoken languages of its inhabitants at the very first sight. The perception of cemeteries as historical sources is not rare,[37] neither is the study of funeral rites and ceremonies as one of the decisive cultural features of different societies.[38] The question remains of how one could approach cemeteries as information sources about the identity of deceased persons.

Richard Jenkins regarded graves as "testaments of identity."[39] Nevertheless, whose identity do they testify to? This chapter focuses on what gravestones manifest on the surface and what remains hidden behind the forms or words. Do gravestones serve as witnesses of the identity of a deceased person?

In order to answer these questions, I carried out two research trips to Medzev in December 2016 and September 2017 for a total duration of three weeks. The fieldwork initially focused on local cemeteries—the cemetery in Medzev, the cemetery in the part of Medzev called *Grund*, and the cemetery in Vyšný Medzev. I analyzed the forms of the graves (stones, crosses of cast iron). However, most importantly, I examined the use of languages (German, Slovak, Hungarian) and

---

37 Albert N. Hamscher, "Talking Tombstones: History in the Cemetery," *OAH Magazine of History* 17, no. 2 (2003): 40–45, https://doi.org/10.1093/maghis/17.2.40; Kühnel, "Der Friedhof als Gradmesser," 154; Lidia Kwiatkowska-Frejlich, *Imputacja kulturowa w polskiej historiografii sztuki 1795–1863: Na przykładzie wypowiedzi o nagrobkach* (Lublin: Wydawnictwo Uniwersytetu Marii Curie-Skłodowskiej, 2014), 247.

38 Ján Botík, ed., *Obyčajové tradície pri úmrtí a pochovávaní na Slovensku s osobitným zreteľom na etnickú a konfesionálnu mnohotvárnosť* (Bratislava: Lúč, 2001); Gabriela Kiliánová, "Rituale als Ausdruck der Veränderung? Beerdigungen in der Slowakei nach 1989," *Anthropological Journal on European Cultures* 12 (2004): 131–56; Jiří Vávra, "Projevy identity v pohřebním ritu obyvatel Bohemky a Veselinovky na Ukrajině," *Český lid* 94, no. 1 (2007): 19–41.

39 Jenkins, *Social Identity*, 17.

the forms of names written on gravestones (first names, endings of the names [*e. g.*, Slovak female ending *-ová*]). During this exploratory part of the research, I conducted an expert interview[40] with the local gravedigger and contacted stonemasons from the neighborhood.

The crucial part of the research was based on biographical interviews with selected members of the *Mantak* language group. During these interviews, narrators retold their life stories and usually touched upon their identity without being asked. These spontaneous references to identity are significant when dealing with identity from a constructivist point of view. As accurately mentioned by Thomas Hylland Eriksen in connection with ethnicity, while also relatable to the concept of identity: "If one goes out to look for ethnicity, one will 'find' it and thereby contribute to constructing it."[41] Therefore, I strictly avoided explicitly asking narrators about their identity, and I let them express the course of their life in their own perceptions and terms. In this way, the biographical interviews revealed the complexity of local identity as well as ambiguous relationships towards the categories of "*Mantak*," "German," "Slovak," or "Hungarian," addressing language groups or even nation states.[42]

The biographical interviews were supplemented by semi-structured interviews with a focus on cemeteries. The narrators were asked about their relationship towards cemeteries, generally, and the graves of their relatives or even their own graves because a significant number of inhabitants of Medzev arrange their graves in advance (or have their names carved on the family grave). They do so before their death either to free their relatives from the duties or to fulfill their own visions of a grave.

In total, I conducted 16 biographical interviews, complemented by 15 semi-structured interviews with the same narrators. The names of narrators are mentioned in the initials, except for those who wanted to be fully anonymized—their statements are quoted under the titles "N1 [Narrator 1]," and "N2 [Narrator 2]." All the narrators have a family grave in one of the three examined graveyards in Medzev or Vyšný Medzev, and often they live in one town and have a family grave in the other.

The narrators were selected through the snowballing method, with other members identifying them as members of the *Mantak* language group. The majority belong to the interwar or war generation, which means that these narrators arranged the graves and decided what should be carved on the gravestones. I also

---

40 Alexander Bogner, Beate Littig, and Wolfgang Menz, "Introduction: Expert Interviews— An Introduction to a New Methodological Debate," in *Interviewing Experts*, eds. Alexander Bogner, Beate Littig, and Wolfgang Menz (Palgrave Macmillan, London, 2009), 2.

41 Eriksen, *Ethnicity and Nationalism*, 218.

42 *Cf.* Lyudmila Nurse, "Biographical Approach in the Study of Identities of Ethnic Minorities in Eastern Europe," in *Realist Biography and European Policy: An Innovative Approach to European Policy Studies*, eds. Jeffrey David Turk and Adam Mrozowicki (Leuven: Leuven University Press, 2013), 115–40.

conducted interviews with middle-aged narrators to capture the process of identity negotiation within families.

All interviews were conducted in the Slovak language, but also contained words or expressions in *Mantakisch* or Hungarian.[43] In addition, I wrote down notes into my research diary from random conversations with visitors of the cemeteries during participant observation in the cemeteries.

Historical Context

This subchapter briefly introduces those historical periods and events, which are still considered important by *Mantaks* in Medzev and constitute one of the significant elements of the local *Mantak* identity. The fundamental component of the individual and collective identity is the idea of common origin, past, and kinship; thus, even the story of the German settlement in Slovakia begins with the search for the places Germans came from.

According to historical scholars, Germans came to the territory of today's Slovakia in several waves. The first significant groups of German settlers arrived in the second half of the thirteenth century at the invitation of King Béla IV of Hungary (1235–1270), whose aim was to improve the economic and cultural situation of the country after the Mongol invasion between 1241 and 1242. The Germans, who came from different parts of the Holy Roman Empire, did not constitute a homogenous group and did not settle in one particular area.[44] Because of that, until today, the German minority is dispersed in several areas of Slovakia.

The town of Medzev belongs to the settlements most probably founded by Germans during the first immigration wave. Several publications about Medzev mention the first village called *Dörfl*, located near today's Medzev.[45] The notions of this first village regularly reappeared in Medzev's history and symbolized the continuity of the German settlement in this area. Another important location for Germans in Medzev is the quarter called *Grund*—part of today's Medzev, considered by locals to be the oldest part of Medzev.

---

43 The narrators spoke Slovak, and I, as the interviewer, Czech. Both languages are mutually understandable. See: Mira Nábělková, "Closely-related Languages in Contact: Czech, Slovak, 'Czechoslovak'," *International Journal of the Sociology of Language* 183 (2007): 53–73, https://doi.org/10.1515/IJSL.2007.004. Sometimes, narrators spoke in *Mantakisch*, and I responded in German, and several times we had conversations in Hungarian. This multilingualism is natural for local inhabitants, and by talking with them in several languages, I could usually gain their trust. The interviews were transcribed without significant intervention and, therefore, may contain colloquial expressions or filler words. All quotations in this text are in original, *i. e.*, the Slovak language, supplemented by an English translation by the author. I did not translate colloquial expressions or filler words.

44 Botík, *Etnická história Slovenska*, 83.

45 Kauer, Schürger, and Wagner: *Metzenseifen—Stoß*, 18; Guzsak, *Bergstädte der Unterzips*, 392; Gedeon and Bistika, *Medzev*, 34.

Dörfl and *Grund,* as the oldest settlements in the area, contribute to the identity building of Medzev's Germans through their status of places of common origin.[46] The second common attribute of the group identity is the blacksmith's heritage. German settlers coming during the thirteenth century gained various privileges from the Hungarian kings, such as the right to live by the German law,[47] independent handling of property and the right to mine almost all ores except gold, silver, and tin.[48] Thanks to all these rights, Germans could bring and use their progressive legal codes or technologies. In Medzev, the metalworking industry in waterwheel-powered trip-hammer works became the primary source of livelihood. The iron hammer works were and, to a certain extent, still are the symbol of Medzev and constitute an important value for the German minority as narrators mentioned in conducted interviews:

Dneska bohužiaľ žije jeden jediný človek ako v celom Medzeve, to je jeden starý dôchodca, ktorý ešte dokáže pravý medzevský kováčsky ryl—ako vykovaný—vykovať. Ja sa do istej miery takto chystám, keď budem ako dôchodca, že aby ma aspoň ten ryl naučil ako tak vykovať. Že by to ostalo, ako by som povedal, ako také nehmotné kultúrne dedičstvo. (N1)[49]

[Today, there is unfortunately only one last person in all of Medzev, it is an old pensioner, who still knows how to make a proper Medzev forged spade. To a certain extent, I am actually getting ready to, when I retire, I would like him to teach me how to forge at least the spade so that it would remain, so to speak, as an intangible cultural heritage.][50]

The third of the features considered to be decisive in identity construction is religion. Nowadays, the dominant religion in Medzev is Roman Catholic. However, the question of religion was much more complicated in the past. During the sixteenth and seventeenth centuries, Medzev was highly influenced by the spreading Protestant Reformation, and the majority of local inhabitants became followers of the Protestant Church.[51] At the end of the seventeenth century, however, the inhabitants of Medzev and its surroundings became Catholics again due to the Counter-Reformation and forced Recatholicization. The entire seventeenth century was also marked by anti-Habsburg uprisings. Medzev inhabitants not only

---

46   See Tamáska, "Stadtbild und Ethnische Identität," 95–99.
47   Mainly Magdeburg rights (*Magdeburger Recht*) and Nuremberg rights, see Botík, *Etnická história Slovenska*, 85.
48   Gedeon and Bistika, *Medzev*, 34.
49   Interview with N1, December 7, 2016.
50   All translations by the author unless otherwise noted.
51   Gašpar *et al., Vyšný Medzev*, 31; Kauer, Schürger, and Wagner, *Metzenseifen—Stoß*, 42–50.

took part in these uprisings but also supplied the insurgent armies with weapons.[52] The participation of Medzev men in the Rákoczi Uprising (1703–1711) influenced even the local folk culture, which was especially evident in the Medzev male folk costumes that resemble the uniforms of the Rákoczi army.[53]

The nineteenth century, a period of growing nationalism and nation-building, is very significant when studying local Medzev identity layers. The revolution of 1848–1849 and, even more, the Austro-Hungarian Compromise of 1867 were important for Medzev, located in the Hungarian Kingdom.[54] The central policy of the Hungarian rule concerning minorities was the enforcement of Magyarization, which was an attempt to unify the state mainly through the propagation of the Hungarian language in schools, official institutions and all fields of public life.[55] Generally, the German minority did not regard Magyarization as problematic and commonly used Hungarian in adapting to the new conditions, which primarily meant the increase of economic and political opportunities.[56]

The adherence of Germans to the Hungarian Kingdom became especially apparent after the break-up of the Austro-Hungarian Empire and the establishment of the Czechoslovak Republic in 1918. On the one hand, the new state guaranteed the rights of national minorities, which, among other results, enabled education in minority languages. On the other hand, Germans in Slovak regions (mainly from the Spiš/Zips region) strongly identified with Hungarian statehood and thus refused to adhere to the newly emerged Czechoslovakia.[57]

The year 1918 started a half-century full of rapid changes for inhabitants of Medzev—border modifications, political regime shifts and ambiguous social status of the German minority. After World War I, the most perceptible problems for the Medzev blacksmiths were losing the Hungarian sales market and their new competition in the solid Czech industry.[58] During 1919 Medzev also faced an

---

52 Gedeon and Bistika, *Medzev*, 38, 41; Guzsak, *Bergstädte der Unterzips*, 394, 396.

53 Margaréta Horváthová, *Nemci na Slovensku* (Komárno, Dunajská Streda: Lilium Aurum, 2002), 103–106.

54 After the Austro-Hungarian Compromise, the Habsburg Empire was divided into two parts—Cisleithania (Austrian part), which was composed of 17 crownlands, and Transleithania (Hungarian part) as a formally unitary state. See: Rogers Brubaker *et al.*, *Nationalist Politics and Everyday Ethnicity in a Transylvanian Town* (Princeton: Princeton University Press, 2008) 27–67.

55 See for example, Frank Henschel, *"Das Fluidum der Stadt..." Urbane Lebenswelten in Kassa/Košice/Kaschau zwischen Sprachenvielfalt und Magyarisierung 1867–1918* (München: Collegium Carolinum, 2017); Joachim von Puttkamer, *Schulalltag und nationale Integration in Ungarn. Slowaken, Rumänen und Siebenbürger Sachsen in Auseinandersetzung mit der ungarischen Staatsidee, 1867–1914* (München: Südosteuropäische Arbeiten, 2003).

56 Kokorák, *Die deutsche Minderheit in der Slowakei 1918–1945*, 33–35; Gabzdilová-Olejníková and Olejník, *Karpatskí Nemci na Slovensku*, 10f.

57 Gabzdilová-Olejníková and Olejník, *Karpatskí Nemci na Slovensku*, 11.

58 Gedeon and Bistika, *Medzev*, 50f.

armed conflict between the Czechoslovak army and the army of the Hungarian Soviet Republic.[59] Traces of this conflict can still be followed today in Medzev's public space—both Czechoslovak soldiers and the soldiers of the Hungarian Red Army killed during the fights in the surroundings were buried in the local cemeteries. However, they were separated after death, the first ones buried in the cemetery in Medzev, the latter in the cemetery of Vyšný Medzev.

A branch of the communist party was founded in Medzev as early as 1921. Its popularity significantly increased during the following years.[60] The communists were repeatedly successful in the interwar elections (1929, 1935, 1938), which not only depicts the popularity of communist ideology in Medzev but also shows the failure of the German national party (*Karpathendeutsche Partei*, after 1938 *Deutsche Partei*[61]) in this area.[62]

The rejection of the German nationalist movement culminated in an attempt to assassinate the leader of the *Deutsche Partei*, Franz Karmasin, during his visit to Medzev in December 1938.[63] The incident was a climax of public demonstrations provoked by the decision of the First Vienna Award in November 1938. According to the treaty, Medzev remained in the territory of Slovakia, cut off from neighboring villages and important routes that became part of Hungary.

After the establishment of the Nazi puppet Slovak State in March 1939, members of the German minority became its citizens. Thus, they were not enlisted in the *Wehrmacht* as, for example, were German inhabitants of Bohemian and Moravian border areas annexed to Hitler's Germany.[64] As German *Reich* citizens, these individuals were obliged to serve in the *Wehrmacht*. Nevertheless, during the war years, the *Deutsche Partei* urged Germans in Slovakia to enter another military organization of Nazi Germany—the *Waffen-SS* units. After the failure of the German military campaign in the Soviet Union in 1943, all ethnic Germans were to be mobilized, and later, during 1944, all German-speaking members of

---

59 The Hungarian Soviet Republic under the leadership of Béla Kun was established in the spring of 1919, and one of its goals was to get back territories seized by the neighboring states. The Hungarian Soviet Republic was defeated already in the summer of 1919.

60 For the description of the establishment of the communist party in Medzev, it is worth viewing the memoirs of Michal Schmotzer: Michal Schmotzer, *Prerody* (Košice: Východoslovenské vydavateľstvo, 1987), 14, 20, 32.

61 The activities of the *Deutsche Partei* were directed from Berlin, the structure and program of the party were based on the NSDAP ones. See: Gabzdilová, "Nemecká komunita v živote slovenskej spoločnosti 1938–1945," 141.

62 Schvarc, "Guľka pre štátneho tajomníka," 42.

63 See the comprehensive analysis of this event in ibid.

64 For more information about the situation in the annexed Moravian borderlands, see the chapter of Anežka Brožová "World War II Monuments and Graves in the Hlučín Region: Fallen Hlučín Soldiers as a Contested Realm of Memory in the Czech Culture of Remembrance" in this volume.

the Slovak army were to be enlisted in the *Waffen-SS* units.[65] As a consequence of these orders, all Medzev men able to fight were recruited for war on the side of Nazi Germany unless they had hidden or joined communist partisan groups that started emerging in 1942.[66]

The consequent post-war categorization of Medzev inhabitants to either "fascists" or "communists" based on their engagement in World War II either in *Waffen-SS* units or in partisan groups is still present in today's Medzev society. Narrators in the interviews frequently talked about the injustice through labeling soldiers of the *Waffen-SS* units as "fascists," because, in their view, inhabitants of Medzev had rarely expressed adherence to that ideology. According to some narrators, the communist regime misused and overused the heroism of the partisans in the postwar period.[67] Others would talk about their fear while hiding from any involvement in the war.[68]

The cohesion of the German community in Medzev was not only influenced by the involvement of men on the battlefields, local fights or soldiers passing through Medzev, but also by the organized "evacuation" of German civilians from the approaching Red Army in September and October 1944.[69] The evacuees from Medzev were usually transferred to Northern Moravia, in the then Nazi Germany (*Reichsgau Sudetenland*). For Germans, who remained in Medzev in subsequent months, the war culminated after the arrival of the Red Army in January 1945. More than one hundred people were taken to labor camps in the Soviet Union.[70]

After the end of World War II, Germans in Medzev were affected by decrees of the Czechoslovak president Edvard Beneš, by which the majority of them were deprived of Czechoslovak citizenship and property.[71] Several persons from Medzev were designated for the official expulsion of Germans. Also, the every-

---

65 Michal Schvarc, "'Každý Nemec uvedených ročníkov sa má bez vyzvania dostaviť pred komisie': Nábor a služba slovenských Nemcov vo Waffen-SS 1939–1945," *Historický časopis* 67, no. 4 (2019): 659–693.

66 Gašpar et al., *Vyšný Medzev*, 42.

67 See Elena Mannová, "Jubiläumskampagnen und Uminterpretationen des Slowakischen Nationalaufstands von 1944," in *Erinnern mit Hindernissen. Osteuropäische Gedenktage und Jubiläen im 20. und zu Beginn des 21. Jahrhunderts,* eds. Rudolf Jaworski and Jan Kusber (Berlin: LIT Verlag, 2011), 201–240.

68 All of these remarks were revealed in biographical interviews with Medzev inhabitants. Those who concentrated on guilt after World War II or spoke emotionally about the dichotomy between "fascists" and "communists" often wanted to remain anonymous.

69 Gabzdilová, "Evacuation of the German Population," 10.

70 Kauer, Schürger, and Wagner, *Metzenseifen—Stoß*, 8.

71 According to the constitutional presidential decree No. 33/1945 August 2, 1945, Czechoslovak citizens of German and Hungarian nationality were deprived of their Czechoslovak citizenship. However, there were exceptions for those who fought for the liberation of Czechoslovakia, signed up for Czech or Slovak nationality during the war, suffered under the Nazi occupation, and other reasons. For detailed information see: Dušan Kováč, *Vysídlenie Nemcov zo Slovenska (1944–1953)* (Praha: Ústav pro soudobé dějiny AV ČR,

day life of Germans in Medzev completely changed—Germans had to declare their nationality as "Slovak" through the so-called Reslovakization, i. e., to Slovakize their names and attend Slovak language classes. Suddenly, using the German language in public became undesirable, and German-speaking children had to begin or continue their education only in Slovak without any previous knowledge of the language.[72]

After the communist takeover in 1947–1948, the official state view of Germans as betrayers of the Czechoslovak Republic did not go in line with the principles of proletarian internationalism. Although Germans regained Czechoslovak citizenship directly by law in 1953, the state still considered them a "potentially dangerous group."[73] Everyday life in Medzev after 1953 slowly stabilized, and the German language was once again used in the streets. Medzev society had been divided not based on spoken language but along political lines. For the next forty years, Medzev communists gained decisive power in the town.

The 1960s symbolized a period of political, social and cultural liberalization for Czechoslovakia and even for the Czechoslovak Germans. The *Kulturverband der Bürger deutscher Nationalität der ČSSR,* the first cultural association of the German minority in Czechoslovakia, was established in 1969, and one of its branches was also founded in Medzev in 1970.[74] However, the Soviet military intervention in Czechoslovakia in 1968 and consequent tightening of the communist regime during the 1970s caused a 20-year halt to the recovery of the German community in Medzev as well as the gradual dissolution of the Medzev cultural association.

For the further development of the Medzev community, especially for its multilingual setting, another event of the 1960s played a crucial role—the significant growth of the state-owned metalworking industry in Medzev. After a new factory, *Tatrasmalt* (later *Strojsmalt*), was opened in 1962, it attracted many Slovak or Hungarian-speaking workers, who resettled to Medzev and changed its predominantly German character up to today.[75]

The "Velvet revolution" in 1989, after which democracy was established in Czechoslovakia, symbolized to the German language group in Medzev a new possibility to publicly manifest their German identity, be it through declaring German nationality and mother tongue in censuses, changing names back to their German form, or founding the Carpathian Germans association and its branch in Medzev in 1990.

2001) or Gabzdilová-Olejníková and Olejník, *Karpatskí Nemci na Slovensku*, 95–99, 159. On Beneš Decrees, see also the chapter by Anežka Brožová.

72   Gabzdilová-Olejníková and Olejník, *Karpatskí Nemci na Slovensku*, 72, 157.

73   Ibid., 159.

74   Katharina Richter-Kovarik, "Kultúra mantáckej minority v období socializmu," *Slovenský národopis* 51, no. 3 (2003): 334; Gedeon and Bistika, *Medzev*, 96.

75   Gabriela Kiliánová, "Predstava o postave smrti—Štúdium kultúrneho javu v slovenskej a nemeckej jazykovej skupine na Slovensku," *Slovenský národopis* 61, no. 2 (2013): 132–33.

Local Context

The previous subchapter shortly outlined the historical periods and events that, until current times, have been perceived by the German minority in Medzev as significant in contributing to the identity construction of this group. However, the primary bearer of the local German identity is mainly the common language—*Mantakisch*. This language is a dialect of German that was introduced by German settlers to this area during the thirteenth century.[76] The dialect functions as the main constitutive attribute of the German language group whose members refer to themselves as *Mantaks*.[77] In general, only the person who is able to speak this dialect can claim to be or can be regarded as *Mantak*. In reality, however, the category of *"Mantak"* means something slightly different for each member of the group. For some, the *Mantak* is the person who speaks *Mantakisch* and has ancestors in Medzev or other German-speaking settlements in the Spiš region.[78] Others see the category more freely as they recognize members of other language groups coming to Medzev:

V niektorých rodinách sa ten jeden člen rodiny úplne prispôsobil a po nejakom čase začal rozprávať *mantácky* úplne. Sú takýto, že boli, pochádzali z maďarskej menšiny a stali sa z nich *Mantáci*. (E. G., *1962)[79]

[In some families, there was one member who fully adapted [to the language spoken in the family], and after some time, they started to speak only *Mantakisch*. There are some, who were, who came from the Hungarian minority and became *Mantaks*.]

The manifestation of the *Mantak* identity through any other way than speaking the dialect[80] is quite problematic because *Mantakisch* has no written form. There are several exceptions, such as pieces of poetry in *Mantakisch*[81] or a *Mantakisch*-Ger-

---

76   German dialects in the Spiš region and in Medzev were examined in, for example: Ladislaus Guzsak, *Vom Puchbald Pis Óffs Mihlhiebl: Gedichte in Gründler Mundart* (Erlangen: Höfer und Limmert, 1959); Kauer, Schürger, and Wagner, *Metzenseifen—Stoß*, 36–41; Werner Besch, *Dialektologie: ein Handbuch zur deutschen und allgemeinen Dialektforschung* (Berlin; New York: Walter de Gruyter, 1982).
77   Kiliánová, "Perception of Differences? One Cultural Phenomenon in Two Language Groups," 140.
78   This was revealed, for example, in the interview with A. B., *1938. September 12, 2017.
79   Interview with E. G., September 11, 2017.
80   However, there are also some cultural specifics such as traditional folk costumes or, for example, *Mantak* recipes.
81   One of the iconic Medzev personalities was the priest Peter Gallus who wrote poetry in *Mantakisch*.

man dictionary,[82] but otherwise, if a member of the *Mantak* language group decides to use a written form, they usually use the standard German language. This ambiguity between the categories of *"Mantaks"* and "Germans" was expressed in the majority of interviews, for example, in the interview with E. S. (*1961):

> To bola vlastne identita tých ľudí, ktorí sa k tomu hlásili, boli to Nemci, v úvodzovkách, Nemci–*Mantáci*, potom kovia Nemcov. (E. S., *1961)[83]

> [This was actually the identity of these people, who professed it, they were Germans, in quotation marks, Germans–*Mantaks*, descendants of Germans.]

In Medzev, the colloquial categorization of *Mantaks* and non-*Mantaks* works simply—according to a popular saying: If two *Mantaks* talk to each other and do not find a common relative within three minutes, then one of them is not a *Mantak*. The field research revealed that in the examined town of Medzev, with its 4,261 inhabitants[84], the majority of the *Mantak* families know each other. The recognition is enabled not just by the small number of the inhabitants, who are familiar to each other, but also by traditional surnames. The most frequented *Mantak* surnames are listed in a publication about Medzev, which aimed to show the prevalence of *Mantak*/German inhabitants of Medzev in the middle of the nineteenth century.[85] Because of the frequency of some surnames, people added nicknames to particular family branches based on various connections. Narrator E. S. described the origin of nicknames in the Schmotzer families:

> Vo Vyšnom Medzeve bolo tých Schmotzerovcov [...] veľmi veľa. A tie rodiny mali taká prímenia, aby sa rozoznávali. [...] Ja som Schmotzer-Schbatza, ako "Schwarzer," ako "čierny," pretože starí rodičia a predkovia sa venovali kováčstvu. (E. S., *1961)[86]

> [There were a lot of Schmotzer families [...] in Vyšný Medzev. And those families had nicknames to recognize each other. [...] I am Schmotzer-Schbatza, like "schwarzer," like "black," because my grandparents and ancestors engaged in blacksmithing.]

---

82 Gabriela Schleusener and Heinz Schleusener, *Wörterbuch der deutschen Mundart in Metzenseifen* (Aachen: Shaker, 2013).

83 Interview with E. S., September 6, 2017.

84 These numbers are taken from the official census of 2011 (See: "Medzev: Obyvateľstvo podľa pohlavia a národnosti," *The 2011 Population and housing census Slovakia*, accessed January 9, 2021, https://census2011.statistics.sk/SR/V%FDchodn%E9%20Slovensko/Ko%9Aick%FD%20kraj/Okres%20Ko%9Aice%20-%20okolie/Medzev/TAB.%20115%20Obyvate%BEstvo%20pod%BEa%20pohlavia%20a%20n%E1rodnosti.pdf).

85 The data were based on the Austro-Hungarian census in 1857. See: Gedeon and Bistika, *Medzev*, 179–183.

86 Interview with E. S., September 6, 2017.

The dichotomy between written German and spoken *Mantakisch*, which was highly influenced by the Hungarian and Slovak language in the course of centuries, is also present in the different written and spoken forms of the first names. For example, the first names in spoken *Mantakisch* regularly get an ending –*é* (such as Filip = Filé, Roland = Rolé), but there are even more complicated uses of names in the multilingual context of Medzev. A typical example is a member of the *Mantak* language group, who speaks *Mantakisch* at home. In official documents, his first name appears in Slovak—Július[87]—but his relatives and friends call him Gyuszi, a diminutive of the Hungarian first name Gyula. The usage of modified first names in everyday communication is one of the signs of the complex linguistic space in Medzev.

Another vital feature of multilinguality is the situational use of particular languages. A foreigner in Medzev is generally addressed in Slovak as it is the official state language. *Mantakisch* is used only among people who all understand the dialect. On some occasions, mainly if a Hungarian arrives in Medzev, the older generation in Medzev (born in the interwar period) also show their fluent proficiency in the Hungarian language. To illustrate the complex image of this multilingual space, the youngest generation sometimes answers in official German when asked a question in *Mantakisch* and, due to the presence of a significant number of Roma minority members, the Romani language is also often heard in the streets of Medzev.

Identity on the Gravestones

There are several ways to analyze cemeteries—from focusing on the placement of gravestones and their forms to studying inscriptions or symbols on the gravestones. I took all of these into account and examined if and how they could represent any form of identity. The placement of graves in a specific graveyard section did not prove particularly relevant in symbolizing adherence to a language group. Instead, graves were usually arranged according to their size (and size connected to financial value) to make the cemetery look neat. There was no division among linguistic lines—gravestones with inscriptions in Slovak, Hungarian or German language are ordinarily placed next to one another.[88] In some cases, the placement of a grave can refer to adherence to a family—gravestones of several family members are placed side-by-side, or the family could even rent a few burial places and surround them with a fence. Grave forms and materials, whether granite or concrete or crosses of cast-iron or wood, do not symbolize membership to a

---

87   The official use of Slovak first names in the *Mantak* language group was predominantly caused by the forced Reslovakization after World War II.

88   The gravestones of the Roma minority are recognizable through decoration. Thanks to conversations with some Roma visitors, I learned that, in some cases, gravestones are different from others and tend to be in one area together.

language group either but rather indicate the financial situation of the deceased person or their descendants.

Thus, only specific symbols and languages used on the gravestone might represent a person's adherence to a group. Because the primary layer of identity under scrutiny in this research is identification with a language group, I predominantly concentrated on gravestones' language use and reflection. The focus lies on inscriptions (such as "rest in peace") and the forms of names (such as Slovak or German forms of first names or possible Slovak female endings attached to German surnames). As for the names, I compared the names written on a gravestone with the names written in official documents and the way people are addressed in a friendly setting.

The crucial question of this analysis was what influenced the language on gravestones? In connection with the often-mentioned high cost of the grave, I asked the gravedigger and stonemasons whether there is a price difference between the carving of Slovak and German inscriptions on gravestones. All respondents explained that, because of automatized carving, language plays no role, and the price depends on the number of letters[89] and the design of the font.[90]

Consequently, I was interested in whether the language on gravestones was affected by historical events in the second half of the twentieth century and their impacts, such as the Reslovakization or the communist takeover. Nevertheless, those who witnessed the rapid changes during and after World War II, and also experienced reslovakization, problems with using German in public spaces, and, sometimes, even persecution by the communist regime, deny any control over or ban of the use of German for gravestones.[91] As one of these narrators put it:

Na náhrobný kameň si mohol každý dať, čo chcel, a nikto nemohol mať námietky. (V. B., *1929)[92]

[Everyone could put what they wanted on the gravestone, and no one could have any objections.]

---

89   For example, the German version of a woman's surname (such as Schmiedt instead of Schmiedtová) would be cheaper because of the smaller amount of letters. However, the people I talked to never mentioned that they would choose German or Slovak inscriptions on gravestones because of a probably slightly different price.

90   Interview and email conversation with local gravedigger and stonemasons during September 2017.

91   The narrators who were asked about the possibility of the language on gravestones would usually emphasize another problem concerning cemeteries: Those who wanted to have a church funeral service during communism could face various obstacles imposed on behalf of officials of the communist party.

92   Interview with V. B., September 8, 2017.

Therefore, the language in the cemeteries was not directly affected by the restrictive policies of Czechoslovak governments, municipal authorities, or possible higher financial expenses. So, what did cause the varied and complex usage of German or Slovak language in the cemeteries of Medzev and Vyšný Medzev? For this research, I developed a typology following the dominant language used on gravestones. I chose graves belonging to families from the *Mantak* language group that were relevant to my research. I divided the graves into three groups based on the dominant language used on a gravestone: (1) Grave inscriptions in the German language, (2) Inscriptions in the Slovak language, and (3) Bilingual gravestones.[93] I compared these manifestations with the identifications and personal motivations that emerged in the interviews.

(1) Grave Inscriptions in German Language

The first type of grave of the *Mantak* language group consists of gravestones with inscriptions predominantly in the German language ("Hier ruhet"; "Ruhet in Frieden"; "Ruhet sanft")[94] and with names in German forms, be it first names (Walter, Johann) or female surnames without the typical Slovak ending *-ová*. A gravestone with German inscriptions is the result of a firm consideration of language use because, in the case of the vast majority of the *Mantaks*, it required regermanizing the official Slovak form of their names. Even though the *Mantak* language group could change their names (after 1945 often Slovakized) in official documents since 1989, only a minor part of the group has done it. The most common reason was that the older generation considered the arrangement process too complicated. Therefore, for those *Mantaks* who decided to use the German language on their gravestones, ordering the inscriptions meant considering the German form of their names and, thus, creating a difference between their official documents and their burial place. This is, for example, the case with the grave of Karl and Viktoria Schmiedt (see Figure 1), who decided to arrange their grave in the Medzev cemetery in advance. On the gravestone, there are two longer inscriptions written in Gothic script ("Hier ruhet"; "Ruhet in frieden" (sic!))[95] and names (Karl Schmiedt and Viktoria Schmiedt, born[96] Gedeon). Viktoria Schmiedt, in official documents Schmiedtová, told me:

---

93 Because of the methodology based on the interviews with the people who obtained the grave or who still remember the deceased person, this research concentrated only on more recent gravestones (maximum 70 years old), which have inscriptions predominantly in German or Slovak. Hungarian is highly present among older gravestones whose owners were affected by Magyarization in the Austro-Hungarian Empire.

94 "Here rests"; "Rest in Peace"; "Rest gently."

95 "Here rests"; "Rest in Peace."

96 In German, "geboren" is abbreviated as "geb."

Ja som si dala nemeckú národnosť. [...]
Meno nie [nezmenila som si], lebo sú
veľké problémy s vybavovačkou. (V. S.,
*1940)[97]

[I took German nationality. [...] No, [I
did not change] the name because there
are big problems arranging it.]

During the interview, the same narrator
expressed strong identification with the
Mantak/German language group and
when asked about her decision to use
German on the gravestone, she said:

Figure 1: Gravestone with German inscriptions.
Source: Author (September 2017).

Ja som taká—ako sa povie—tvrdohlavá *Mantáčka*. My sme taký *Mantáci*, keď nás
nedonutia [použiť na náhrobku slovenský jazyk], my to neurobíme. (V. S., *1940)[98]

[I am—as they say—a stubborn *Mantak* woman. We are *Mantaks*; if they do not
force us [to use the Slovak language on the gravestone], we do not do it.]

She not only chose to use German but the Gothic script too, which she associated
with the German culture and by which she wanted to emphasize her "German-
ness."[99] Therefore, in this case, the gravestone manifests the identity of the people
who will be buried there.

A similar case is the gravestone of Gaspar and Margarete Meder in the cemetery of Vyšný Medzev (see Figure 2). The names of the deceased persons are in
German form, written in Gothic script. A close relative of the deceased Meder
couple described the language situation in their family as follows:

U nás je jednoznačne nemčina a ja som jednoznačne *Manták*. Takže u nás proste je
takáto tradícia, alebo že národnosť si človek nevyberá, ale národnosť sa dedí. (N1)[100]

[In our [family], it is clearly German [language], and I am clearly *Mantak*. So, we
[our family] simply keep this tradition because one does not choose nationality, but
nationality is inherited.]

---

97   Interview with V. S., September 6, 2017.
98   Ibid.
99   Golden script on a black stone can also be regarded as typical for "German" graves.
100 Interview with N1, September 7, 2017.

Figure 2: Gravestone with German inscriptions.   Figure 3: Gravestone with German inscriptions.
Source: Author (September 2017).   Source: Author (September 2017).

This expression also refers to the ambiguity mentioned earlier between the categories, "German" and "*Mantak.*" In this case, by using the category "German," the narrator referred to the language spoken in his family. He interpreted the category of "*Mantak*" as the "ethnic group" as he defined the category when he started thinking about cemeteries:

> Ja si takisto prajem nemecký alebo latinský nápis [na náhrobku]. [...] Ja aj po smrti chcem demonštrovať príslušnosť k môjmu etniku. (NI)[101]

> [I also wish for a German or a Latin inscription [on the gravestone]. [...] Even after death, I want to demonstrate belonging to my ethnic group.]

The narrator's spontaneous usage of categories such as "ethnic group" is unique among the other narrators and might be explained through his academic education. On the other hand, the idea of "inherited" membership of the *Mantak* group is generally widespread even in relation to gravestones. Another narrator, a member of the Bistika family and respected amateur historian of Medzev, explained his motivation to write his name on the gravestone in Medzev (see Figure 3) in the German form as follows:

> Rodičia tak isto majú [nápisy na náhrobku] po nemecky, to *geboren*, my sa nebudeme odlišovať od nich, ale pokračujeme normálne v tom jazyku starých predkov našich, tak sa to berie. (V.B., *1929)[102]

> [My parents also have [inscriptions on the gravestone] in German, that [word] *geboren*. We will not be different, but we will normally continue [to use inscriptions] in the language of our old ancestors; that's how it is.]

---

101 Ibid.
102 Interview with V.B., September 8, 2017.

However, in many cases, there are no suitable alternations to the Slovak names in official documents; mistakes appear in the transcription or people do not consider the Slovak form of the first name to be an obstacle to the identity manifestation as in the case of the grave of Július Pöhm. His wife declared German nationality and has even changed her name from the Slovak form Pöhmová to the German form Pöhm (with the support of her husband). When asked about the grave inscriptions in German, his wife said that they were never really thinking about the Slovak form of the name Július as problematic. Thus, again there is a dichotomy between the name written in the documents and the name appearing in grave inscriptions:

> Viete čo, že nás to nenapadlo. [...] Každý mu hovoril Gyuszi[103], no a Gyuszi nenapíšem na toto [náhrobok], viete. A Gyuszi mi skôr pripadá ako v maďarčine. (M. P., *1941)[104]

> [You know, this did not occur to us. [...] Everyone called him [my husband] Gyuszi, but I will not write Gyuszi on it [gravestone], you know. After all, Gyuszi feels more Hungarian to me.]

Other narrators are rather displeased when seeing the names of their close relatives on gravestones with mistakes considered to be made by the stonemason. This is the case of the gravestone of Johan Schmotzer and Terezia Schmotzer born (in German "geboren" abbreviated as "geb.") Lang. There is one longer inscription on the gravestone—"Ruhet sanft."[105] Ervín Schmotzer talks about the grave of his grandparents (see Figure 4):

> JohaNN by tam malo byť, [...] to je také skomolené. To tiež nemôže byť Terezia, [... má to byť..] Theresia. [...] Nie som s tým spokojný. (E. S., *1961)[106]

> [There should be JohaNN, [...] it is distorted. It also cannot be Terezia [...], [it is supposed to be ...] Theresia. [...] I am not satisfied with that.]

Therefore, German inscriptions on gravestones usually refer to the intentional use of the language to manifest personal identity. On the other hand, mistakes or Slovak/Slovakized names often appear on gravestones with German inscriptions, thus in some cases leading to the dissatisfaction of bereaved persons from the *Mantak* community. However, other *Mantaks* showed indifference to the mis-

---

103 A diminutive form of the Hungarian name Gyula, in Slovak—Július.
104 Interview with M. P., September 10, 2017.
105 "Rest gently."
106 Interview with E. S., September 6, 2017.

Figure 4: Gravestone with German inscriptions.   Figure 5: Gravestone with Slovak inscriptions.
Source: Author (September 2017).   Source: Author (September 2017).

takes, Slovakization of names, or even predominant use of Slovak on gravestones as the following subchapter shows.

(2) Grave Inscriptions in the Slovak Language

The second type of gravestones of the members of the *Mantak* language group consists of gravestones with inscriptions predominantly in Slovak ("Odpočívaj v pokoji"; "Kto v srdci žije, neumiera")[107] and with names in Slovak forms, be it first names (Ján) or female surnames with the typical Slovak ending -*ová* (Gedeonová). These graves are typical for contemporary linguistically mixed families, where *Mantaks* usually adapt to their Slovak-speaking partner.[108] In these cases, the categorization is exercised based on the language groups or the place of origin. In Medzev and its surroundings, there is a somewhat simple categorization of people according to their town or village of origin. *Mantaks* are assumed to live in Medzev, Vyšný Medzev and Štós, whereas Slovaks are to live in Poproč, and Ruthenians in Hačava. This came up in one of the random conversations in the cemetery of Vyšný Medzev. When talking about the grave of Viera, born Rostášová, (see Figure 5) with its Slovak inscriptions ("manželka"; "Kto v srdci žije, neumiera"),[109] her relative said that she was "an original Slovak from Poproč," and he, as a *Mantak*, did not want to "offend" her by German inscriptions on the common grave.[110] Several times, the interviewee stressed that he was not a nationalist, and even though it was possible to use German language on a gravestone (as it is, for example, the case with the gravestone of his brother), he decided to use Slovak, showing respect to his beloved relative [Viera].

107 [Rest in Peace; Those who live in hearts do not die].
108 Some narrators mentioned that, when Medzev was predominantly inhabited by the *Mantaks* (until 1945), different language-speaking newcomers learned and spoke *Mantakisch*.
109 [Wife; Those who live in hearts do not die].
110 Notes in the author's research diary.

The complex linguistic and historical context of Medzev became evident again in the interview with Michal Brösztl (*1931).[111] He repeatedly explained that his name is a Magyarized form of a traditional Medzev name Bröstl. Michal Brösztl's mother tongue was *Mantakisch*. He could not yet speak Slovak when he started school, yet he later spoke Slovak with his children, because he had needed to master the language to get a better job. On the gravestone of his wife in Vyšný

Figure 6: Gravestone with Slovak inscriptions. Source: Author (September 2017).

Medzev (see Figure 6) that already bears his name [Michal Brösztl] all inscriptions are in Slovak ("Odpočívajte v pokoji")[112] and only the Magyarized German name refers to the *Mantak* origin of my interviewee. The gravestone manifests the multilinguality of the place, where an inscribed personal life story completes the local image that conveys the situational use of languages and the shifting adherence to a particular language group.

I also explored the situational use of languages during the process of arrangement of graves. Until now, I only analyzed the cases of graves of people who either pre-arranged their grave before their death or died of natural causes in later life. This fact enabled people to order a gravestone once they had managed to reconcile to a certain extent with the death of their close relative or family member. However, I also talked to people who had lost a loved one suddenly. In these cases, I found it necessary to behave cautiously and gently and not increase the sadness of the narrators. In this manner, I talked with a bereaved person at the grave of Adrián Schürger, who died at the age of 39. Even though the name refers to a *Mantak* family, the inscriptions on the gravestone (see Figure 7) are in Slovak ("Kto v srdciach žije, neumiera").[113] The relative told me that the language question was not important when they had to arrange the grave.[114] The described situation again shows the situational use of language on a grave without any intent to manifest identity.

Slovak language on gravestones was also used according to political orientation, as one narrator claimed; only *Mantak*-communists have gravestones in Slovak.[115] This notion is connected with the unsettled status of the *Mantaks* during the communist period when the usage of the *Mantak* dialect in public or any offi-

---

111 Interview with M. B., September 8, 2017.
112 [Rest in Peace].
113 [Those who live in hearts do not die].
114 Notes in the author's research diary.
115 Notes in the author's research diary.

Figure 7: Gravestone with Slovak inscriptions. Source: Author (September 2017).

Figure 8: Gravestone with Slovak inscriptions and a star as a communist symbol. Source: Author (September 2017).

cial connection to *Mantak*/German culture was a contested issue. However, in the cemetery in Vyšný Medzev, the grave of Michael Schmotzer, a long-time member of the communist party and a partisan fighter during World War II, showed a completely different picture. On the one hand, the gravestone bore a star (see Figure 8), and, on the other, it had inscriptions in German ("Ruhet in Frieden"),[116] and a *Mantak* (!) form of the female first name (Kathe).[117]

Ambiguities still exist between the *Mantaks*, who were members of the communist party, and those, who were either persecuted by the communist party or simply did not agree with its ideology. Nevertheless, the case of Schmotzer's grave shows that this dichotomy has not had a demonstrable influence on the usage of language on the gravestones. More likely, this case verifies the claim that the language of inscriptions was never subjected to any official control or censorship.

(3) Bilingual Gravestones

I consider gravestones with inscriptions in both languages as bilingual gravestones. These are rare in the examined cemeteries yet represent a remarkable case. A unique example of a bilingual gravestone is the grave (see Figure 9) of the deceased Jozef Göbl and Gabriela born Gajdošová, who is still alive. There are two longer inscriptions on the gravestone—one in German next to the name

---

116 [Rest in Peace].
117 One narrator, V.S., commented on the given *Mantak* form of the first name, wondering why the wife of a communist official wanted to be remembered as *Mantak*. The inscriptions had probably been made as the wife died in 1992, after the fall of the communist regime. However, she is remembered as the wife of a communist official who discouraged *Mantaks* from using German language in public and, therefore, according to the narrators, should not have declared German affiliation.

of Jozef Göbl ("Hier ruhet")[118], and the
second one next to the name of Gabriela born (in Slovak "rodená" abbreviated as "rod.") Gajdošová in Slovak
("Odpočívaj v pokoji").[119] The name
of Jozef Göbl is also complemented by
another identification sign important
for the *Mantaks* in Medzev—the nick-
name Hanzal. Therefore, the gravestone
emphasizes the *Mantak* identity of the
man and the Slovak identity of his wife.
This bilingualism of the gravestone was
explained to me by the couple's son:

Figure 9: Bilingual gravestone. Source: Author
(September 2017).

> Moja mama neni tu rodáčka z Medzeva a neni Mantáčka. Takže ona sa necíti ani do
> dneska *Mantáčka*. [...] Otec sa cítil ako Nemec. (E. G., *1962)[120]

> [My mother was not born in Medzev, and she is not a *Mantak*. To this day, she does
> not feel like a *Mantak*. [...] My father felt German.]

This case clearly shows that linguistically mixed families have different strategies when choosing the language for their gravestones. Some members of the
Mantak language group adapt to the Slovak language—the language of the partner and the state language; others choose to emphasize their different origin,
mother tongue and identity by using both German and Slovak language on one
gravestone.

Conclusion

The aim of this chapter was to explore public manifestations of identity of the
German/*Mantak* language group in the Eastern Slovak town of Medzev. Local
cemeteries—places that provide a picture of history, culture, and identity—were
chosen as a medium that can display local identity/-ies. The field research in
Medzev and the subsequent analysis focused on the question of whether gravestone inscriptions manifest the identity of Germans/*Mantaks* in Medzev and if
yes, to what extent was it an intentional decision of the deceased or the relatives.
A comparison of inscriptions on gravestones with their reflection in biographic
and semi-structured interviews with local *Mantaks* confirmed the hypothesis

---

118 [Here rests].
119 [Rest in Peace].
120 Interview with E. G., September 11, 2017.

that gravestones can expose the identity of the deceased members of the *Mantak* language group. However, gravestones manifest only one part of the multi-layered *Mantak* identity, where particular layers are relevant for each member of the group in different circumstances.

Therefore, gravestones serve as a tool for the manifestation of the *Mantak* identity for some members of the German/*Mantak* language group. Those people wish to express their *Mantak* origin, adherence to their *Mantak* family and heritage. However, the chapter has shown that the wish to express identity on gravestones depends greatly on individual experiences and context. Some narrators, who arranged their graves in the German language and even the Gothic script in advance, showed indifference to minor mistakes or the Slovak/Slovakized form of their names. This could be a sign of unwillingness to deal with the stonemason again (due to additional financial expenses caused by re-writing), or, more importantly, as a sign of loose boundaries between the languages used in everyday life.

The examination of the gravestones of *Mantaks* with inscriptions in Slovak, as was the case mainly in the linguistically mixed families, exposed the situational use of various layers of identity. As confirmed by the interviews, entirely used Slovak inscriptions or Slovakized names do not mean that a person has a Slovak identity. I argue that language change in the multilingual space of Medzev in Eastern Slovakia does not always mean the change of identity. It could also refer to an adaptation to a particular situation. My research has shown how fluid the boundaries between language groups are and how problematic the concept of identity as an analytical tool for multilingual areas can be.

Therefore, the findings of this research bring us back to the theoretical assumptions of Rogers Brubaker. Similar to Brubaker,[121] my research confirmed that the categories based on different languages (which were used as analytical categories) are not strictly bounded and impenetrable. The individuals, perceived as members of a specific language group, adjust their degree of adherence to a particular group according to their everyday experiences. At the same time, interviews with members of the *Mantak* language group have shown that identification based on language or nationality need not be relevant in a multilingual area. These categories may have a conditional meaning for each member of the community. Research of such a variety of identities and their public manifestations is crucial to understanding the reality of coexistence in language-mixed areas.

Interviews

Narrator A. B. (*1938), interview with the author, September 9, 2017.
Narrator V. B. (*1929), interview with the author, September 8, 2017.
Narrator M. B. (*1931), interview with the author, September 8, 2017.

---

121 Brubaker, *Nationalist Politics.*

Narrator E. G. (*1962), interview with the author, September 11, 2017.
Narrator M. P. (*1941), interview with the author, September 10, 2017.
Narrator N1 (*1956), interview with the author, September 12, 2017.
Narrator V. S. (*1940), interview with the author, September 6, 2017.
Narrator E. S. (*1961), interview with the author, September 6, 2017.
All original recordings and informed consents of the narrators are stored in the author's archive.

Other primary sources

Author's Research Diary, Author's Archive.

Selected Bibliography

Brubaker, Rogers, Margit Feischmidt, Jon Fox, and Liana Grancea. *Nationalist Politics and Everyday Ethnicity in a Transylvanian Town.* Princeton: Princeton University Press, 2008.

Gabzdilová-Olejníková, Soňa, and Milan Olejník. *Karpatskí Nemci na Slovensku od druhej svetovej vojny do roku 1953, Acta Carpatho-Germanica 12.* Bratislava: Spoločenskovedný ústav SAV, Múzeum kultúry karpatských Nemcov, 2004.

Jenkins, Richard. *Being Danish: Paradoxes of Identity in Everyday Life.* Copenhagen: Museum Tusculanum Press, 2016.

Kováč, Dušan. *Vysídlenie Nemcov zo Slovenska (1944–1953).* Praha: Ústav pro soudobé dějiny AV ČR, 2001.

Pešek, Jan, ed. *V tieni totality: Politické perzekúcie na Slovensku v rokoch 1948–1953.* Bratislava: Historický ústav SAV, 1996.

Zückert, Martin, Michal Schvarc, and Jörg Meier, eds. *Migration—Zentrum und Peripherie—Kulturelle Vielfalt: neue Zugänge zur Geschichte der Deutschen in der Slowakei.* Leipzig: Peter Lang, 2016.

Narrating Boundaries: The Cartographical Approach to Upper Lusatian Cemeteries

MICHAŁ PIASEK

Introduction

One may observe that sepulchral culture in Germany is constantly changing. Notably in Eastern Germany, on former German Democratic Republic (GDR) territory, it has changed a lot throughout history. Nowadays, this region has the highest rate (over 70 percent) of atheists and one of the highest cremation rates in Europe.[1] The reason for this situation lies in historical and political changes and shifting borders that accompanied it.

Hornja Łužica/Oberlausitz (Upper Lusatia) in Saxony is the center of the Upper Sorbs, a small Slavic ethnic group[2] and one of the four recognized minorities in Germany. Since the Lutheran reformation, Sorbs have been religiously divided into Protestants and Catholics with each having a different number of speakers.[3] According to the Sorbian umbrella organization *Domowina* there are 40,000 Sorbs

---

1   Matthias Petzold, "Zur religiösen Lage im Osten Deutschlands. Sozialwissenschaftliche und theologische Interpretationen," in *Woran glaubt die Welt. Analysen und Kommentare zum Religionsmonitor,* ed. Bertelsmann Stiftung (Gütersloh: Verlag Bertelsmann Stiftung, 2008), 125–50.

2   The term *Volksgruppe* [ethnic group] is used, since the Saxon Sorbs Act (*Sächsisches Sorbengesetz (SächsSorbG), Gesetz über die Rechte der Sorben im Freistaat Sachsen, 31. März 1999*) defined it this way. §1 states about Sorbian ethnicity: "One belongs to the Sorbian people if they choose to belong to the given group as such. The choice is free. It may neither be denied nor reviewed. This orientation may not cause any disadvantage." All translations by the author unless otherwise noted.

3   There are no statistics of the Sorbian-speaking population documenting a specific ethnic affiliation nor the number of its speakers. The data merely estimate the number of speakers or non-speakers of Sorbian. Martin Walde postulates that it would be simpler and more politically correct to leave to each individual the choice of which "nationality" they belong to. Martin Walde, "Demographisch-statistische Betrachtungen im Oberlausitzer Gemeindeverband 'Am Klosterwasser'," *Lětopis* 51, no. 1 (2004): 3–27. See also: Ludwig Elle, "Wie viele Sorben gibt es—noch? Oder: Kann und soll man Minderheiten zählen?," in *Dialogische Begegnungen: Minderheiten—Mehrheiten aus hybridologischer Sicht, Hybride Welten,* eds. Elka Tschernokoshewa and Ines Keller, Band 5 (Münster: Waxmann, 2011), 209–23.

in Upper Lusatia.[4] Further historical events amplified the divergent linguistic development, which has always been closely tied to religion.[5] Subsequently, distinct Sorbian dialects spoken in specific regions have evolved based on the prevalent denomination.[6] Cemeteries display these dialectal differences, together with the linguistic transition (Sorbian to German) within the Upper Sorbian group. This transition also led to a changing appearance of cemeteries and changing burial practices within the German- and Sorbian-speaking area of Upper Lusatia.

A small area north-west of Budyšin/Bautzen, in the so-called catholic-triangle (Wojerecy/Hoyerswerda–Budyšin/Bautzen–Kamjenc/Kamenz) represents an exception.[7] Here the inhabitants maintained their burial practices and their use of Sorbian.

Consequently, I distinguish three areas in Upper Lusatia:

1) Northern Upper Lusatia, where Sorbian inscriptions are almost non-existent. North of the Prussian-Saxon border (see Map).

2) Upper Lusatia (around Budyšin/Bautzen area), where several cemeteries with Sorbian inscriptions exist.

3) the Catholic-triangle, where the majority of gravestones have Sorbian inscriptions.

Throughout history, these three areas have undergone very specific historical and religious changes, which I aim to make visible through a cartographic[8] approach. I combine this method with the *phantom borders*[9] theory. It is a new approach showing how shifting borders and religion are entangled with current use of the Sorbian language on gravestones. This approach facilitates reading history on maps and provides insights on the distribution of Sorbian in Upper Lusatia from

---

4   Franz Schön, Dietrich Scholze, Susanne Hose Maria Mirtschin, and Anja Pohontsch, *Sorbisches Kulturlexikon* (Bautzen: Domowina-Verlag, 2014). See also: Ludwig Elle, "Sorben—demographische und statistische Aspekte," in *Minderheiten als Mehrwert,* ed. Matthias Theodor Vogt (Frankfurt am Main: Lang, 2010), 309–18.

5   Martin Walde, "Katholisches versus evangelisches Milieu bei den Sorben," *Lětopis* 53, no. 2 (2006): 15–28.

6   Heinz Schuster-Šewc, "Zur schriftsprachlichen Entwicklung im Bereich des Sorbischen," *Sociolinguistica* 6, no. 1 (1992): 65–83, https://doi.org/10.1515/9783110245110.65.

7   Peter Kunze, "Geschichte und Kultur der Sorben in der Oberlausitz—Ein geschichtlicher Abriss," in *Geschichte der Oberlausitz: Herrschaft, Gesellschaft und Kultur vom Mittelalter bis zum Ende des 20. Jahrhunderts,* ed. Joachim Bahlcke (Leipzig: Leipziger Univ.-Verl, 2004), 280.

8   Marie-Laure Ryan, Kenneth E. Foote, and Maoz Azaryahu, *Narrating Space/Spatializing Narrative: Where Narrative Theory and Geography Meet* (Columbus: The Ohio State University Press, 2016).

9   Béatrice von Hirschhausen, Hannes Grandits, Claudia Kraft, Dietmar Müller, and Thomas Serrier, *Phantomgrenzen: Räume und Akteure in der Zeit neu denken* (Göttingen: Wallstein Verlag, 2015).

a completely different point of view. It shows what impact the historicity[10] of the borders has on the current cemetery situation and how the cemetery situation mirrors political structures that no longer exist. Marko Zajc put it succinctly by saying that "the core idea behind the concept is as simple as it is intricate: *phantom borders* are political borders that once were, are no more, but—nevertheless—somehow still are."[11] The method of cartographic reading provides an alternative way of presenting language use and vitality within communities of small-language speakers.

Funerary inscriptions reveal linguistic and cultural affiliation of the deceased and the bereaved.[12] This capacity of a grave to tell something about a person or community implies narrating/storytelling qualities. This applies both to the choice of language and the symbols used on gravestones. The narrative form of graves is intertwined with space and—according to the work of Marie-Laure Ryan *et al.*[13]—space is characterized by location, position, design, distance, direction, orientation and movement. Space and narrative, in turn, are connected with maps. They include selected data in its reduced form. For example, ethnic, linguistic, tourist, road, or topographical maps.[14] Whereas, ethnic and linguistic maps are mostly based on the outcome of a census and depict the language distribution and use only roughly and inaccurately. As a consequence, maps are often considered speculative or manipulative because it is hardly possible to create an ideal 1: 1 map.[15]

Following the concept of *phantom borders* elaborated by Beatrice von Hirschhausen *et al.*,[16] borders can withdraw as physical entities but prevail in the form of political and historical processes over a particular period of time. The stronger the impact on a particular region, the more visible such a phantom border becomes. After all, not only do the traces of no longer existing political structures remain tangible, but they also affect future development of a specific region.[17]

---

10 Eric Hirsch and Charles Stewart, "Introduction: Ethnographies of Historicity," *History and Anthropology* 16, no. 3 (2005): 261–74.

11 Marko Zajc, "Contemporary Borders as 'Phantom Borders': An Introduction," *Südosteuropa* 67, no. 3 (2019): 298.

12 Eva Reimers, "Death and Identity: Graves and Funerals as Cultural Communication," *Mortality* 4, no. 2 (1999): 147–66. I do not elaborate further on the concept of *identity*. More on that matter, see the chapter by Tereza Juhaszová, "'Bien Mantaakn': The Manifestation of Identity in Cemeteries in the Eastern Slovak Town of Medzev" in this volume.

13 Ryan, *Narrating*, 7.

14 Ibid., 45.

15 Jeremy W. Crampton, *Mapping: A Critical Introduction to Cartography and GIS* (Chichester: Wiley-Blackwell, 2010); Denis Wood, John Fels, and John Krygier. *Rethinking the Power of Maps* (New York: Guilford Press, 2010).

16 Hirschhausen von, *Phantomgrenzen*.

17 Đorđe Tomić, *Phantomgrenzen und regionale Autonomie im postsozialistischen Südosteuropa. Die Vojvodina und das Banat im Vergleich* (Göttingen: Wallstein Verlag, 2016).

Various scholars have used this concept to identify phantom borders linked to electoral votes. In particular, Jarosław Jańczak compared the electoral outcome in the Voivodeships Pomorskie (Pomerania) and Wielkopolskie (Greater Poland), a territory in which regional and state borders shifted many times between 1772 and 1945.[18] Beatrice von Hirschhausen and her collaborators followed up on that and showed the electoral share between the former partitioned territories in Poland during the Presidential elections in 2015. They demonstrated the diverging electoral votes within these regions. In addition, they also highlighted the physical appearance of infrastructure by illustrating the railroad network infrastructure in the early 1950s, which showed the density within former Prussian territories, in contrast to the Russian and Austrian territories.[19]

By using this method, I will address the following research questions: What influence do political borders and religion have on the historical use of the Sorbian language? How is it possible to connect spatial narratives to language use and how does the language reflect on gravestones in Upper Lusatia. Finally, how can this information be implemented on a map?

This offers an alternative approach to define micro-areas within a region with distinct languages and religions through a map considering these parameters. It shows the impact of different states and their individual language policies in addition to topographical changes caused by extensive coal mining and the subsequent decreasing use of Sorbian in these areas.[20] This approach, linked with historical events will help identify linguistically mixed areas and make phantom borders visible again.

Methodology

While there is Lower and Upper Lusatia, I dealt with the latter, as it has a much larger number of speakers as well as a distinction between Catholic and Protestant Sorbs. Up to now, Ernst Tschernik has made the most important attempt after World War II at identifying Sorbian-speaking areas. In the early 1950s, he performed a demographic and statistical research of the Sorbian speaking population in Upper and Lower Lusatia based on previous data from the nineteenth

---

18 Jarosław Jańczak, "Phantom Borders and Electoral Behavior in Poland Historical Legacies, Political Culture and their Influence on Contemporary Politics," *Erdkunde* 69, no. 2 (2015): 125–137.

19 Béatrice von Hirschhausen, "Phantomgrenzen als heuristisches Konzept für die Grenzforschung," in *Grenzforschung: Handbuch Für Wissenschaft Und Studium,* eds. Dominik Gerst, Maria Klessmann, and Hannes Krämer (Baden-Baden: Nomos, 2021): 175–189.

20 More information on coal-mining: Jeremias Herberg, Konrad Gürtler, David Löw Beer, "Strukturwandel als Demokratiefrage—Der Lausitzer Kohleausstieg, ein Ausstieg aus der Transformationsblockade?," in *Berliner Debatte Initial* 30, no. 4 (2019): 113–124.

century.[21] On the grounds of this data, he conducted a linguistic analysis by himself in the mid-1950s to estimate the number of Sorbian speakers.[22] Tschernik's research method would no longer be possible today, as he conducted his research in Sorbian speaking areas by knocking on doors and asking people about their Sorbian language skills. Current German privacy policy laws do not allow such an approach. Regardless, his data remains very useful, as I used it to determine the main research area in Upper Lusatia.

With this data, I created a corpus including 109 visited cemeteries in Upper Lusatia during several visits in 2016 and 2017. All visited cemeteries are located in today's officially recognized settlement area of the Sorbs.[23]

I, in contrast, connect Sorbian grave inscriptions at cemeteries with Sorbian language use and implement the data onto a map. I use the *phantom borders* theory and spatial narratives to develop a concept that relates to linguistic geography. As far as possible, I extracted information from linguistic qualities, lettering types and an anthroponymic analysis to provide the most accurate possible representation of the deceased. Inscriptions serving as spatial narratives can provide specific information such as what language was used or what origin the descendants had. For example, using a distinct type of grave (wooden cross or stone) or symbols. I gathered further information during random encounters at cemeteries. I used this information to quantify and illustrate the use of Sorbian on graves on the map.

The map depicts all visited cemeteries as well as the (historical) *phantom borders* and administrative borders. The light-colored pins depict cemeteries with less than 30 percent Sorbian inscriptions, whereas the dark pins represent cemeteries with over 30 percent Sorbian inscriptions. The northern dark colored border is today's administrative border between Brandenburg and Saxony. The brightly colored border in the south is the historical Prussian-Saxon border, which existed

---

21 Ernst Tschernik, *Die Entwicklung der Sorbischen Bevölkerung von 1832 bis 1945: Eine demographische Untersuchung* (Berlin: Akademie-Verlag, 1954). In the first step, Tschernik summarized Arnošt Muka's data from the nineteenth century and used it for his historical overview of the Sorbian people. In a second step, he began his own demographical statistics. Presumably Tschernik's data was not published until the 1990s out of fear of losing minority rights. The numbers were much lower than what Muka's research showed. Furthermore, the GDR censorship did not allow him to ask anything related to ethnicity/nation. That reduces his research outcome enormously and limits it to only active Sorbian speakers. His data is only available in Ludwig Elle's publication, see Footnote 22.

22 Data in Ludwig Elle, *Sprachenpolitik in der Lausitz. Eine Dokumentation 1949–1989* (Bautzen: Domowina-Verl. 1995), 241. Tschernik's data was supposed to be a purely demographic survey of 750 villages in Lusatia The data was never published and was only accessible in the Sorbian Cultural Archive in Budyšin/Bautzen. Tschernik's research can be considered critically from a scientific point of view, but it serves to illustrate the Sorbian-speaking area.

23 The area is described in the Saxon Sorbs Act. See Footnote 2.

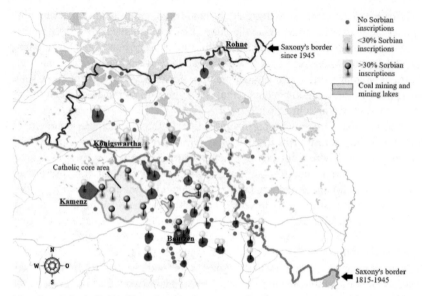

Map: Cemeteries in Sorbian Upper Lusatia. Source: OpenStreetMap and contributors, CC-BY-SA, www.openstreetmap.org. Edited by the author.

between 1815 and 1945. Furthermore, I marked the coal mining areas and artificial lakes, which divided Sorbian settlements, made the area uninhabitable and created another *phantom border*.

Upper Lusatia in Historical Context

Upper Lusatia has been exposed to several significant events in its history, mirroring the current cemetery situation which is characterized by multi-linguistic grave inscriptions as well as homogenous gravestones influenced by GDR policies. The Lutheran Reformation in 1517, which marked the beginning of religious division had the first far-reaching impact on the Sorbs, with its subsequent change of territory playing a further role. In 1526, Upper Lusatia and Bohemia came under Habsburg rule.[24] Only around 10 percent of the Sorbs remained Catholic, and the rest converted to the Lutheran Church.[25] Consequently, the so-called Catholic triangle emerged.[26]

---

24 Kunze, *Geschichte*, 279.
25 Martina Lindseth and Angelika Soldan, "The Sorbian Population Before and After German Reunification," *Journal of Contemporary Central and Eastern Europe* 8, no. 2 (2000): 149–61.
26 See Footnote 7.

In 1635, after signing the Peace of Prague, the Bohemian Crown handed over Upper Lusatia to Saxony. Henceforth, the Lower Sorbian center, Cottbus, went to Prussia, causing a further division of the Sorbian settlement area. To compensate for the population loss caused by the Thirty Years' War and plague, German-speaking settlers came to Upper Lusatia.[27] Similarly, the expulsion of some 150,000 Protestant religious refugees from Bohemia brought another change into the Sorbian population structure.[28] Both events of the seventeenth century amplified the use of German due to the new linguistically mixed area.

After the Congress of Vienna in 1815, the borders were redrawn once again. Saxony lost the entire area of Lower Lusatia and northern parts of Upper Lusatia. The latter had been divided among Silesia and Brandenburg. Out of the estimated 250,000 Sorbs, only about 50,000 remained in Saxony.[29] The division also meant separation and reconstruction of the parishes, which influenced both the religious milieu and the Sorbian-speaking population. Forthwith, the use of German became stronger.

After the founding of the German Reich in 1871, Otto von Bismarck aimed to achieve an inner unity, both denominational and cultural. His goal was to build a strong German national identity.[30] Thereupon, the Prussian government pursued a rather hostile policy towards the Sorbian language. The legislation in the Prussian part of Upper Lusatia even prohibited Sorbian in schools in 1875.[31] In 1885, most of the Protestant parishes in Prussia held all church-related activities in German, which largely succeeded by 1914.[32]

Contrastingly, in Saxon Upper Lusatia, schools offered Sorbian, and Sorbs used the language regularly. The Catholic Church played a significant role in this, since it saw the preservation of Sorbian as its task and declared the family as an important institution for maintaining traditions and the language.[33] A very stable Sorbian-speaking, Catholic milieu emerged. There were close to no religiously mixed marriages until 1945 in this milieu,[34] which has kept up a strong confessional boundary until today.

The influx of German-speaking workers coupled with other non-Sorbian speakers who arrived in the late nineteenth century to work in the extensively rising

---

27 Kunze, *Geschichte*, 282.
28 This was a result of the liberal religious policy of Saxon Electors.
29 Kunze, *Geschichte*, 288.
30 Walde, *Katholisches*, 15.
31 Soldan Lindseth and Konstanze Glaser, *Minority Languages and Cultural Diversity in Europe: Gaelic and Sorbian Perspectives* (Clevedon: Multilingual Matters, 2007), 105.
32 Peter Barker, "Kirchenpolitik und ethnische Identität: Das Beispiel der evangelischen Kirche in der DDR," in *Die DDR in Europa—zwischen Isolation und Öffnung*, ed. Heiner Timmermann (Münster: Lit, 2005), 269–80.
33 Walde, *Katholisches*, 18.
34 Ibid.

brown coal mines, linguistically influenced the Sorbian speaking population.[35] Mining often caused the demolition of entire villages, completely eradicating them from maps. Industrialization and urbanization also meant increased use of German, as people considered it a common language. Not to mention that the merchants and workers did not speak any Sorbian at all.

After 1933, the Nazi regime tried to bring the Sorbs into line (*Gleichschaltung*). Because of the strong resistance from the Sorbs, the Nazi-regime changed its policy and banned Sorbian and all of its associated institutions in 1937, causing Sorbian to completely vanish from the public sphere.[36] In 1940 the regime re-classified the Sorbs as Slavs which resulted in the forceful relocation of Sorbian clergy and teachers to other parts of Nazi Germany. Many were even sent to concentration camps.[37]

In 1950, around 750,000 German expellees from East- and South-East Europe arrived in Saxony.[38] Accordingly, the German language reinforced its role as the church service language. At the same time, the use of Upper Sorbian within predominantly Protestant areas further declined. Despite tensions and arguments between Catholic German expellees and Sorbs, Catholic church services remained Sorbian.[39] According to the statistics gathered by Ernst Tschernik in 1956, 17,876 Catholics were living in Upper Lusatia. Among them, 11,382 were Sorbs.[40]

Until 1974, the GDR-regime did not yet recognize Sorbs as a minority, but only as a "fremdsprachiger Volksteil" [foreign-language speaking part of the nation].[41] In the second constitution of 1974, the regime granted the Sorbs the status of a nation.[42]

The communist regime opposed religion and introduced several measures to decrease religious activities and, hence, the use of Sorbian. For example, the *Jugendweihe* [youth consecration][43] and the steady increase of the cremation rate

---

35 Gerald Stone, *Slav Outposts in Central European History: The Wends, Sorbs and Kashubs* (London: Bloomsbury, 2016), 269.

36 Lindseth and Glaser, *Minority languages;* Kunze, *Geschichte*, 301.

37 Lindseth and Glaser, *Minority languages*, 106.

38 Konstanze Gebel, *Language and Ethnic National Identity in Europe: The Importance of Gaelic and Sorbian to the Maintenance of Associated Cultures and Ethno Cultural Identities* (London: Middlesex University, 2002), 84.

39 Peter Barker, "Refugees, Expellees and the Language Situation in Lusatia (1945–7)," in *German Life and Letters* 57, no. 4 (2004): 396.

40 Data in Tomasz Kowalczyk, *Die katholische Kirche und die Sorben: 1919–1999* (Bautzen: Domowina-Verlag, 1999), 33.

41 *Die Verfassung der Deutschen Demokratischen Republik* (Berlin: Amt f. Information d. Regierung d. Deutschen Demokratischen Republik, 1949), Art. 11.

42 *Verfassung der Deutschen Demokratischen Republik: [vom 6. April 1968 in der Fassung des Gesetztes zur Ergänzung und Änderung der Verfassung der Deutschen Demokratischen Republik vom 7. Oktober 1974]* (Berlin: Staatsverlag der DDR, 1974), Art. 40.

43 A secular coming-of-age ceremony not aligned to any religion.

significantly reduced religious gatherings.[44] In 1960, the *Institut für Kommunal-wirtschaft* (Institute for municipal Economy, hereafter referred to as IfK) was founded in Dresden. Among other things, the institute was responsible for the cemetery and funeral system of the GDR.[45] The collectivization of cemeteries had practical reasons. One of them was the introduction of new cemetery policies. Lacking resources, namely stones which the regime needed to rebuild the infrastructure and housing led to the relocation of labor forces and resources no longer needed at the cemetery. Cutting back the resources and labor led to increasing cremation rates. Nevertheless, the official reason, apparently, was to promote the "sozialistisches Lebensgefühl" [socialist attitude to life] since the GDR-regime considered cremation as an ethically and hygienically perfect burial method.[46] In a 1970 study, the IfK questioned the funeral habits of Catholic Sorbs. They criticized Sorbs rarely resorting to state funeral homes. The local parish or village community carried out all activities. At the time, most Catholic Sorbs had not yet learnt that the Vatican had started allowing cremations.[47]

Despite the rigid socialist system and its authorities, Catholic funerals in Upper Lusatia took place with a priest, a cross-bearer, flag bearers, organists, and a cantor. As most of them were pupils, the schools allowed them to join the funerals. This resulted from the social structure among the Catholic Sorbs, who held the Sorbian clergy in high regard and had close ties with their parish, which defied the socialist leadership ideology of forming an atheist country.[48] This was unique for the whole GDR and saved Catholic traditions and Sorbian in this particular area, contrary to the Protestant areas, where religious ties loosened and the tradition to offer Sorbian church services had (mostly) been given up leading to a decreased use of Sorbian in the private sphere.

The Socialist Cemetery

In the following, I elaborate on some of the aforementioned arguments about the socialist cemetery by giving examples from Saxony or Upper Lusatia to show the influence of both coal mining and the 1815 Prussian-Saxon border on cemeteries in this Protestant part of Upper Lusatia.

---

44 Felix Robin Schulz, *Death in East Germany, 1945–1990* (New York: Berghahn, 2013).

45 Barbara Happe, "Grabdenkmale in der DDR—Der erzwungene Abschied vom persönlichen Grabmal," in *Grabkultur in Deutschland: Geschichte der Grabmäler*, eds. Reiner Sörries and Barbara Happe (Berlin: Reimer, 2009), 189.

46 Ibid., 190.

47 Stephan George, *Bestattung und katholische Begräbnisliturgie in der SBZ/DDR. Eine Untersuchung unter Berücksichtigung präskriptiver und deskriptiver Quellen* (Würzburg: Echter, 2006), 104.

48 Ibid., 285.

The communist regime aimed to establish a classless cemetery and, thus, it decisively interfered in the religious freedom and rights of its citizens.[49] Death and mourning were to become a state-controlled sphere and questions related to death were not supposed to arise.[50] The regime considered death as a lack of socialist progress and, therefore, the regime had very high expectations of medicine. For example, there was no entry for "death" in the *Philosophisches Wörterbuch* [*Philosophical Dictionary*], which did not resemble a classical encyclopedia, but a multivolume rule book of Marxist-Leninist theory.[51] In socialist speech, anything related to death was known as "Lebensbegleitende sozialistische Rituale" [lifelong socialist rituals].[52]

Noteworthy is the fact that the the cemetery laws the GDR applied, were almost identical to those of Nazi Germany. This included the ban on establishing or extending churchyards, a law originally introduced in 1933.[53] The regime also planned to keep burial expenses at the pre-war level of 1936. As this goal was not always possible to achieve, the result was decreased material quality, and people could not maintain their traditional gravestones or crosses. Resultingly, the regime increased cremation rates.

In 1956, the linguistic situation within the Sorbian-speaking areas worsened because of increasing brown coal mining. Mining companies destroyed villages and people had to move to other regions, mostly in newly built neighborhoods in larger cities like Wojerecy/Hoyerswerda or Dresden. These measures created a visible landscape boundary between the Lower and Upper Sorbs because those areas became uninhabitable. It separated not only the Lower Sorbs from the Upper Sorbs, but also cut off northern parts of Upper Sorbian settlement areas (see Map and coal mining markers). Between 1945 and 1989, 46 villages and 27 districts inhabited by Sorbs totally vanished due to coal mining.[54] According to Stone, the authorities repeatedly re-housed around 22,300 mostly Sorbian-speaking people outside of Lusatia in that period.[55] This also caused the huge loss of many Sorbian-speaking priests, who were crucial for language preservation.

In the early 1950s, 85 percent of the believers in Upper Lusatia were Protestants.[56] The regime concentrated on minimizing this number and constructing

---

49 This afflicts particularly the Protestant church, which lost its influence in the Sorbian-speaking community due to the language shift from Sorbian to German. Moreover, after adapting and adjusting to the new circumstances under socialism, the sense of community was not as strong as was the case within Catholic communities.

50 Schulz, *Death*.

51 The encyclopedia had been published between 1964 and 1987 in Verlag des Bibliographischen Instituts in Leipzig.

52 Schulz, *Death*, 62.

53 Ibid., 89.

54 Kunze, *Geschichte*, 306.

55 Stone, *Slav Outposts*, 338.

56 Schulz, *Death*, 89.

Ulbricht's "Gesellschaft ohne Türme" [society without [church] towers].[57] The Catholics, having strong social and religious ties and living in remote rural areas, were not affected by this as much as the Protestants. As a result, the latter noticed a fall in numbers of their faithful in 1956.[58]

The authorities completely transformed and changed cemetery traditions. The aim was to discourage people from staying at the cemetery longer than needed. Therefore, they removed benches and older parts of the cemetery were often subject to "reconstruction," which in no way meant restoration of the original grave. Rather, it was a contemporary redesign of the cemetery, after which the old graves irrevocably disappeared.[59] These "model cemeteries" were all meant to look the same and contain lying gravestones to avoid the "Unerträglichkeit der Unterschiede" [unbearable differences].[60]

The GDR-regime shortened the resting periods considerably. In large parts of the GDR, the periods lasted only 15 years.[61] Although rural cemeteries and churchyards in Upper Lusatia remained partially untouched by the so-called aesthetic revolution,[62] the Slepo/Schleifer region (Northern Upper Lusatia) proves an exception.[63]

The trend from the GDR period continued even after the political transformation in 1989/1990. In 1999, the newly formed federal states in the former GDR achieved a cremation rate of 75.3 percent (160,988 burials, of which 39,784 were coffin burials).[64] Thus, the cremation rate roughly equates to the proportion of the population not belonging to any denomination (in former East Germany: around 80 percent). In Saxony, the cremation rate in 1996 was about 81 percent.[65] It is not unusual that church attendance in urban areas is usually lower or steadily decreasing, whereas in rural areas the rate is traditionally higher. Most of the researched cemeteries have mainly secular gravestones. Anonymous burials did not exist within the Catholic Sorbian-speaking population whatsoever.[66]

---

57   Ibid., 91. Specifically meaning churches.
58   Ibid., 98.
59   Happe, *Grabdenkmale*, 192.
60   Schulz, *Death*, 98.
61   Ibid., 145.
62   Ibid.
63   The cemeteries in this micro-region show typical elements from the socialist cemetery, see: Schulz, *Death*.
64   Ibid., 152.
65   Data in Robin Sircar, "Untersuchung der Emissionen aus Einäscherungsanlagen und der Einsatzmöglichkeiten von Barrierenentladungen zur Verringerung des PCDD/F-Austrages" (PhD diss., Halle an der Saale: Univ. 2002).
66   George, *Bestattung*, 279.

Cemeteries in Protestant Upper Lusatia

The phantom border divides Upper Lusatia into former Prussian and Saxon Upper Lusatia (see Map). According to my findings, in Prussian Upper Lusatia, there are nine cemeteries with only a few Sorbian gravestones and 32 cemeteries with none. Former Prussian Upper Lusatia has three boundaries. The first is the historical Prussian border, the second is today's administrative border with Brandenburg and the third, a topographical boundary comprising mining lakes, which result from extensive coal mining.

I will elaborate on the cemeteries in Rowno/Rohne and Łaz/Lohsa at a later stage, as they are historically valuable to the Sorbs, but due to coal mining and mining lakes, both are cut off from the Upper Sorbian settlement area. Below this border, there are at least 24 cemeteries with Sorbian inscriptions.[67] Twenty cemeteries do not have any graves with Sorbian inscriptions.

One reason for the disappearance of Sorbian graves is the traditional use of wooden crosses. Between 1840 and 1880 the cemeteries consisted almost exclusively of wooden crosses (see Figure 1), which did not last long because of weathering.[68] This type of cross still exists today, albeit used only occasionally and mostly in Catholic cemeteries.

Another typical, nowadays declining, characteristic of Sorbian cemeteries concerns the usage of historical lettering styles.[69] Both, Catholic and Protestant Sorbs, used a distinct Gothic fractured font called the *Schwabacher*[70] on their gravestones. The Protestants used a German influenced orthography and the Catholics a Czech influenced one.[71] This proves a greater influence of German on the language of Sorbian Protestants than on that of Sorbian Catholics. The different orthography also contains a narrative element, which allows one to identify and show religious affiliation on the map (see Map). Although the Nazis forbade

---

67 Below the historical Prussian-Saxon border, there are 29 cemeteries in total. Five are inside the Catholic core area.

68 Erich Schneider, "Das Holzgrabkreuz in der sächsischen Oberlausitz," *Lětopis* 26, no. C (1983): 3–37.

69 There is a difference between Upper Sorbian Catholic and Protestant orthography and lettering styles. See: Helmut Faßke, "Zur Herausbildung einer einheitlichen Graphik und Orthographie des Obersorbischen im 19. Jahrhundert," *Zeitschrift für Slawistik* 29, no. 6 (1984): 873. Helmut Faßke elaborates that between 1862 and 1937 Sorbs predominantly used the Protestant orthography and two types of lettering: Latin Antiqua and German Fraktur (Ibid., 878).

70 Ibid.

71 Roland Marti, "Ein 'Kulturkampf' in der Slavia romana: 'Deutsch' vs. 'Slavisch' in Schrift und Schreibung," in *Slavic Alphabets in Contact*, eds. Vittorio Springfield Tomelleri and Sebastian Kempgen (Bamberg: University of Bamberg Press, 2015), 159–87.

the use of fractured lettering types in 1941[72], after 1945 the Sorbs renewed previous practices of using fractured lettering.

The research in Protestant Upper Lusatia did not reveal any cemeteries having over 10–15 gravestones with Sorbian inscriptions. Today, this area is religiously characterized by a high number of atheists. Especially during my random conversations with local pastors or church chaplains, I learned that the number of church visitors is continuously decreasing. The local churches offer Sorbian-speaking services only occasionally.[73]

Figure 1: New cemetery in Njeswačidło/Neschwitz, before World War II. Characteristic wooden crosses. Source: SLUB/Deutsche Fotothek.

Many cemeteries in Protestant Upper Lusatia with no Sorbian inscripted graves still bear evidence of a Sorbian heritage. Countless deceased have Germanized Sorbian names. In Upper Lusatia, Sorbian (sur-)names always have a German pendant and *vice versa*. For example, Sorbian Krawc corresponds with Krautz/Schneider [tailor] and Wowčer with Wowtscher/Schäfer [shepherd]. This means there is a German phonetic translation or the actual meaning of the word. In this case, as in most others, the surname represents an occupation, typically some form of craftsmanship. However, there is a difference between the Protestant and Catholic cemeteries. In the Protestant area, gravestone inscriptions often reveal information on the deceased person's occupation. Many of the municipal cemeteries still have the typical look of the GDR's model cemetery. They often comprise row of graves, with the gravestones in similar colors, and the inscriptions are limited to only the first and last name and the date of birth and death and sometimes they also display Christian symbols like flowers. At the municipal cemeteries, there are hardly any graves older than 20 or 25 years.

Regarding the physical appearance of the cemeteries, such as inscriptions and symbols, the Protestant area reveals a variety of symbols. And yet, the variety significantly decreases from the south (Budyšin/Bautzen area) to the north (Slepo/ Schleife area). The symbols are of Christian origin only in the broadest sense.

---

72 Peter Rück, "Die Sprache der Schrift—Zur Geschichte des Frakturverbots 1941," In *Homo scribens*, eds. Jürgen Baurmann, Hartmut Günther, and Ulrich Knoop (Berlin, New York: Max Niemeyer Verlag, 2011), 231–72. The lettering type is considered to be German because German public administration used this font from the sixteenth century until 1941. The Sorbs used it, too, as they did not adapt any other lettering type and Upper Lusatia has been under German administration for several centuries.

73 I gathered the information during my field trips.

The decrease is particularly evident in the villages between Wojerecy/Hoyerswerda and Běła Woda/Weißwasser. These include Bórk/Burk, Bórkhammer/Burghammer, Nowe Město/Neustadt Spree, Slepo/Schleife and others. This area displays neither a significant amount of occupational information nor a wide variety of symbols. There are hardly any crosses, which is due to the very high number of atheists. The most common symbols were flowers and roses, followed by wheat grains and, occasionally, praying hands. The only indicators of Sorbian origins were a few surnames, such as Kilian, Sprejz and Nakoinz. These cases show the German spelling of originally Sorbian surnames.[74]

Figure 2: Cemetery in Hrodźišćo/Gröditz. Traditional wooden cross with a linden leaf as symbol. Source: Author (February 2017).

South of the former Prussian border, however, several inscriptions indicated occupations. Most of these were exclusively at municipal cemeteries. The occupational groups include craftsman professions and jobs that require technical education and training. Some examples are craftworkers, master painters, master carpenters and butchers. The cemeteries south and east of Budyšin/Bautzen display mostly Christian symbols. Graves without crosses mostly include engraved roses or flowers.

On graves with Sorbian inscriptions, there is less occupational information than on German graves. The majority of the existing Sorbian inscriptions are dedicated to important or famous Sorbian personalities like writers, composers, chairpersons of the Sorbian umbrella organization *Domowina* and also pastors. The typical symbols are either a cross, Jesus or the symbol of the Sorbian people, a linden leaf, which appear in Bukecy/Hochkirch (at both cemeteries), Hrodźišćo/Gröditz and Kubšicy/Kubschütz.

From a linguistic point of view, there are only a few noteworthy cases.[75] This means that inscriptions were limited to usual phrases like "Here rests in God" and

74 Walter Wenzel, *Lausitzer Familiennamen slawischen Ursprungs* (Bautzen: Domowina-Verlag, 1999).
75 It has to be kept in mind that the descendants decide on the inscriptions and gravestones in the end. If one of them does not speak Sorbian the inscriptions will probably be in German.

the names and dates. The Upper Sorbian Protestant dialect is often used along with the German Fraktur lettering. Two examples from Rakecy/Königswartha:

Tu wotpočuja w bozy Hanka Laser, geb. Würgatsch, 1918–1986

[Here rests in God Hanka Laser, born Würgatsch, 1918–1986]

Tuhdy wotpočujetaj w Bozy naša luba mać a wowka Lejna Lukasowa, rodź. Šewčikec, z Komorowa, 1874–1957

[Here rest (sic!) in God our beloved mother and grandmother Lejna Lukasowa, born Šewčikec, from Komorow, 1874–1957]

The spelling of "bozy," which lacks the diacritic ž, and the extra *h* in "tuhdy" are typical Protestant dialectal forms of Upper Sorbian and thus could not be regarded as mistakes. The only mistake I observed was the wrong use of the grammatical dual verb form[76], as in the last example "wotpočujetaj," although only one person is included on the epitaph. It remains unknown if the person was married or planned to share her grave with a relative. If this was the case, the form would be correct.

Other important features are bilingual gravestones or family graves, where certain members have chosen either German or Sorbian inscriptions. Sorbian inscriptions with German names are a different case. The reasons, among others, lie in mixed marriages or the lack of Sorbian proficiency. With this in mind, a gravestone in the old churchyard in Bukecy/Hochkirch reads:

Tu wotpočuja w bozy Hanka Laser, geb. Würgatsch, 1918–1986
Ruth Nilius, geb. Würgatsch, 1922–1987
Gerhart Laser, Pfarrer, 1910–1992

[Here rest in God Hanka Laser, born Würgatsch, 1918–1986
Ruth Nilius born Würgatsch 1922–1987
Gerhart Laser pastor 1910–1992]

Gerhart Laser (1910–1992) was a well-known Sorbian-Protestant pastor in Bukecy/ Hochkirch between 1959–1979. His Sorbian name was Gerat Lazar, however, the gravestone includes only the German spelling.

---

76 Most of the Slavic languages have the Singular–Plural system. However, historically there was also a dual verb form, which always means two persons/objects. Besides Upper Sorbian, the dual verb form is also used in Lower Sorbian and Slovene. See also: Tatyana G. Slobodchikoff, *The Evolution of the Slavic Dual: A Biolinguistic Perspective* (Lanham: Lexington Books, 2019).

In the Protestant area, the cemeteries have a very high number of surnames of Sorbian (or Slavic) origin. In the majority of villages, the most common name is Kschieschank. It derives from the Upper Sorbian *kśižan/křižan* [Christian or cross-bearer]. The following different spellings of the name are common: Kschischang, Kschischan, Kschieschenk, Zieschang, Zieschank[77]

Figure 3: Cemetery in Rowno/Rohne. There are twelve old gravestones from the late nineteenth and early twentieth centuries. Source: Author (February 2017).

It is followed by the name Mirtschink, which comes from the Sorbian Měrćin [Martin]. The modifications are: Miertschink, Mirtschin, Martschink.[78] Other examples include the names Mittasch,[79] from Upper Sorbian *mjetać* [to throw], Wowtscherk[80] from Upper Sorbian *wowčer* [shepherd], Wujanz[81] from Upper Sorbian Wujanc, Symmank[82] from Upper Sorbian Syman [Simon].

In Rakecy/Königswartha there is a German-Sorbian mixture of the same surname. For example, there is a form of the German-spelled surname Wukasch on two different graves. On the one hand Wukaš from Upper Sorbian Łukaš [Lucas][83] and on the other hand Lukasowa, the female form, but without diacritics. Both families came from Komorow/Commerau, hence they were possibly somehow related, as both deceased were born around 1870.

In Contrast, the variety of Sorbian surnames is substantially lower in northern Upper Lusatia, above the phantom Prussian border. Nakoinz, a typical Lower Sorbian name, is one of the few examples found in Slepo/Schleife. In Sorbian, it is spelled Nakóńc and means "top, end of the village."[84] Furthermore, Niemz,[85] Upper Sorbian Němc [a German] is also present on several gravestones. The latter examples show signs of mixed Lower and Upper Sorbian names.

In my research, I paid special attention to two cemeteries in former Prussian Upper Lusatia. The first is the cemetery in Rowno/Rohne, which faced possible relocation until March 2017, when the mining company *Lausitz Energie AG*

77   Wenzel, *Lausitzer Familiennamen*, 147.
78   Ibid., 177.
79   Ibid.
80   Ibid., 277.
81   Ibid., 265.
82   Ibid., 243.
83   Ibid., 264.
84   Ibid., 183.
85   Ibid., 185.

decided against expanding the mining area.[86] The other cemetery is in Łaz/Lohsa. These two exceptions are directly located in the coal mining area and still contain Sorbian inscriptions.

The cemetery in Rowno/Rohne was founded in 1863, a year before the old churchyard closed.[87] This happened at a time when Sorbs still formed the majority of the population. The cemetery existed until 1919. Then, locals established a new cemetery near the old one. The local population did not care and neglected the old cemetery. By the 1980s it was heavily overgrown and damaged. In the late 1980s and early 1990s, activist and scholars recovered about sixty old Sorbian gravestones from the old cemetery.[88] The stones had been ignored for a long time until the Sorbian scholar Trudla Malinkowa cataloged them and eventually the authorities placed them in the new cemetery. During my research trip in 2017, twelve gravestones had been erected as a memorial (see Figure 3). In 2019, this number increased by another fifty newly recovered and reconstructed gravestones.[89] The inscriptions are written in the Sorbian Schleifer dialect.[90] They include several linguistic mistakes and Malinkowa assumed locals had used the spoken language in their writing instead of the norm. Additionally, she discovered that German stonemasons had made the inscriptions, which could explain further mistakes.[91] These twelve gravestones also prove that the inscriptions used to be significantly longer than nowadays.

The cemetery with this memorial also includes three other contemporary Sorbian gravestones of people who died between 1978 and 2007. Noteworthy is the fact that only one grave has a complete Sorbian inscription. The other two graves contain German language. The inscription on Lenka Nowakova's (born Čižikec) grave is in Sorbian. It reads that she was the chairperson of the Sorbian umbrella organization *Domowina* in Rowno/Rohne from 1978–1990 and worked in preserving the language. Her husband's grave, though, has his name writ-

---

86 Tilo Berger, "Mulkwitz, Rohne und Schleifes Süden werden nicht abgebaggert," *Süddeutsche Zeitung,* March 30, 2017, accessed August 31, 2022, https://web.archive.org/web/20170331115956/http://www.sz-online.de/nachrichten/mulkwitz-rohne-und-schleifes-sueden-werden-nicht-abgebaggert-3649320.html.

87 Trudla Malinkowa, *Der alte Friedhof in Rohne. Eine Dokumentation—Stare pohrjebnišćo w Rownom* (Bautzen: Lusatia-Verl. 2011), 6.

88 Ibid., 7.

89 Andreas Kirschke, "Begräbniskultur für die Nachwelt bewahrt," *saechsische.de*, May 12, 2019, accessed August 31, 2022, https://www.saechsische.de/plus/begraebniskultur-fuer-die-nachwelt-bewahrt-rohne-5068161.html.

90 It is a transitional dialect between Lower and Upper Sorbian. More on the dialect: Arnulf Schroeder, *Die Laute des wendischen (sorbischen) Dialekts von Schleife in der Oberlausitz (Lautbeschreibung)* (Köln: Böhlau-Verlag, 1958); Hélène Brijnen, "Die phonologische Entwicklung des Schleifer Dialekts im 19. und 20. Jahrhundert," *Studies in Slavic and General Linguistics* 24 (1998): 93–123.

91 Malinkowa, *Der alte,* 21.

ten in German spelling—Erich Noack.
In another case, only the first saying
"wěcne spominanje" [rest in peace] is
in Sorbian. The second is not and the
name is written in German.
The other significant example is the
cemetery in Łaz/Lohsa. The village
lies between flooded opencast mining
pits in northern Upper Lusatia, south-
west of Rowno/Rohne and displays a
contrasting way of dealing with its Sorbian heritage. This might seem ironic,
considering that it is the place of birth

Figure 4: Cemetery in Łaz/Lohsa. A pile of rubble with old gravestones and crosses. The cross
reads: "Zassowidženie!" [Goodbye]. Source:
Author (February 2017).

of the Sorbian folk poet Handrij Zejler, who is often quoted on Sorbian-inscribed
graves. Apart from Zejler's grave, there are three other Sorbian gravestones in
this cemetery. One belongs to the Sorbian pastor Georg Mahling. Another grave
is that of Sorbian composer Jan Pawoł Nagel and lastly, there is a grave of a person with a German name and a Sorbian phrase on her gravestone:

Spitaj w božim měrje, Anneliese Roblick, geb. Batzke, 1921–2006

[Rest in God's Peace, Anneliese Roblick, born Batzke, 1921–2006]

Unlike Rowno/Rohne, this cemetery contained a Sorbian-inscribed cross among
a pile of rubble and, hence, the insensitive dealing with its past and heritage (see
Figure 4). It proves that not too long ago, there were more Sorbian gravestones.

Given these points, it is important to record the low number of Sorbian inscriptions within the Protestant areas of Upper Lusatia. The area is also very heterogeneous, as it contains more cemeteries without than with Sorbian inscriptions.
The latter form small spots on the map and, therefore, also phantom borders to
non-Sorbian cemeteries. Nonetheless, there are still Sorbian traces, revealed by
the names from the anthroponymic analysis, as well as old, recovered gravestones, which now serve as monuments or, in contrast, as piles of old stones with
Sorbian inscriptions, probably ending up on a waste disposal site. The most striking difference between historical Prussian and Saxon Upper Lusatia is the very
low number of Sorbian grave inscriptions. The only exceptions are Łaz/Lohsa
and Rowno/Rohne.

Figure 5: Cemetery in Radwor/Radibor, 1928. Source: SLUB Dresden / Deutsche Fotothek / Max Nowak.

Figure 6: Cemetery in Radwor/Radibor in 2017. The number of wooden crosses is much lower than in 1928 (see Figure 5), even so, most of the gravestones have Sorbian inscriptions. Source: Author (October 2017).

Cemeteries in Catholic Upper Lusatia

Scholars often refer to the Catholic-Sorbian core area as the "Catholic triangle,"[92] which roughly extends between Budyšin/Bautzen, Kamjenc/Kamenz, and Wojerecy/Hoyerswerda. In addition, there are four other small Catholic enclaves, including Kulow/Wittichenau in the north, Kamjenc/Kamenz in the west, Radwor/Radibor and Zdźěr/Sdier in the east and Budyšin/Bautzen in the southeast area of this core (see Map).

As Martin Walde points out, the church plays an important role for Catholic Sorbs.[93] Michael Hainz emphasizes that the Catholic milieu proves to be a common good that strengthens group affiliation.[94] Moreover, the Sorbian Catholic clergy were already using religion at the end of the nineteenth century to preserve the Sorbian language. Over time, this produced close ties between the parish and the community.

The Catholic area was not spared by the changes, though. This is visible in Njeswačidło/Neschwitz and Radwor/Radibor, where the wooden crosses have almost disappeared (see Figures 5 and 6).[95] In Radwor/Radibor, both in 1928 and 2017, most of the inscriptions were in Sorbian.

The village Zdźěr/Sdier is religiously mixed and according to Ernst Tschernik's research, 63 percent were Sorbs in 1954.[96] During my field research

---

92 See Footnote 7.
93 Walde, "Demographisch-statistische Betrachtungen."
94 Michael Hainz, "Kirchlichkeit im sorbisch-katholischen Siedlungsgebiet," *Lětopis* 46, no. 1 (1999): 104–14.
95 In Njeswačidło/Neschwitz there are only two newer Sorbian and some pre-World War II graves left.
96 Hainz, *Kirchlichkeit*, 246.

in 2017, there were 21 Sorbian and three mixed-language gravestones among the 59 total graves. It might point to a language shift towards German, which would eventually exclude Zdźěr/Sdier from the Catholic-triangle. Budyšin/ Bautzen is, unquestionably, the cultural center of the Sorbs. There are not as many Catholics, yet the oldest Catholic cemetery in the region is situated here. The Catholic Nikolai Friedhof is historically important because it was traditionally the main cemetery for Catholics in Budyšin/Bautzen and the remaining Catholics from nearby villages. Nowadays, there are still about fifty Sorbian graves (out of around 200). The cemetery also has the graves of notable Sorbian personalities, such as Michał Hórnik,[97] Georg Wuschanski,[98] Filip Rězak[99] and Jan Bulank.[100] Those are the older graves, of which some have inscriptions in old Catholic Sorbian orthography.[101]

At the Catholic cemeteries, symbols are very diverse. In most cases, there are crosses, grapes, a grain of wheat, a Christ monogram and praying hands. In contrast to the Protestant cemeteries, fewer flowers are used. There was no information or any symbols regarding profession except in the case of well-known Sorbian personalities.

A striking observation is also the fact that the gravestones of female deceased that carry Sorbian inscriptions also display their birth name, which suggests the importance of their origin. However, German gravestones do not or only occasionally have this information. It is also uncommon for German gravestones to bear information about the origin of the deceased. Exceptions are found in the cemeteries in Radwor/Radibor and Zdźěr/Sdier, where many German-inscribed graves show the origin of the deceased. Such examples occur often, as most villages, where the deceased came from, are partially Catholic without either their own Catholic cemetery or any cemetery at all. In Zdźěr/Sdier, the following inscriptions are two significant examples that exemplify the situation:

Tu wotpočujetaj w Božim mjenje, Monika Hantschick, 1925–2008, Brehmen

[Here rests in God's name, Monika Hantschick, 1925–2008, Brehmen]

Rosynek Paul, 1934–2012, Crosta

Both deceased mentioned above were not from Zdźěr/Sdier, but from surrounding religiously mixed villages with no cemetery. The phrase in the first example is in Upper Sorbian and yet the name and place of origin are in German. The

---

97 Sorbian priest (1833–1894).
98 Titular bishop (1839–1905).
99 Priest and author (1859–1921).
100 Composer and conductor (1931–2002).
101 See the subchapter "Cemeteries in Protestant Upper Lusatia" and the footnotes 69–72.

second example is German, but shows the origin too, as Sorbian graves usually do. Gravestones in Radwor/Radibor in particular have inscriptions referring to the place or the surrounding villages, such as Bronjo/Brohna, Chelno/Cölln and Boranecy/Bornitz. These villages are religiously mixed, but have no cemetery.

Generally, in the Catholic cemeteries, the Sorbian inscriptions, like the German ones, are kept mostly in the present tense. Therefore, most of them start with "Tu wotpočuje w Bohu" [Here rests in God] or "Tu wotpočujetaj w Božim pokoju" [Here rests in God's peace]. The prospective forms are not common. There are only a few with the following type: "Tu wočakuja zbóžne zmortwychstanjenje" [Here they await glorious resurrection]. And a few retrospective forms, like "Pósli pruhu jasnosće z Božeje nam krasnosće" [The ray of brightness passed from God of glory].

The spelling of surnames in the Catholic areas is noteworthy because there are different spelling combinations. Usually, the Sorbian-inscribed gravestones have Sorbian names on them. But there are cases where inscriptions are mixed German-Sorbian or only in German. Correspondingly, there are many names and surnames of Slavic origin. Among them, Nowottny from Upper Sorbian and Polish Nowotny [new, modern],[102] Robel from the Upper Sorbian *wrobl*[103] [sparrow], Sauer[104] or Schur from Upper Sorbian and Polish *žur*[105] [sourdough]. Kubank from Sorbian or West Slavic represents the Christian baptismal name Jakub.[106]

After conversations with randomly met visitors at the cemeteries, I was able to assume that a certain percentage of German-inscribed gravestones are also related to the Sorbs. Ultimately, in the researched Catholic cemeteries in the core area, the share of Sorbian inscriptions varies between 30 and 90 percent in each location. There are surnames of Slavic or Sorbian origin, as in the same way there is a significant number of German expellees—with German surnames—from Hungary, Sudetenland, and Silesia. Only the inscriptions might suggest their origins. In Baćoń/Storcha, there is the following example:

Unsere lieben Eltern
Karl Schreier, Oberhohenelbe, Riesengebirge, 1895–1946,
Berta Schreier, 1902–1980,
Ruhet in Frieden

---

102 Wenzel, *Lausitzer Familiennamen*, 187.
103 Ibid., 212.
104 A randomly met cemetery visitor confirmed this in the cemetery of Radwor/Radibor in 2017, which bears the last name after her Sorbian husband Sauer. Her parents-in-law have German inscriptions, however, she showed me the grave of her brother-in-law, which has a Sorbian inscription and the last name Žur.
105 Wenzel, *Lausitzer Familiennamen*, 227.
106 Ibid., 148.

[Our beloved parents,
Karl Schreier, Oberhohenelbe, Giant Mountains 1895–1946,
Berta Schreier 1902–1980,
Rest in Peace]

Another example of a deceased person from Upper Silesia in Zdźěr/Sdier:

Hier harrt der Auferstehung Maria, Paul geb. 15.3.1912 in Kreuzburg, Oberschlesien, gest. 27.9.1989, Unvergessen

[Here awaiting the resurrection of Maria, Paul born March 15, 1912 in Kreuzburg, Upper Silesia, passed away September 27, 1989, Unforgotten]

Based only on the names, it would be impossible to determine where the deceased persons came from. These examples suggest that after World War II there was a large influx of German expellees into the Catholic Sorb areas.[107]

I previously mentioned that in the Catholic cemeteries, some of the German-inscribed graves presumably belong to the Sorbian-speaking population. Passers-by were mostly not able to provide reasons for the choice of German language. Some reasons they did give included that the people were no longer fluent in Sorbian, they were afraid that the stonemason could not write in any other language than German or they simply had not figured out that the stone could have Sorbian inscriptions.

One specific Catholic cemetery has to be highlighted, though. It is very significant for the Catholic Sorbs because it represents the so-called perfect Catholic cemetery where every buried person is equal, has the same gravestone and almost identical inscription. It is the churchyard in Ralbicy/Ralbitz. This cemetery comprises about 300 white wooden crosses. Even the GDR-regime declared it a national monument in 1981. Its general appearance has remained unchanged since its restoration in 1948, after it had been heavily damaged during World War II. All crosses look the same and stand in exact rows. However, during my visit in 2016 none of them had been erected before 1996. This is a result of strict regulations regarding resting periods which prove to be very short. However, in this case it is linked to the cemetery's size, as it has only 300 burial spaces and the deceased are buried in a specific order.[108]

All crosses look the same (figure 7), the only difference among them being the inscriptions on the small oval plaques. Almost all plaques begin with the phrase "Tu wotpočuje w Bohu" [Here rests in God] and predominantly end with this saying: "Spi w božim měrje!" [May sleep in God's peace], "Wotpočuj w

---

107 See also footnote 39.
108 No one can choose the space at the Ralbitz-cemetery. Every spot is assigned in a specific order.

měrje!" [Rest in Peace] or "Wotpočuj w pokoju!" [Rest in Peace]. There are only around a dozen German inscriptions. Often, it remains unclear why German in these specific cases. With attention to this, the following example serves as an illustatration:

Hier ruht in Frieden unser lieber Vater, Bruder und Opa Beno Lulak z Koslowa. Aus Gottes Hand in Gottes Hand!

Figure 7: Cemetery in Ralbicy/Ralbitz. Source: Author (October 2016).

[Hier rests in peace our beloved father, brother, and grandfather Beno Lulak from Koslow/Caßlau.
From God's hand into God's hand]

The entire text is kept in German except for the place of origin and the corresponding Sorbian preposition. It remains unclear why they used "z Koslowa" instead of "aus Caßlau." The surname, Lulak (German equivalent Lulag, Lullack), provides an indicator that the deceased has Sorbian roots. It derives from Upper Sorbian "lulać" [lull into sleep]."[109]

Other German inscriptions correspond to the Sorbian ones because they also start with: "Hier ruht in Gott" [Here rests in God] or "Ruhe in Frieden" [Rest in peace]. It follows personal information related to the deceased.

My analysis of the collected data precedes the quantitative evaluation of the proportion of Sorbian inscriptions in each location. All things considered the original naming of the Catholic triangle proves to be difficult. The triangle steadily decreased, hence, only a significant core area with six corner points is left. These are: Baćoń/Storcha, Wotrow/Ostro, Njebjelčicy/Nebelschütz, Šunow-Konjecy/Schönau-Cunnewitz, Ralbicy/Ralbitz and Wětrow/Wetro (see Map). This core area contains a total of six cemeteries, in which graves with Sorbian inscriptions still form a majority. Only the one in Smječkecy/Schmeckwitz[110] represents an exception with its low proportion. Hence, the triangle forms a homogenous Catholic area and a phantom border to the non-Catholic villages. Two other spots on the map (Radwor/Radibor and Zdźěr/Sdier) were revealed as Catholic villages in the midst of non-Catholic areas, forming two enclaves.

---

109 Wenzel, *Lausitzer Familiennamen*, 163.
110 In 1956, Ernst Tschernik counted only 63.6 percent Sorbs in this village. Among the main reasons for such a low proportion, the local sanatorium and the influx of German expellees were named. See Elle, *Sprachenpolitik*.

Conclusion

The research of the spatial, temporal and linguistic characteristics of religious affiliation in Upper Lusatia produced a specific mapping of religious and linguistic affiliation that contributes to the understanding of Sorbian Upper Lusatia. It is an attempt to create a map that contains no census data, but is based solely on cemetery data. The research showed the historicity of phantom borders and narrowed the Catholic triangle down to a more precise circle. It also proved the ongoing change regarding the funeral culture. The large number of Sorbian inscriptions on gravestones in Catholic cemeteries shows Catholicism is still strongly tied to Sorbian language use and although Ernst Tschernik's data confirmed a significant number of Sorbian-speaking people in Protestant areas, the number of Sorbs in these parishes has decreased visibly in the last seventy years.

Despite using German inscriptions many graves still indicate a Sorbian heritage by Sorbian surnames, use of symbols (linden leaf) or specific wooden crosses. The information (inscriptions, symbols, objects) triggered a story that allowed the creation of a map, which is defined as a structured cartographic representation of information. It is necessary to stress that maps are only temporary, and they merely depict the current state of the cemeteries and religious situation in Upper Lusatia. The situation might change as soon as a cemetery administration decides to replace old gravestones with newer ones that do not carry Sorbian inscriptions or to shorten resting periods.[111] This might make the phantom borders on the map disappear. Still, this research contributes significantly to the understanding of geographies of small languages and religiously mixed areas. It provides a foundation for ongoing research into the role of religion linked with language use and its mirroring in cemeteries. However, the method functions only in multilingual areas in which distinct non-majority speakers live. Nevertheless, it gives an idea how vital Upper Sorbian still is and in which areas the language is rarely or no longer used. Ultimately, political (regime change), economical (coal mining) and historical (migration) processes led to the current linguistical situation in Upper Lusatia.

Selected Bibliography

Barker, Peter. "Refugees, Expellees and the Language Situation in Lusatia (1945–7)." *German Life and Letters* 57, no. 4 (September 2004): 391–400.

Gebel, Konstanze. *Language and Ethnic National Identity in Europe: The Importance of Gaelic and Sorbian to the Maintenance of Associated Cultures and Ethno Cultural Identities.* London: Middlesex University, 2002.

---

111 Barbara Happe, "Grabmalgestaltung in Der DDR—Der Erzwungene Abschied Vom Persönlichen Grabmal," in *Grabkultur in Deutschland: Geschichte der Grabmäler*, ed. Arbeitsgemeinschaft Friedhof und Denkmal / Museum für Sepulkralkultur, Kassel (Berlin: Reimer, 2009), 189–213.

Hirsch, Eric, and Charles Stewart. "Introduction: Ethnographies of Historicity." *History and Anthropology* 16, no. 3 (2005): 261–274.

Hirschhausen, Béatrice von. "Phantomgrenzen als heuristisches Konzept für die Grenzforschung." In *Grenzforschung: Handbuch Für Wissenschaft Und Studium,* eds. by Dominik Gerst, Maria Klessmann, and Hannes Krämer, 175–189. Baden-Baden: Nomos, 2021.

Hirschhausen, Béatrice von, Hannes Grandits, Claudia Kraft, Dietmar Müller, and Thomas Serrier. *Phantomgrenzen: Räume und Akteure in der Zeit neu denken.* Göttingen: Wallstein Verlag, 2015.

Jańczak, Jarosław. "Phantom Borders and Electoral Behavior in Poland Historical Legacies, Political Culture and Their Influence on Contemporary Politics." *Erdkunde* 69, no. 2 (2015): 125–137.

Kunze, Peter. "Geschichte und Kultur der Sorben in der Oberlausitz—Ein geschichtlicher Abriss." In *Geschichte Der Oberlausitz: Herrschaft, Gesellschaft Und Kultur Vom Mittelalter Bis Zum Ende des 20. Jahrhunderts,* edited by Joachim Bahlcke, 267–314. Leipzig: Leipziger Univ.-Verl, 2004.

Lindseth, Soldan, Konstanze Glaser. *Minority Languages and Cultural Diversity in Europe: Gaelic and Sorbian Perspectives.* Clevedon: Multilingual Matters, 2007.

Ryan, Marie-Laure, Kenneth E. Foote, and Maoz Azaryahu. *Narrating Space/Spatializing Narrative: Where Narrative Theory and Geography Meet.* Columbus: The Ohio State University Press, 2016.

Schulz, Felix Robin. *Death in East Germany, 1945–1990.* New York: Berghahn, 2013.

Stone, Gerald. *Slav Outposts in Central European History: The Wends, Sorbs and Kashubs.* London: Bloomsbury, 2016.

Wood, Denis, John Fels, and John Krygier. *Rethinking the Power of Maps.* New York: Guilford Press, 2010.

"A Threatened Majority":[1]
From Unwanted to Welcome Members of the
Community—The Danube Swabians in the
Southeastern Banat, Serbia

SNEŽANA STANKOVIĆ

Introduction

In 1766, the village of Omoljica (see Figure 2) assumed the particular function of
a quarantine station, where all travelers coming from the Ottoman Empire had
to spend at least fourteen days to undergo rigorous medical examinations.[2] The
village played an important role in the security infrastructure within the fortified
and militarized zone of the Habsburg Empire, the *Militärgrenze/Vojna Krajina*
[Military Frontier], by guarding against the possible expansion of the Ottomans
and acting as a health surveillance outpost. Its inhabitants initially served as border guards—*Grenzer/Graničari*, where many of them belonged to the migrants
who came to the Frontier within the settlements ("colonization") organized by
the Habsburg Empire. The majority of these newcomers were German-speaking
groups who had been settling there in dispersed waves from different regions of
the Habsburg Monarchy and the Holy Roman Empire.[3]

Today, situated in the Southeastern Banat region of Serbia that shares a border
with Romania, the village of Omoljica does not reveal the former existence of
a German-speaking group. According to the picture (see Figure 1), it is almost
impossible to conclude that there was once a local German cemetery, which "dis-

---

1   For the reference to Arjun Appadurai's discussion on minority groups as threatening
     "small numbers" see Footnote 33.
2   Rudolf Haag, *Ortsgeschichte von Omoljica (Homoliz), Großgemeinde in der Wojwo-
     dina (Süd-Banat) des Königreichs Jugoslawien: 1766–1938* (Novi Vrbas: Novi Vrbas,
     1938); Срећко Милекер, Историја Банатске Војничке границе *1764–1873* (Панчево:
     Историјски архив. Књижара Прота Васа, 2006 [1926]).
3   See Jelena Ilić Mandić, *Banatska vojna krajina: 1764–1800* (Beograd: Istorijski institut,
     2020); Mirna Zakić, *Ethnic Germans and National Socialism in Yugoslavia in World War
     II* (Cambridge: Cambridge University Press, 2017).

appeared" after World War II, when the
number of Germans/Danube Swabians[4] clearly decreased in the new state
of Socialist Yugoslavia. The landscape
depicted above metonymically leads to
the historical events that affected the
German minority.[5]

How their absence has been transposed onto the public since World War
II forms the central question of this
chapter. The analysis follows oral interviews conducted during research walks

Figure 1: Omoljica, Southeastern Banat, Serbia,
former German cemetery. Source: Author (October 2015).

between 2013 and 2017 through the German cemeteries in five villages and one
town in the Southeastern Banat. Because of sensitivity that may arise when dealing with inter-ethnic coexistence, each interview partner has been assigned a
pseudonym. However, the author uses the original toponyms where memorial
sites were recorded and cemetery conversations took place.

The author hopes to challenge the concept of minority and majority groups, thus
shedding light on common attitudes towards the Hungarian and Muslim minorities. Even though the given information about the author's interests directed the
topic towards the German minority, the Hungarian and Muslim minorities were
present as a constant comparative field when talking about self/selves and the
other(s).

Following Marianne Kamp, the author avoids the analytical category of *collective memory*,[6] which seems to lump together disparate levels of the experienced,

---

4   The German geographer Hermann Rüdiger coined the appellation Donauschwaben (Dan-
     ube Swabians) in 1922 to differentiate between the "ethnic Germans" and the so-called
     Transylvanian Saxons, coming from the former Kingdom of Hungary. See Zoran Jan-
     jetović, *Between Hitler and Tito. Disappearance of the Ethnic Germans from the Vojvodi-
     na* (Beograd: SD Publik, 2005).
5   The paper sometimes uses appellatives like "Danube Swabians"/"Germans"/"German mi-
     nority," "Banat Bulgarians", "Muslims" or "Serbs" as *pars pro toto* to refer to speakers of
     the given language and self-defined ethnicity and also, because both categories often im-
     ply emotional (self-)definition. Pieter Judson avoids such naming because of its normativ-
     ity, in the way he points to speakers of some languages, like "German speakers." Pieter M.
     Judson, *Guardians of the Nation. Activists on the Language Frontiers of Imperial Austria*
     (Cambridge, Massachusetts, London: Harvard University Press, 2006). However, speak-
     ing of languages as clearly distinct systems might imply ideological notions in the spirit of
     romantic nationalist movements. See Jan Blommaert and Ben Rampton, "Language and
     Superdiversity," *DIVERSITIES* 13, no. 2 (2011): 1–21. Furthermore, German-speaking
     groups included not only Germans, but also Jews. See Janjetović, *Between Hitler and Tito*.
6   Marianne Kamp, "Remembering: National Narratives and Mundane Moments in Uzbek
     oral histories," in *History Making in Central and Northern Eurasia. Contemporary Actors
     and Practice*, ed. Svetlana Jacquesson (Wiesbaden: Reichert, 2016), 41–58.

remembered and transmitted. Instead, the author uses "mediated knowledge" to look at "portions of the past," which are "learned about rather than experienced or remembered."[7]

Accordingly, this chapter suggests a different angle on the research on historical work among the societies that physically and mentally coexist(ed) side-by-side while being ethnically, confessionally, and linguistically mixed. Thus, border theory accompanies the study in emphasizing the social "iconographies of boundaries" that arise out of "emotional bordering[s]."[8]

Figure 2: Omoljica, Southeastern Banat, Serbia, previously the location of the quarantine station. Source: Author (August 2017).

The chapter is comprised of three sections. The first subchapter discusses some methodological and theoretical choices. The second part focuses on how the minority and majority groups have been dealing with their pasts and their histories from the 1940s onwards. Finally, by reflecting on some general conclusions, the study opens up a field for new questions and possible future discussions.

Methodological and Theoretical Considerations

Preserved, abandoned, vandalized, destroyed or "disappeared" German cemeteries and monuments and oral interviews represented a source of narratives about the absent German minority in the Southeastern Banat. The author has reconstructed these narratives through interviews that often occurred spontaneously during the cemetery visits in both rural and urban areas over the course of four years (2013, 2014, 2015, 2017). Conversations at cemeteries can be regarded as a hybrid genre of semi-oral literature with fluid boundaries since it can oscillate between talking about/telling (personal) biographies, (local) histories and even legends.[9]

7   Svetlana Jacquesson, "Introduction," in *History Making in Central and Northern Eurasia. Contemporary Actors and Practice,* ed. Svetlana Jacquesson (Wiesbaden: Reichert, 2016), 12.

8   David Newman and Anssi Paasi, "Fences and Neighbours in the Postmodern World: Boundary Narratives in Political Geography," *Progress in Human Geography* 22, no. 2 (1998): 197; Anssi Paasi, "Borders and Border crossings," in *The Wiley-Blackwell Companion to Cultural Geography,* eds. Nuala Johnson, Richard Schein, and Jamie Winders (London: Wiley-Blackwell, 2013), 478–93.

9   Љубица З. Ђурић, "Контекстуализација језичких пејзажа српских гробова у региону реке Мориша," Исходишта 3 (2017): 135.

A fieldwork topology where encounters can happen suddenly means that the roles of the researcher and their interlocutors change in such a way that the performative research stage exists only within the awareness of the researcher. In turn, this means that the information gained during the "semi-natural," non-performative cemetery conversation can be interpreted as illustrating the context of the study, yet with no tendency to claim a general representational value. Nevertheless, the presence of the researcher as an outsider impacts the manner and content of the conversation to a certain degree—in the sense that the encountered interviewee might try to adjust to them.[10]

The ethnic, linguistic, and confessional backgrounds of the interviewees were as highly diverse as were the grave inscriptions themselves: Hungarian, Banat Bulgarian,[11] Romanian, Slovak, BCMS,[12] and German; with mostly Protestant, Catholic, Orthodox or some other (ideological and theological iconography.[13] The conversations were carried out mainly in BCMS/Serbian and in Slovak, due to the native languages of the speakers as well as the language competence of the author and her field family.[14] Although German is still a visible language in cemeterial landscapes, it was never used in the conversations.

Therefore, the research on multilingual cemeteries can implicitly say a great deal about what is called *conviviality*. The author uses this term by adopting the

---

10 Драгана Ратковић, "Разговор на гробљу. Језик Свете Ратковића," in Бањаши на Балкану. Идентитет етничке заједнице, ed. Биљана Сикимић (Београд: Балканолошки институт САНУ, 2005), 202; Биљана Сикимић и Мотоки Номаћи, "Језички пејзаж меморијалног простора вишејезичних заједница: Банатски Бугари/Палћани у Србији," Јужнословенски филолог 72, no. 1–2 (2016): 7–31.

11 *Banátsći balgare* [Banat Bulgarian] is also known as "Pavlikian" or "Paulician.". As Motoki Nomachi has shown, the question of whether Banat Bulgarian is a separate language or a dialect remains open. In contrast to Bulgarians from Bulgaria, who are predominantly Orthodox Christians, Banat Bulgarians are Catholics. They emigrated in the seventeenth and eighteenth centuries to what is today known as Romanian and Serbian Banat. See Motoki Nomachi, "The Rise, Fall, and Revival of the Banat Bulgarian Literary Language: Sociolinguistic History from the Perspective of Trans-Border Interactions," in *The Palgrave Handbook of Slavic Languages, Identities and Borders*, eds. Tomasz Kamusella, Motoki Nomachi, and Catherine Gibson (London, New York, Shanghai: Palgrave Macmillan, 2016), 394–428.

12 The abbreviation "BCMS" designates the Bosnian-Croatian-Montenegrin-Serbian language. When "Serbian" is used apart from this, it refers to the perspective of the research participants from the Serbian part of the Banat.

13 Here, the author refers to the use of heraldry symbols, *e. g.*, five-pointed (red) star, flags, crowns, leaves.

14 The author carried out all the field research with the family who lives in Bavanište, one of the villages in Southeastern Banat. Thanks to their presence and familiarity with the locations and people, the encounters occurred more spontaneously. Most of our interview partners were over the age of forty-five, most of them born at the end of World War II.

notions of Magdalena Nowicka and Steven Vertovec.[15] They frame it as coexistence within everyday life and define it through both friendly and conflictingly shared realities where personal contacts exist in a very diffuse, liquid space that is neither friendly nor conflicting, where ethno-confessional-linguistic markers are not always crucial. From an eighteenth-century perspective, the Banat was a world with overlapping ways of grouping (by locality, ethnicity, religion, tradition), resulting in different convivialities.

Fields of Conviviality

Towards the end of World War II, from mid-1944, when the Red Army was advancing, German defeat was evident, and the Nazi government decided to evacuate as many Germans as possible from Central and Eastern Europe. Those who happened to stay in the post-war states were collectively considered Nazi supporters and collaborators. In August 1945, the Potsdam Agreement between the Allied Powers issued the organized transfer of Germans from Poland, Czechoslovakia, and Hungary to Germany. In the wake of agricultural reforms and repopulation of empty areas once inhabited by Germans (i. e., "colonization"), the newly established Socialist Federal Republic of Yugoslavia, although not covered by the Potsdam agreement, also implemented a German exodus. They were subjected to execution, resettlement, evacuation, expulsion and deportation to labor camps in the USSR. The remaining Germans were placed in local internment camps. After the dissolution of the camps by 1948, those Germans who remained had to adjust to conditions in the new Yugoslavia under Josip Broz Tito.[16] They had to witness the closing of schools and institutions, the renaming of streets and places and the prohibition of any use of the German language.

After dissolving the local camps for the Yugoslav Germans in 1948,[17] the state tried to reintegrate the remaining Germans. Nevertheless, at the same time, the historiography, literature, and cinematography of Yugoslavia constructed a rather negative representation of Germans as an occupying force.[18]

---

15 Magdalena Nowicka and Steven Vertovec, "Comparing Convivialities: Dreams and Realities of Living-with-difference," *European Journal of Cultural Studies* 17, no. 4 (2014): 341–56.

16 Zoran Janjetović, *Nemci u Vojvodini* (Beograd: INIS, 2009); Arnold Suppan, *Hitler— Beneš—Tito: Konflikt, Krieg und Völkermord in Ostmittel- und Südosteuropa* (Vienna: Verlag der Österreichischen Akademie der Wissenschaften, 2014); Ulrich Merten, *Forgotten Voices: The Expulsion of the Germans from Eastern Europe after World War II* (London: Routledge, 2017); Zakić, *Ethnic Germans and National Socialism in Yugoslavia in World War II.*

17 Helena Rill and Marijana Stojčić, *On the Trail of the Danube Swabians in Vojvodina* (Belgrade, Sarajevo: Centre for Nonviolent Action, 2016), 56–57.

18 See also the chapter by Anežka Brožová, "World War II Monuments and Graves in the Hlučín Region: Fallen Hlučín Soldiers as a Contested Realm of Memory in the Czech

A closer look at the German civil and military cemeteries in urban and rural locations in the Banat (see Figures 1 and 3), such as those in the villages of Omoljica and Mramorak, provides a glimpse of the life circumstances of the German minority during the post-war years in Yugoslavia. The minority's selective presence has been preserved in the silenced memories of people who have listened to accounts of or witnessed the past events.

Forced to be "outwardly" invisible, the few remaining Germans had to become invisible from the "inside" as well. Interviews brought out a narrative of the forbidden language. Mathilde, born in the Southeastern Banat in 1940, and imprisoned with her family after World War II, explained:

Bili smo mi na nemačkom, ali kad nas je ujak odveo tamo [u Belu Crkvu], onda nam je nije dalo da pričamo nemački, nego samo srpski je l' se bojao i on nama nije dao. [...] Kolko puta sam se vratila iz škole sa pocepanim knjigama i pokidanom tašnom, i to je bilo čudo. To nije laž, to je živa istina. [...] Bogami smo bežali mi dosta. ... Bilo je šezdesetih. Kolonisti kad su došli. A počeli su tako, šezdeset prve i druge su grobnice rušili. Jeli znam da je došao deda Mitar i kazao je, ajde, Milanko, da idemo da uzmemo cigle, ništa ne naplaćuju s nemačkog groblja, kaže, možemo da zidamo ovo-ono. Moj svekar je rekao, Bože me sačuvaj, moja kuća kakva je takva je, daće Bog da zaradim da moja deca [imaju].[19]

[We spoke [literary: were in] German at home, but when our uncle took us there [to Bela Crkva], he did not allow us to use the language—only Serbian, because he was afraid. ... How many times I used to come back from school with destroyed books and a ripped bag, and that was strange. It is not a lie. It is a true story. [...] Oh God, we were fleeing from places a lot. [...] In the sixties, when the colonists came. They started to demolish the tombs in 1961 and 1962. One day, grandpa Mitar came to us and invited my father-in-law to take some good stone material from the German cemetery, because it was free and we could also use it for some construction. My father-in-law said, God forbid, my house is as it is, God will help me to earn that my children [have enough].

Talking of her daily childhood experiences, Mathilde emphasized her memories about the forbidden language and the new settlers—"*kolonisti*" [colonists] who created a "*čudna atmosfera*" [strange atmosphere] in the village, a story the author often encountered during her research. The newcomers were sent from different parts of Bosnia, Macedonia, Montenegro, and Serbia to replace the departed Germans by using their empty houses and farms. Mathilde's story is about being

---

Culture of Remembrance" in this volume.

19 Interview with Mathilde Müller, Mramorak, November 23, 2013. All translations by the author unless otherwise noted.

targeted as "the other:" The newcomers appeared responsible for the fate of the local cemetery (see Figure 3) that was demolished, with crosses and tomb- stones removed, and some stones even used as construction material.

Figure 3: Mramorak, Southeastern Banat, Ser- bia, abandoned German cemetery. Source: Au- thor (November 2013).

Mimicking the majority culture, Germans ceased to use their language in the public sphere. During the initial post-war years, until 1948, the German language had to be replaced by Serbian, Croatian, or Hungarian. After 1948, German schools were reopened in those places which still had German-speaking children and teachers. Later they were closed, since many of the Germans who survived left the country. All these conditions also led to the elimination of the use of the German language at home. The remaining Germans tried to transcend these invisible barriers by linguisti- cally fitting into their surrounding society. Adaptation to the majority culture and language, giving up traditional ceremonies such as burials became some of their codes of survival. As one of the interview partners reported:

[…] Je l' kod mene kući, ona [majka] je iz Skorenovca, bez obzira što je i Nemica, ona je vaspitana u, pošto je tamo, bilo je samo četiri, pet ili šest nemačkih porodica, sve je vaspitano u mađarskom duhu. Sve je vaspitano u mađarskom duhu. […] I onda sam svuda bio Mađar. Jer Nemac u ono vreme nije mogao da ide u školu.[20]

[[…] Because, at my home—she [my mother] is from Skorenovac, and despite being German, she was raised, everyone was raised in the Hungarian spirit, because there [in Skorenovac] were only four or five German families. […] When I went to high school, I was always a Hungarian. And everywhere, I was Hungarian. Because, at that time, a German could not attend school.]

While talking of the "Hungarian spirit" of the village of Skorenovac, Robert defined the *majority culture,* to which the Yugoslav Germans had been adapt- ing. Professing a totalizing explanation about how "a German could not attend school," he indicated a public denial of every German. Therefore, it is possi- ble to say, following the notes of Christian Promitzer on *hidden minorities,* that *majority* is a set of "self-aware and publicly recognized"[21] cultures or groups. In

---

20 Interview with Robert Tischler, Kovin, March 15, 2013.
21 Christian Promitzer, "Small is Beautiful: The Issue of Hidden Minorities in Central Eu- rope and the Balkans," in *(Hidden) Minorities: Language and Ethnic Identity between*

direct contrast to Mathilde's story about destroyed books and demolished German tombs in Mramorak, the majority of members are not bound by notions of "cultural otherness."

In this context, the fact that Hungarians in Serbia succeeded in escaping revenge measures also brings a new perspective on othering. Zoran Janjetović assumes that one of the reasons could lie in the different quantities of land owned by Germans and Hungarians. The German properties were much bigger and were used to reward colonizing partisan veterans.[22] The Yugoslav state did indeed pay pivotal attention to the new ("colonizing") settlers by giving them the right to receive land and houses, thus acknowledging their heroism and loyalty.[23] In this way, empty German houses were later inhabited by new settlers whose stories about abandoned, destroyed and vanished cemeteries and churches would often follow the course of local rumors and fears. Miroslav, whose family was resettled from Central Serbia into the village of Mramorak, recalled in a whisper a similar case:

Ja se sećam kao dete, to [Evangelistička crkva] se rušilo [...] nismo smeli da priđemo. [...] Sve kuda gazimo, bilo je groblje.[24]

[I remember, when I was a child, it [the Protestant church] was being demolished. [...] We were forbidden to come closer. [...] All over the place where we are walking now it was a cemetery.]

Miroslav's words describe ways of remembering and conveying knowledge in post-war Yugoslavia where the remaining members of the German minority existed as "hidden: by the authorities" during the initial post-war years and then, later, by themselves.[25] This short description reflects "an overall plot" created and, subsequently mediated as collaborative knowledge between various groups

---

Central Europe and the Balkans, eds. Christian Promitzer, Klaus-Jürgen Hermanik, and Eduard Staudinger (Münster: Lit Verlag, 2010), 89.

22   The Hungarian Communists appealed to the Yugoslav government not to expel the members of the Hungarian minority, who were not as numerous as the Germans, so they were not perceived as a real danger to the state. On the other hand, the fact that some Hungarians supported the partisan movement also explains the different attitude of the state towards the given minority. See, for example, Zoran Janjetović, "Proterivanje nemačkog i mađarskog življa iz Vojvodine na kraju Drugog svetskog rata," *Hereticus* 1 (2007): 106–18.

23   This policy added another dimension of the importance of access to education and enlightenment for the financially weakened internally displaced migrants from the remote mountain areas of Bosnia, Macedonia, Montenegro, and Serbia.

24   Interview with Miroslav Đurić, Mramorak, November 7, 2013.

25   Promitzer, *Small is Beautiful*, 77.

that build on mutual recognition.[26] At the same time, such togetherness can imply the exclusion of another group. Taking as a point of reference some of the observations made by Gordon Allport within the contact theory, this boundedness of the defined majority requires a "line, fence, or boundary" that "marks off an inside from an outside."[27] As he quotes Susan Isaacs, "the existence of an outsider is, in the beginning, an essential condition of any warmth or togetherness within the group."[28] Although debatable, this paper argues that such standpoint is closely related to the concept of conviviality as defined by Tilmann Heil—as a process that "addresses the in-between, the fleeting, the superficial and the unremarkable."[29]

Today's historians from ex-Yugoslav countries are divided about Yugoslav-German history after World War II. Revisionist narratives on the recognition of collaborators' pasts attempt to create an anti-memory of Yugoslavia as a failed and dictator state. In her study (2019), Jelena Đureinović discusses political transformations of World War II memories in present-day Serbia. She explains that the fall of Milošević diminished the myths of partisan resistance against fascism and liberation in bringing četniks onto the scene—as real heroes and liberators as well as the unrecognized victims of communism.[30] This order of victims has also turned the attention to Yugoslav Germans in the search for secret graves of people killed after the 1944 liberation.[31]

The fieldwork cemetery conversations and arranged interviews about the absent German minority exposed a shift from silence to a longing for the common past that upheld the values of togetherness. "High culture," "hard-working, honest people," "good neighbours," "very educated"—those were the formulaic descriptions of the former German neighbors. In a similar vein, Jovana, at that time in her 80s, shared the world she experienced, in which: "these Germans went to our [Orthodox] church, and they spoke Serbian. [Also] [...] among themselves, as if they were Serbs. [...] and I never felt somehow separated, that they spoke German among themselves. No, me never! I was a member of their family."[32] Jovana's reminiscence clearly introduced the above-mentioned change in the local remembrance suggesting that there were different cultural (*i. e.*, religious) groups that,

---

26 Elisabeth Davenport and Hazel Hall, "Organizational Knowledge and Communities of Practice," *Annual Review of Information Science and Technology* 36, no. 1 (2002): 170–227.

27 Gordon W. Allport, *The Nature of Prejudice* (Addison-Wesley: Reading MA, 1954), 42.

28 Ibid.

29 Tilmann Heil, "Conviviality: (re)Negotiating Minimal Consensus," in *Routledge International Handbook of Diversity Studies*, ed. Steven Vertovec (London, New York: Routledge, 2015), 319.

30 See also the chapter by Martina Mirković, "The (Newly) Negotiated Remembrance of the *Bleiburška Tragedija*: Parallels and Discontinuities" in this volume.

31 Đureinović, *Ethnic Germans and National Socialism in Yugoslavia in World War II*, 91.

32 Interview with Jovana Đurić, Mramorak, November 23, 2013.

nevertheless, attended the same church, used the same language and lived similar lives. She did not mention the absence of a Catholic or Protestant church in the village of Bavanište because this fact was not essential for her nostalgic memory of the convivial past. Regretfully, her concluding statement also echoes the new apologetic course of the remembrance of the German minority: "What can I say … I am very sorry for them. I am very sorry for them."

"We got on well with the Swabians" is a recurring statement throughout most conversations. When addressing memories, collective remembrance and mediated knowledge, the memory of the past relates to the field of personal experience that later gets recalled, retold and reshaped. It thus becomes knowledge both for those who lived it and for the others who received it as a story. In the given settings, always framed by the state, most of those who recall appear as storytellers, listeners, and mediators. Here, reaching majoritarian status does not always entail belonging to the same nation or ethnic group, but it is also conditioned by becoming bound by the same attitudes and values. Therefore, "incomplete purity" appears as a constant source of fear, as Arjun Appadurai puts it when talking about "a threatened majority." Minority groups (ethnic, religious, sexual, social) are "small numbers" that pollute the whole and create a "sense of incompleteness."[33]

It is a paradoxical situation, for minorities represent an overflow—an additional part that upsets the majoritarian hegemony. However, following Alport,[34] it can be argued that this paradoxical surplus is a much-needed constituent. As Germans became the acceptable members of the majority, a replacement of the memory of the missing by the new content had to occur.[35] Therefore, it is no longer "the Germans" who hamper the majoritarian whole, but the "Hungarians" and the "Muslims" who have to stay outside the desired narrative. They emerge as "others" who do not fit into the framework of the ordinary and close.

The Hungarians are viewed with strong negative connotations. While remembrance and knowledge of collaborative actions undertaken by the local Germans during the war have seemingly evaporated, the behavior of the Hungarian neighbors is still remembered. Although forming part of stories that the locals have inherited from their parents, the atrocities in the Vojvodina of the *Hortijevci* [Horthy militias] against the Jews, Romani, and Serbs[36] were mostly personified in the narration of the interviewees.

33 Arjun Appadurai, *Fear of Small Numbers: An Essay on the Geography of Anger* (Durham/ NC: Duke University Press, 2006), 8, 55.

34 Allport, *The Nature of Prejudice*.

35 See Luisa Passerini, "Memories between Silence and Oblivion," in *Contested Pasts. The Politics of Memory*, eds. Susannah Radstone and Katharine Hodgkin (London: Routledge, 2003).

36 See Павле Шосбергер, *Jevreji u Vojvodini: Kratak pregled istorije vojvođanskih Jevreja* (Нови Сад: Прометеј, 1998).

Apart from their negative historical experiences and knowledge, the interview partners somewhat bitterly emphasized the current cultural alienation of the Hungarians from the others. According to the conversations, "the Hungarians" have mostly attained their detachment because of their linguistic indifference to the other surrounding languages.[37] The Hungarian minority features as a monolingual insulated community. Yet multilingualism works in a certain way, because (only) Banat Bulgarian-, (also) Hungarian-, Romanian- and Slovak-language speakers are fluent in at least two other languages spoken in Vojvodina (Serbian as the majority language and some other minority language), as opposed to the Serbs/Serbian-speaking majority, whose knowledge is mainly restricted to their own language.

Muslims reappear as unpleasant neighbors who constitute a "different world." In the words of Jelena from the village of Mramorak: "Banatski Brestovac … it is a dead village. A Muslim village. There are the Muslims. And they are a different world. They are enclosed, and it's better not to trust them."[38] In Jelena's worldview, Banatski Brestovac is a "mrtvo selo" [lifeless village], "a different world" because it is inhabited by Slavic speaking Muslims.

While her attitude concerned the (culturally foreign) atmosphere of the place, other views, like those of Vladimir from Omoljica, were guided by notions of "religion," "nation," and "culture." A lot of Muslims living in the Banat were according to him "Poturice" [the Turkicized] and the traitors, as: "they have forgotten that they were Serbs. They just made up their culture, their nation. But the big ones are supporting them."[39] Muslims are erstwhile Serbs who converted to Islam and forgot their actual origins. This widespread image of the "Poturice" bears traces of the Serbian nineteenth-century nationalism and parallel state-building. Both interview partners defined themselves as belonging to the Serbian(-speaking and orthodox) majority, convinced of the truth of the doctored narratives about the disloyal Balkan Muslims. The closing thought on the support the "big ones" are providing to the Muslims is an echo of the recent Yugoslav wars and denied genocidal atrocities against the Bosnian Muslims/Bosniaks committed under the military command of *Republika Srpska* (Serbian Republic), proclaimed in 1992, and the Republic of Serbia.[40]

---

37 In 2018, a daily newspaper Политика [Politics] published an article on the education of Serbian as a foreign language in the Vojvodina. Only in 2018, in Subotica (near the Serbia-Hungary border), schools started with specially developed programs for non-native BCMS/Serbian speakers. See: Александар Исаков, "Нови програм учења српског језика за националне мањине," Политика, October 7, 2018, accessed August 31, 2022, https://www.politika.rs/scc/clanak/412693/Novi-program-ucenja-srpskog-jezika-za-nacionalne-manjine.

38 Interview with Jovana Đurić, Mramorak, November 23, 2013.

39 Interview with Vladimir Tomić, Omoljica, August 25, 2017.

40 Željana Tjunić and Snežana Stanković, "Unearth Not. Gestures of Concealment and Zlatko Paković's Theater of Reveal in Post-Yugoslav Serbia," *Performance Research* 26, no. 8 (2021): 41–51.

Hungarians as "tricky people" and
Muslims "the untrustworthy ones," on
the one side, and "good Germans," on
the other, reflect the conviviality comprising the spectrum of attitudes towards
a proximate neighbor: indifference,
refusal, tolerance, or acceptance. We
may conclude that the majority refers to
a "cross-group friendship"[41] that carries
an overall narrative(s). In this type of
distinction, the author finds a renewed
interest in the question of whom the
majority is when talking about those
who create and spread general narratives about other groups, minorities, and
communities. Dealing with the majority's views on the other neighbors, *i.e.*,
Germans, Hungarians, and Muslims, it
is possible to speak of a "community of
practice.[42]

Figure 4: Bavanište, Southeastern Banat, Serbia.
Source: Radiša Brković (October 2013).

Being "re-accepted" after the fall of Milosević's regime in 2000, Germans
from all corners of the world started to gather in their former homeland to commemorate their past. Preserved, abandoned, vandalized, or destroyed and vanished cemeteries became main gathering points. In this spirit, living members
of the former German community of Mramorak, as well as their descendants,
would meet every year[43] at the memorial site in the neighboring village Bavanište,
where a group of Germans underwent internment and were the victims of mass
shootings in 1944 (see Figure 4).

Hier ruhen 110
unserer deutschen
Mramoraker Landsleute
20.10.1944
Sie ruhen
in Gottes Hand
HOG Mramorak

41 Thomas F. Pettigrew, "Intergroup Contact Theory," *Annual Review of Psychology* 49
    (1998): 76.
42 Davenport and Hall, *Organizational Knowledge and Communities of Practice*, 2002.
43 Before the COVID-19 pandemic.

Овде почива 110
Мраморачких Немаца
20.10.1944
Почивајте у миру
Са Божјом помоћу

[Here lie 110
our German fellow countrymen.
October 20, 1944.
May they rest in peace God [literary: in God's hand]].[44]

These annual reunions and encounters have impacted the attitudes of the local residents towards the German culture (customs, language, religion, monuments, past, and history) to the degree that it has become a mutual legacy. Where once the post-war Germans had to submit to a specific culture of disgrace, Germano-phobia later emerged because of the "reconstruction, modification and actualization of handed down images of the enemy."[45] Today, their cultural revival occurs as a mission of the state itself through the official support expressed to new memorials and museums[46] commemorating the "German victims" of the Yugoslav National Liberation Army and the Communist Regime.

In other words, similar to the stories during the cemetery visits, these moments testify of the goal to retell the past and thus rewrite history. Until recently, they were clearly supposed to convey the message of reconciliation, friendship and "commitment to European values." In the moment of writing down the closing lines of this chapter, the Russian invasion of Ukraine has transformed the contemporary political context of the Republic of Serbia. The future will bring new meanings to or, more likely, re-introduce the old meanings of (cultural and religious) "loyalty" and "friendship."

---

44 Serbian saying differs from the German by directly addressing the dead [May you rest in peace with (the help of) God] and not mentioning the organization of the village of Mramorak.

45 Holm Sundhaussen, "Ethnonationale Gewalt auf dem Balkan im Spiegel der Goldhagen-debatte," in *Politische und ethnische Gewalt in Südosteuropa und Lateinamerika*, eds. Wolfgang Höpken and Michael Riekenberg (Köln, Weimar, Wien: Böhlau Verlag, 2001), 48.

46 In May 2017, the Serbian president, Aleksandar Vučić, unveiled a new memorial to the Danube Swabians in the village of Bački Jarak (Bačka, Central Vojvodina). Miodrag Sovilj, "Spomen-obeležje Podunavskim Švabama u Bačkom Jarku," *Vesti N1*, May 6, 2017, accessed August 31, 2022, https://rs.n1info.com/vesti/a247004-spomenik-podunavskim-sv-abama-u-backom-jarku/.

Conclusion

After World War II, half of the surviving Germans were imprisoned, evacuated, resettled or expelled, and a great number of them fled the country voluntarily. However, such absences and their empty spaces retain traces of their presence and value in the eyes of the majority.

We can follow the appearance of the new boundaries, *i. e.*, bonds through the annual gatherings, revived cemeteries, monuments installed and memorials, which serve as a spatial affirmation of communal togetherness. The duality of presence-absence has a disproportionate correspondence to the processes of forgetting and remembering: the denial of the visibly and physically close Hungarian and Muslim minorities works in favor of the affirmation of the absent and invisible German minority.

In this spirit, some scholars of border studies suggest "the principle of thinking from the border" regarding non-material boundaries, demarcation practices and diversity of orders.[47] For borders indeed "demarcate at least two orders on [...] multiple 'insides' and 'outsides',"[48] the reciprocal research on culturally and socially different neighborhoods, *i. e.*, convivialities, is necessary. The questions on how the members of the Hungarian and Muslim minority in the Banat perceive their neighbors (*i. e.*, Serbs, Slovaks, Pavlikians, who, in our case, represent the majority) and what attitudes and narratives they keep and hand down would complement the concerns of this chapter.

Selected Bibliography

Appadurai, Arjun. *Fear of Small Numbers: An Essay on the Geography of Anger.* Durham/NC: Duke University Press, 2006.

Bossong, Raphael, Dominik Gerst, Imke Kerber, Maria Klessmann, Hannes Krämer, and Peter Ulrich. "Complex Borders: Analytical Problems and Heuristics." In *Advances in European Borderlands Studies*, edited by Elżbieta Opiłowska, Zbigniew Kurcz, and Jochen Roose, 65–84. Baden Baden: Nomos, 2017.

Davenport, Elisabeth, Hazel Hall. "Organizational Knowledge and Communities of Practice." *Annual Review of Information Science and Technology* 36, no.1 (2002): 170–227.

Ђурић, Љубица З. "Контекстуализација језичких пејзажа српских гробова у региону реке Мориша." Исходишта 3 (2017): 129–40.

---

47   Raphael Bossong, Dominik Gerst, Imke Kerber, Maria Klessmann, Hannes Krämer, and Peter Ulrich, "Complex Borders: Analytical Problems and Heuristics," in *Advances in European Borderlands Studies*, eds. Elżbieta Opiłowska, Zbigniew Kurcz, and Jochen Roose (Baden Baden: Nomos, 2017), 75.

48   Ibid.

Heil, Tilmann. "Conviviality: (re)Negotiating Minimal Consensus." In *Routledge International Handbook of Diversity Studies*, edited by Steven Vertovec, 317–24. London, New York: Routledge, 2015.

Ilić Mandić, Jelena. *Banatska vojna krajina: 1764–1800*. Beograd: Istorijski institut, 2020.

Janjetović, Zoran. *Between Hitler and Tito. Disappearance of the Ethnic Germans from the Vojvodina*. Beograd: SD Publik, 2005.

Judson, Pieter M. *Guardians of the Nation. Activists on the Language Frontiers of Imperial Austria*. Cambridge, Massachusetts, London: Harvard University Press, 2006.

Merten, Ulrich. *Forgotten Voices: The Expulsion of the Germans from Eastern Europe after World War II*. London: Routledge, 2017.

Newman, David, Anssi Paasi. "Fences and Neighbours in the Postmodern World: Boundary Narratives in Political Geography." *Progress in Human Geography* 22, no. 2 (1998): 186–207.

Passerini, Luisa. "Memories between Silence and Oblivion." In *Contested Pasts. The Politics of Memory*, edited by Susannah Radstone and Katharine Hodgkin, 238–54. London: Routledge, 2003.

Promitzer, Christian. "Small is Beautiful: The Issue of Hidden Minorities in Central Europe and the Balkans." In *(Hidden) Minorities: Language and Ethnic Identity Between Central Europe and the Balkans*, edited by Christian Promitzer, Klaus-Jürgen Hermanik, and Eduard Staudinger, 75–106. Münster: Lit Verlag, 2010.

Rill, Helena, Marijana Stojčić. *On the Trail of the Danube Swabians in Vojvodina*. Belgrade and Sarajevo: Centre for Nonviolent Action, 2016.

Zakić, Mirna. *Ethnic Germans and National Socialism in Yugoslavia in World War II*. Cambridge: Cambridge University Press, 2017.

About the Authors

Anežka Brožová is a Ph.D. candidate in Modern History at Charles University (Prague). She is also a participant in a project supported by the Czech Science Foundation (GACR) at the Institute of Ethnology, Czech Academy of Sciences. She studied Area Studies with a focus on Germany and Central Europe in Prague and Regensburg (B.A.) and Prague and Cracow (M.A.).

Tereza Juhászová is a Ph.D. student in Modern History at Charles University (Prague). She studied Area Studies (B.A.) and Balkan, Eurasian, and Central European Studies (M.A.) at Charles University. Her research focuses on the modern history of Slovakia and Hungary, marginalized communities, and memory studies. She received scholarships from the Leibniz Institute for East and Southeast European Studies (IOS) in Regensburg, Corvinus University of Budapest, and the Institute of Social Sciences of the Slovak Academy of Sciences.

Ferdinand Kühnel is an affiliated researcher at the Austrian and Central European Center (*Österreich und Ostmitteleuropa Zentrum*) at the Institute of East European History at the University of Vienna and currently works as a publication coordinator of the Austrian-Slovene History Book at the Austrian Academy of Sciences (*Österreichische Akademie der Wissenschaften*). He studied History (M.A.) and Political Science (M.A.) at the Universities of Vienna and Warsaw. He also holds a Ph.D. in History from the University of Vienna.

Soňa Mikulová, Ph.D., gained all her degrees at the Faculty for Social Sciences, Charles University (Prague). Currently, she is a postdoctoral researcher at the Max Planck Institute for Human Development, Center for the History of Emotions in Berlin. Her research interests range from memory studies to the history of emotions, focusing on the twentieth Century in Central Europe.

Martina Mirković studied history (Bachelor of Arts) and economic and social history (Master of Arts) at the University of Vienna. Between autumn 2017 and October 2021, she was a member of the Doctoral College for Central European History at Andrássy University Budapest. Currently, she is a researcher at the Institute of East European History at the University of Vienna.

Michał Piasek is a Ph. D. candidate at the Department of Slavic Studies at Humboldt University of Berlin. His research explores memory processes in multi-ethnic and multi-religious regions through monuments and cemeteries.

Snežana Stanković is a postdoctoral researcher at the Friedrich Schiller University Jena in Germany. Her research concerns aging in environments battered by post-war precarity. She brings medical humanities, environmental studies, literary theories of narration, and the history of emotions into dialogue while following aging, forced (im-)mobilities and trans-local care networks.

Studies on Language and Culture in Central and Eastern Europe (SLCCEE)

Edited by Christian Voß

Band 19 STERN, Dieter: Tajmyr-Pidgin-Russisch. Kolonialer Sprachkontakt in Nordsibirien. 2012.

Band 20 KERSTEN-PEJANIĆ, Roswitha; RAJILIĆ, Simone; VOSS, Christian (Hrsg.): Doing Gender – Doing the Balkans. Dynamics and Persistence of Gender Relations in Yugoslavia and the Yugoslav successor states. 2012.

Band 21 BOBRIK, Marina (Hrsg.): Slavjanskij Apostol. Istorija teksta i jazyk. 2013.

Band 22 BESTERS-DILGER, Juliane (Hg.): Kommentierter Apostolos. Textedition und Kommentar zur Edition. (= Die großen Lesemenäen des Metropoliten Makarij Uspenskij Spisok.) Unter Mitarbeit von V. Halapats, N. Kindermann, E. Maier, A. Rabus. 2014.

Band 23 ILIĆ, Marija: Discourse and Ethnic Identity. The Case of the Serbs from Hungary. 2014.

Band 24 HLAVAC, Jim; FRIEDMANN, Victor (Hrsg.): On Macedonian Matters: from the Partition and Annexation of Macedonia in 1913 to the Present. A Collection of Essays on Language, Culture and History. 2015.

Band 25 HLAVAC, Jim: Three generations, two countries of origin, one speech community: Australian-Macedonians and their language(s). 2016.

Band 27 TYRAN, Katharina Klara: Identitäre Verortungen entlang der Grenze. Verhandlungen von Sprache und Zugehörigkeit bei den Burgenländischen Kroaten. 2015.

Band 28 LORMES, Miriam: „Among good musicians there has never been an ethnical divide". Interkulturalität und politisches Engagement in Musikerdiskursen im postjugoslawischen Makedonien. 2013.

Band 29 GLANC, Tomáš und VOSS, Christian (Hrsg): Konzepte des Slawischen. 2016.

Band 30 GEHRKE, Stefan: Jedwabne und die Folgen. Eine semantische Analyse der Debatte über Juden in der polnischen Presse 2001–2008. 2018.

Band 31 STERN, Dieter; NOMACHI, Motoki; BELIĆ, Bojan (eds.): Linguistic regionalism in eastern europe and beyond. Minority, Regional and Literary Microlanguages. In memoriam Jiří Marvan. 2018.

Band 32 RAJILIĆ, Simone: Weiblichkeit im Serbischen. Weibliche Genderspezifizierungen zwischen Gewalt und Widerstand. 2019.

Band 33 SCHELLER-BOLTZ, Dennis: Grammatik und Ideologie. Feminisierungsstrategien im Russischen und Polnischen aus Sicht der Wissenschaft und Gesellschaft. 2020.

Band 34 FRIEDMAN, Victor; JANEV, Goran; VLAHOV, George (eds.): Macedonia & Its Questions. Origins, Margins, Ruptures & Continuity. 2020.

Band 35 MUJADŽEVIĆ, Dino (ed.): Digital Historical Research on Southeast Europe and the Ottoman Space. 2021.

Band 36 DANOVA, Tsvetomira: John of Damascus' Marian Homilies in Mediaeval South Slavic Literatures. 2020.

Band 37 JOURAVEL, Anna; MATHYS, Audrey (eds.): Wort- und Formenvielfalt. Festschrift für Christoph Koch zum 80. Geburtstag. Unter Mitarbeit von Daniel Petit. 2021.

Band 38 ČAPO, Jasna: Zwei Zuhause. Kroatische Arbeitsmigration nach Deutschland als transnationales Phänomen. 2022.

Band 39 VOSS, Christian; FOTIADIS Ruža: Sprachliche Grenzziehungen in der griechisch-mazedonischen Kontaktzone im 20. Jahrhundert. 2023.

Band 40 VOSS, Christian; JUSUFI, Lumnije; REUTER, Evelyn (eds.): Innovative Paths of Albanology. Proceedings of the Early Career Researcher Conference on 14th and 15th October, 2021. 2023.

Band 41 KÜHNEL, Ferdinand; MIKULOVÁ, Soňa; STANKOVIĆ Snežana (eds.): East Central European Cemeteries. Ethnic, Linguistic, and Narrative Aspects of Sepulchral Culture and the Commemoration of the Dead in Borderlands. 2023.

www.peterlang.com

Printed in Great Britain
by Amazon